Jacob Richards Dodge

West Virginia

Its farms and forests, mines and oilwells

Jacob Richards Dodge

West Virginia
Its farms and forests, mines and oilwells

ISBN/EAN: 9783744723572

Printed in Europe, USA, Canada, Australia, Japan

Cover: Foto ©Andreas Hilbeck / pixelio.de

More available books at **www.hansebooks.com**

ITS

FARMS AND FORESTS, MINES AND OIL-WELLS;

WITH A GLIMPSE OF ITS SCENERY, A PHOTOGRAPH OF ITS
POPULATION, AND AN EXHIBIT OF ITS
INDUSTRIAL STATISTICS.

BY

J. R. DODGE

OF THE U. S. DEPARTMENT OF AGRICULTURE.

PHILADELPHIA:
J. B. LIPPINCOTT & CO.
1865.

PREFACE.

THE oak that graces the mountain-slope has come from an acorn planted by an errant squirrel. From a seed as small, dropped in a Kanawha Valley mail-bag in equal unconsciousness of hidden germ-life, this volume has grown, little by little. Like the forest oak, its growth has been natural, without pruning or "pinching back," or artistic fashioning of any sort. The only aim has been to make it true to nature and to life, however homely its phase.

A single letter with a striking reference to mineral resources, followed by other correspondence, a tour of observation in behalf of the Department of Agriculture, exploration of State archives and national census schedules, and free conferences with intelligent business men of West Virginia, led to the exhibit made in the United States Report of Agriculture for 1863. Enterprising citizens of other States, attracted by these resources, wished to know more of their character and extent. In answer to such demands, from all sections of the North, the author has been induced to prepare this little volume, as intervals of leisure afforded opportunity.

It was a virgin territory, practically unknown to industrial writers, without records of its natural wealth or reported transactions of agricultural or geographical societies. Hence this is but a partial and cursory survey, preliminary in its nature, and by no means exhaustive of the subject. As such it is presented, and not as a mature and full exhibit of the natural resources and industrial condition of West Virginia.

To the following persons, among many others, acknowledgments for valuable information and suggestions are gratefully tendered: Hons. W. T. Willey, P. G. Van Winkle, J. G. Blair, K. V. Whaley, and C. D. Hubbard, representing the State in Congress; United States District Attorney, Benjamin H. Smith; United States Assessor, A. G. Leonard; Governor, A. I. Boreman; Hon. John M. Phelps, President of the State Senate; Senators Burley, Carskadon, Stevenson and Young; Delegates, McGrew, McWhorter, Ruffner, and Crawford; Messrs. W. P. Smith and J. B. Ford, of the Baltimore and Ohio Railroad; Messrs. H. Hagans, J. H. D. Debar, C. S. Richardson, A. W. Campbell, and J. E. Wharton. The favors of others, however small, are held in equal remembrance.

J. R. D.

WASHINGTON, D. C., August, 1865.

CONTENTS.

CHAPTER I.
WEST VIRGINIA.—CRADLED IN CONVULSION.—A STURDY RACE.—OLD JEALOUSIES.—REORGANIZATION.—NEW LAWS.—FINANCES.—HER BOYS IN BLUE. . . . Page 7

CHAPTER II.
ORIGINAL SETTLEMENT.—WHERE VIRGINIANS EMIGRATE.—TOBACCO AND THE BLUE LAWS.—LANDS.—THE "TOMAHAWK RIGHT."—HOW THE PIONEERS LIVED.—GETTING MARRIED.—PROGRESS.—POPULATION. 23

CHAPTER III.
LOCATION.—VALUE OF LANDS.—STOCK GROWING.—FERTILITY.—NO WASTE AREAS.—COMPARISON WITH MARYLAND, MINNESOTA, AND NEW HAMPSHIRE. 39

CHAPTER IV.
CLIMATE.—ALTITUDE.—TEMPERATURE.—RAIN-FALL.—SALUBRITY.—SCENERY. . . 54

CHAPTER V.
TOPOGRAPHY AND STATISTICS OF COUNTIES.—THE VALLEY GROUP. 68

CHAPTER VI.
SURVEY OF COUNTIES CONTINUED.—THE MOUNTAIN GROUP. 79

CHAPTER VII.
SURVEY OF COUNTIES CONTINUED.—THE "PANHANDLE." 87

CHAPTER VIII.
SURVEY OF COUNTIES CONTINUED.—THE RIVER DISTRICT. 101

CHAPTER IX.
SURVEY OF COUNTIES CONTINUED.—THE KANAWHA VALLEY. 112

CHAPTER X.
SURVEY OF COUNTIES CONTINUED.—THE SOUTHERN GROUP. 123

CHAPTER XI.
SURVEY OF COUNTIES CONTINUED.—THE CENTRAL GROUP. 128

CONTENTS.

CHAPTER XII.
STATISTICS OF PRODUCTION. 142

CHAPTER XIII.
INTERNAL IMPROVEMENTS.— ROADS AND TURNPIKES.— SLACKWATER NAVIGATION.— OHIO AND CHESAPEAKE CANAL.— BALTIMORE AND OHIO RAILROAD.— OTHER RAILROADS. . 149

CHAPTER XIV.
MINERAL WEALTH.— COAL. 160

CHAPTER XV.
IRON.— SALT.— LIMESTONE.— OTHER MINERALS. 168

CHAPTER XVI.
PETROLEUM.— ITS WIDE DISTRIBUTION.— DISCOVERY IN WEST VIRGINIA. . . . 176

CHAPTER XVII.
HOW ORIGINATED.— POPULAR AND UNPOPULAR THEORIES. 185

CHAPTER XVIII.
WHERE FOUND.— HOW TO FIND IT. 192

CHAPTER XIX.
USES.— QUANTITY USED. 206

CHAPTER XX.
WELL BORING.— OIL DISTILLING.— REFINING. 213

CHAPTER XXI.
THE ERA OF OIL WELLS.— THE BURNING SPRINGS DISTRICT.— THE LITTLE KANAWHA. . 220

CHAPTER XXII.
THE HUGHES' RIVER REGION.— OIL RUN OF GOOSE CREEK.— HORSENECK AND COW CREEK. 229

CHAPTER XXIII.
THE CENTRAL AND NORTHERN OIL REGION. 237

CHAPTER XXIV.
THE GREAT KANAWHA OIL BASIN.— THE VALLEYS OF THE GUYANDOTTE AND BIG SANDY. 243

CHAPTER XXV.
PETROLEUM COMPANIES OF WEST VIRGINIA. 250

CHAPTER XXVI.
PETROLEUM PROSPECTS. 265

WEST VIRGINIA.

CHAPTER I.

WEST VIRGINIA.—CRADLED IN CONVULSION.—A STURDY RACE. — OLD JEALOUSIES. — REORGANIZATION. — NEW LAWS.—FINANCES.—HER BOYS IN BLUE.

THE "logic of events" is but the dictum of Deity. It shows how God disposes of what man proposes. The "*pride*" that "goeth before destruction" is sometimes only the Christian name of the *madness* inspired by "the gods" in their victims. The humbling of the pride of Virginia secession was largely wrought, so far as accomplished by human means, by her own people through the agency of her own constitution. As "when a man's pride is thoroughly subdued, it is like the sides of Mount Etna," so the treasonable state sovereignty eruption was "terrible while it lasted, and the lava flowed; but when that is passed and the lava is turned into soil, it grows vineyards and olive trees up to the very top."

Nor was this political eruption — thus made the occasion of purification — a matter either of surprise or wonder, when viewed in its native character. When statesmen degenerate into politicians, and the principle of states' rights is prostituted to the uses of treason, it is eminently fit and in accordance with the law of compensation, that the madness of the present hour should open to patriotism a door of escape from inequality and organized oppression, to future industrial advancement, political independence, and a superior civilization.

The "Old Dominion" of our fathers, eldest in the family of States, and fairest in all that constitutes the highest natural attractions of the sisterhood, has committed the *hari kari*, or "happy despatch," under the influence of the demon of secession — is disembowelled and rent in twain. But she is immortal, and while East Virginia writhes in penitential agony, West Virginia not only lives, but is beginning to put forth a hitherto unknown vigor, and promises a career of glory and benefaction, a full maturity of beauty and pride, and a name of honor among the most illustrious of States in all coming time.

The new State has had her birth in the era of revolution, and has been baptized in blood, in the name of law and liberty; yet her most ardent aspiration was always for a peace unsullied by cowardice or injustice — for an honorable diversion from the "war path" to the path of progress in the arts of industry — for a higher and purer life, that shall animate and elevate every human being within her borders, and bless, with prosperity, education, refinement, and religion, myriads of happy homes.

Other States may boast of broad savannas that bask in placid beauty, and soils of interminable depth and richness. West Virginia acknowledges a rough exterior, but claims for her hills the adornment of majestic and comely forest growths; for her vales a permeable and fruitful soil; for her rivers a wealth of water power; for her mines a heritage illimitable, and for her broad domain the insignia of strength, enduring vitality, and sturdy independence — the proud characteristics of her people.

Their fathers were taught in a school of manly self-reliance, noble endurance, and intrepid daring. With Washington they risked the covert perils of the wily Indian's arrow, and sought and founded homes to be defended with the constant rifle, and beautified with the strength of the labor of many years. The sons of these pioneers, lured by the general rush of population to the fruitful prairies, and conscious that the poor man was not in the line of promotion according to feudal prerogative obtaining in Virginia, joined the general throng that followed the guidance of the star of empire. Thus were many of the bravest and noblest of her children lost to her fame and her material progress. Thus were sylvan homes left unadorned; the sweetest herbage scantily depastured; giant frames of great ships in vain awaiting the woodman's axe by the river side; the hill sides ready to flow with wine; and the oil lubricating a passage to the surface from the caverns beneath; while the minerals, in rich variety and still richer profusion, offered in vain their seductive charms to the fugacious proprietor of all this wealth. Yet with all these drawbacks, substantial progress was made, so that when this section became a State, it assumed at once a strong and influential position among her sisters.

The political jealousies between East and West Virginia, and the oppressions and injustice of the East, had a very early beginning. In the revolutionary period, Jefferson complained that the tide-water region, having but eleven thousand two hundred and five out of one hundred and twenty-one thousand five hundred and twenty-five square miles, claimed as occupied Virginia territory, and but nineteen thousand and twelve of forty-nine thousand nine hundred and seventy-one fighting-men, possessed one-half the representation in the Senate, and seventy-one of the one hundred and forty-nine members of the House of Delegates; and objected that "these nineteen thousand, therefore, living in one part of the country, give law to upwards of thirty thousand living in another, and appoint all their chief officers, executive and judiciary," regarding the want of four members to make a majority as more than compensated practically by the vicinity of their residence to the seat of government.

Not only was there an inequality of representation, but, in later years at least, a want of magnanimity and true chivalry on the part of the majority; which hesitated not to legislate further inequality — taxing, for instance, only nominally the negro property, of which the West had little, and piling the burdens of state upon Western interests, making them pay *pro rata* for building railroads and constructing other internal improvements in the East, to the exclusion of all recognition of the trans-Alleghanian territory.

It would seem that the East regarded that rich domain of mines and of forests much as an overprudent father looks upon a son of free and generous impulses, injudiciously and unjustly curbing his actions and thwarting his desires. As the youth at last cuts loose from such leading strings, so was the auspicious moment of paternal infidelity and disloyalty improved; and it will be fortunate if the progress of the youthful disenthralled should not become slightly too *fast*, in obedience to the law of precedents.

The story of separation and organization as a new State, in the mode prescribed by the Constitution of the United States, is briefly told.

On the 13th of May, 1861, twenty-four days after the adoption of secession by the convention at Richmond, delegates from twenty-five counties met at Wheeling and passed resolutions in condemnation of the traitors and the treason of Richmond, and providing for a convention of all the counties adhering to the Union.

On the 11th of June, representatives from forty counties assembled at Wheeling, on invitation to all loyal men of Virginia, and declared independence of the action of the State convention, announced an interregnum in the State government, and took measures for the establishment of a provisional government.

On July 2d, the legislature, duly elected, convened at Wheeling, and elected United States Senators, passed a stay law, and voted two hundred thousand dollars for carrying on the war, and the same amount for the operations of the State government. October 24th the action of the legislature was approved by the people in a vote almost unanimous.

WEST VIRGINIA.

A convention met at Wheeling, November 26th, 1861, and framed a State constitution, and on the 3d of May, 1862, that constitution was approved and adopted by the qualified voters of the proposed State. On the 13th day of May, the legislature of Virginia gave its consent to the formation of a new State within the jurisdiction of Virginia.

On the 31st of December, 1862, the President approved the act of Congress for the admission of the State of West Virginia into the Union, to comprise the counties of Hancock, Brooke, Ohio, Marshall, Wetzel, Marion, Monongalia, Preston, Taylor, Tyler, Pleasants, Ritchie, Doddridge, Harrison, Wood, Jackson, Wirt, Roane, Calhoun, Gilmer, Barbour, Tucker, Lewis, Braxton, Upshur, Randolph, Mason, Putnam, Kanawha, Clay, Nicholas, Cabell, Wayne, Boone, Logan, Wyoming, Mercer, McDowell, Webster, Pocahontas, Fayette, Raleigh, Greenbrier, Monroe, Pendleton, Hardy, Hampshire, and Morgan, to which have been subsequently added Berkeley and Jefferson, making fifty counties, including a total area of about twenty-four thousand square miles. Provision is also made for the admission of Frederick, with the consent of its voters.

This act took effect in sixty days after the proclamation of the President stating the fact of its ratification by the people, and the adoption of the following in place of the clause in the Virginia constitution respecting slavery:

"The children of slaves born within the limits of this State after the fourth day of July, eighteen hundred and sixty-three, shall be free; and all slaves within the said State who shall, at the time aforesaid, be under the age of ten years, shall be free when they arrive at the age of twenty-one years; and all slaves over ten and under twenty-one years shall be free when they arrive at the age of twenty-five years; and no slave shall be permitted to come into the State for permanent residence therein."

This remnant of slavery remained until the third day of February, 1865. The amendment to the Constitution of the United States, abolishing slavery forever, had just been adopted by Congress. It had been ratified the day before by the Legislature of West Virginia. Now it was proposed not to await the ratification by the requisite three-fourths of the States, but to consummate the disenthralment of West Virginia at once. A bill to that effect had passed the House of Delegates on the same day of the ratification, by a large majority; and now the Senate, by the decisive majority of seventeen to one, removed the last obstacle to the free ingress of skilled labor, enterprise and capital, so much needed for the full development of inexhaustible natural resources. Thus peacefully was legally buried that which was already regarded as essentially and utterly dead. Thus became the new State, "without an if or a but," a free State!

The Executive power of the State is vested in a Governor who is elected biennially. The Secretary of State, Treasurer, Auditor and Attorney-General, are elected at the same time with the Governor, holding office for the same period. The fourth Thursday October is designated for the election of State and County officers, and members of the Legislature. The Governor receives a salary of $2000; the Secretary of State, $1300; Treasurer, $1400; Auditor, $1500; Attorney-General, $1000.

The Legislative power is vested in a Senate and House of Delegates. The former consists of twenty-two members, elected for two years; the latter, of fifty-seven Delegates, elected for one year. The sessions commence on the third Tuesday of January, are annual and limited to forty-five days, unless otherwise ordered by two-thirds of both Houses. The pay of Senators and Delegates is $3 per day, and ten cents per mile of travel, going and returning; the President of the Senate and Speaker of the House, $5 per day; Clerk of the Senate, $8; Clerk of the House, $9.

The Judicial system includes a Supreme Court of Appeals, Circuit and Inferior Courts. The former consists of three judges, elected by the people, to hold office for twelve years, one to retire every fourth year. This court has original jurisdiction in cases of *habeas corpus, mandamus,* and *prohibition;* appellate jurisdiction in civil cases, involving pecuniary values exceeding two hundred dollars, exclusive of costs; in questions of land title or boundary, the probate of wills, the appointment or qualification of a personal representative, guardian, committee or curator, or concerning a mill, road or ferry, or the right of a corporation or county to levy tolls or taxes, or in cases involving freedom or the constitutionality of law, or in criminal cases in which conviction for felony or misdemeanor has been reached in a Circuit Court. It is also invested with the jurisdiction and powers which could have been exercised by the Supreme or District Courts of Virginia respecting any suit or proceeding in West Virginia. Two sessions of this Court are held yearly at Wheeling, beginning respectively on the second Thursday of January, and the second Thursday of July.

First District.—Hancock, Brooke, Ohio, and Marshall Counties.

Second District.—Monongalia, Preston, Tucker, and Taylor Counties.

Third District.—Marion, Harrison, and Barbour Counties.

Fourth District.—Wetzel, Tyler, Pleasants, Ritchie, Doddridge, and Gilmer Counties.

Fifth District.—Randolph, Upshur, Lewis, Braxton, Webster, and Nicholas Counties.

Sixth District.—Wood, Wirt, Calhoun, Roane, Jackson, and Clay Counties.

Seventh District.—Kanawha, Mason, Putnam, and Fayette Counties.

Eighth District.—Cabell, Wayne, Boone, Logan, Wyoming, and Raleigh Counties.

Ninth District.—Pocahontas, Greenbrier, Monroe, Mercer, and McDowell Counties.

Tenth District.—Pendleton, Hampshire, Hardy, and Morgan Counties.

Eleventh District.—Frederick, Berkeley, and Jefferson Counties.

The seal of the State bears the legend, "State of West Virginia," with the motto, "*Montani semper liberi,*" ("Mountaineers always free,") in the circumference. In the centre is a rock, over which ivy is twined, emblematic of stability and continuance. On the face is inscribed, as with the point of a diamond, the date, "June 20, 1863." On the right of the rock stands the farmer-hunter, as denoted by the primitive hunting-shirt — the pioneer blended in the citizen — his right arm resting on plough-handles, his left supporting an axe; at his right a cornstalk and sheaf of wheat. On the left of the rock is a miner, with oil-barrels and fragments of minerals at his feet, and flanked by an anvil and sledge-hammer. In front of the rock two rifles, crossed, surmounted at the place of contact by the cap of Liberty, ready at a moment's warning to be taken up for the maintenance of that freedom and independence which they have helped to win.

The present State officers are as follows: Governor, A. J. Boreman; Secretary of State, Granville D. Hall; Treasurer, Campbell Tarr; Auditor, Joseph McWhorter; Attorney-General, Ephraim B. Hall.

The Judges of the Supreme Court of Appeals are: R. L. Berkshire, James H. Brown, and William A. Harrison. Salary, $2000 each. Clerk, Sylvanus W. Hall; salary, $1000 and fees.

The Judges of the Circuit Court are: First District, Elbert H. Hall, Moundville; Second District, John A. Dille, Kingwood; Third District, Thomas W. Harrison, Clarksburg; Fourth District, Chapman J. Stuart, West Union; Fifth District, Robert Irvine, Weston; Sixth District, James Loomis, Parkersburg; Seventh District, Daniel Polsley, Mason County; Eighth District, Henry J. Samuels, Guyandotte. The Ninth, Tenth and Eleventh Districts, are at present vacant. John W. Kennedy, of Berkeley Springs, presided in the Tenth, but was removed by the last legislature.

The first session of the Legislature, in 1863, in the

midst of civil war, in the peculiar circumstances attending the birth of the new State, involved an immense amount of labor, requiring wisdom, energy, and boldness. From a few days' observation of this Legislature, the earnestness, loyalty, intelligence, and practical wisdom of the great majority of its members were strikingly apparent for a body suddenly thrown together by the convulsions of a revolution.

The laws of this session are comprised in a volume of more than three hundred pages, and considerable additional legislation has been perfected in the two subsequent sessions.

One of the first enactments was a law appropriating fifty thousand dollars for procuring arms and munitions of war.

Early in the first session provision was made for the prosecution and trial of colored persons charged with crime, in the same mode, and with the same punishment, upon conviction, as in the case of whites.

An act "to prevent the encouragement of invasions and insurrections" visited with fine and imprisonment any advocacy or justification of armed rebellion, by public speaking, printing, or writing.

Early action was taken to secure the benefit of the national provision for industrial colleges. The grant for this State amounts to one hundred and fifty thousand acres. The fund realized is required to be invested in United States stocks, the interest only to be used, no portion of which may be expended upon buildings; and the State is made responsible for the loss of any portion of the fund.

In nothing is the spirit of improvement, which has taken possession of the new State, more obvious, than in the school system adopted. The act contemplates the instruction of "all the youth in the State, in such fundamental branches of learning as are indispensable to the proper discharge of their social and civil duties." A board of education is provided for each township, fully empowered to act for the highest interests of the schools, and required to furnish facilities for a full course of common English education; and they may call a township meeting for an authorization of a High School, when the interests of education in their district seem to demand the establishment of such an institution. Schools are also provided for colored children. A State superintendent is placed at the head of the system, with a salary of fifteen hundred dollars, and County superintendencies are likewise created. Five grades of teachers' certificates are made by the county superintendents in the examination of teachers, but the lowest grade can never be granted to the same person a second time, and three No. 1 certificates entitle a teacher to a professional certificate, good for life, except in case of proven immorality or disloyalty. Provision is made for a building fund, land may be condemned for a site, and money may be borrowed for building purposes upon the credit of the fund. The constitution provides that the school fund shall be replenished from proceeds of forfeited, delinquent, and unappropriated lands; grants and bequests to the State for educational or unspecified purposes; the State's share of the Literary Fund of Virginia; the proceeds of escheated estates or those of persons dying without an heir; proceeds of money paid as exemption from military duty; and such sums as may be from time to time appropriated by the Legislature. The interest of this fund only can be expended, and any unexpended balance, at the end of a fiscal year, must be added to the principal.

This law, as appears from the report of W. R. White, the Superintendent of Free Schools, is going into operation as rapidly as circumstances will permit. Enrolments of children have been made in seventeen counties, the aggregate number enrolled being forty-seven thousand seven hundred and seventy-five. Twenty-five counties have elected county superintendents. "The old regime," says the superintendent, "left us a legacy of dilapidated buildings, incompetent teachers, and artificial modes of instruction. There are some noble exceptions, but the general aspect of school affairs, as hitherto presented, is deplorable in the extreme." One of the first acts of this officer, indicative of improvements to be inaugurated, was the distribution to county superintendents of copies of "Barnard's School Architecture." He suggests the necessity of establishing one or more State "normal schools" for the education of teachers, and urges legislators to "see that the republic receive no detriment from incompetent teachers."

A general law authorizing the formation of corporations, applies to associations for manufacturing, mining, insuring, for education or benevolence, and for other purposes, exclusive of banks of circulation, companies for internal improvement, or for the purchase of lands for re-selling at a profit. The capital may not exceed one million dollars; not less than five directors are required; the existence of the corporation is limited to twenty years, except in the case of educational or benevolent associations; no officer or director may act as a proxy; the company must organize in six months after obtaining a charter, and is dissolved if suspended for two years; and the legislature reserves the right to alter or amend the charter. The law is very full in its provisions, embracing sixty-six sections, with several subsequent acts in amendment of the original.

The finances of the State are highly creditable to its government. Like a child deserted of its natural protector, the young dominion stood forth self-reliant, and bravely set up business upon the most scanty patrimony, unwillingly left by the fugacious "governor."

The fiscal year ends September 30. The following are the sources and amount of income received during the year ending in September last:

From the Commonwealth of Virginia,	$45,771 46
" redemption of lands,	701 21
" court and military fines,	1,177 65
" miscellaneous sources,	1,064 95
" notarial seals,	297 32
" railroad, turnpike, and express companies,	436 98
" deeds, seals, etc.,	3,328 80
" licenses,	16,761 35
" banks and insurance companies,	30,848 26
" taxes,	172,908 50
Total,	$273,296 48

Of the taxes received, (from collections made only

in twenty-five counties,) $132,864.03 were for taxes levied for the fiscal year.

The present condition of the Treasury is thus shown:

Balance in Treasury, September 30, 1863,	$138,659 46
Receipts for the year ending September 30, 1864,	273,296 48
Total receipts,	$411,955 94
Disbursements during fiscal year,	232,926 10
Balance in Treasury, October 1, 1864,	$179,029 84
Receipts from October 1, 1864, to January 1, 1865,	144,553 54
Aggregate,	$323,583 38
Disbursements from October 1, 1864, to January, 1, 1865,	26,372 51
Balance in Treasury, January 1, 1865,	$297,210 87

The Governor states in his annual message, that he had paid, for expenses of organizing a militia force to protect the border, from money furnished on his own checks by the banks, $23,907.06, in addition to the appropriation for that object.

The report of the Adjutant-General shows that twenty-six thousand five hundred and forty soldiers have been furnished to the armies of the United States, from an enrollment of thirty-three thousand seven hundred and seventy-four men. If any State can show a better military record, it can only be done by exhibiting the entire arms-bearing population under arms, and marching to the music of the Union! Governor Boreman properly says of them:

"They have evinced a bravery and soldierly bearing that is alike creditable to them and honorable to the State. Led on by our own noble officers, in immediate command, they have endured the hardships and privations of active service without complaint; have eagerly sought the enemy, and, wherever found, they have assaulted him with an intelligence, determination and bold impetuosity, that have not been surpassed by any troops in the history of the war, and have resulted in their triumph on many a hard-fought field."

By an act of Congress, the provisions of the land grant act for colleges of agriculture and the mechanic arts has been extended to West Virginia, by which scrip for one hundred and fifty thousand acres of public lands is secured to the State. The Legislature has already accepted the trust.

CHAPTER II.

ORIGINAL SETTLEMENT. — WHERE VIRGINIANS EMIGRATE. — TOBACCO AND THE BLUE LAWS. — LANDS. — THE "TOMAHAWK RIGHT."— HOW THE PIONEERS LIVED. — GETTING MARRIED. — PROGRESS. — POPULATION.

SETTLEMENTS began to extend across the mountains immediately after the close of the revolutionary war. Localities in Greenbrier and Berkeley, and other counties, were settled before its close. Virginia, in 1781, had already a population of five hundred and sixty-seven thousand six hundred and fourteen — almost double the present population of West Virginia. It was rapidly increasing, doubling its population in twenty-seven years; this rate of increase having long existed with great regularity, Jefferson, assuming the same ratio of advance, predicted the attainment of a population of four million five hundred and forty thousand nine hundred and twelve in 1863. This he regarded as a "competent population," which would be seventy-three to the square mile, and less than the present population of Massachusetts, Rhode Island, Connecticut, New York, and New Jersey, and equal to that of Maryland. In 1790 the population was seven hundred and forty-eight thousand three hundred and eighteen, verifying Jefferson's calculations. In 1808 it should have been one million one hundred and thirty-five thousand two hundred and twenty-eight; it was actually but one million sixty-five thousand one hundred and twenty-nine in 1820, and in 1860 it was one million five hundred and ninety-six thousand one hundred and eighteen, little more than one-third of Jefferson's assumed population.

This calculation was by no means unreasonable. If Virginia had continued to be the most densely populated State in the Union, its population would, in 1860, have been nine million six hundred and eighty-three thousand one hundred and eighty-six. Nor is it due to superior natural resources that a half dozen other States have a denser population than Jefferson expected for his native State, for Virginia exceeds them all in natural wealth, and stands upon an equality with the most favored in point of climate.

It is fair, then, to ask, why has not West Virginia been peopled? When the last census was taken, there were found three hundred and eighty-nine thousand eight hundred and nine inhabitants of other States born in Virginia. How many, in the past, had died away from their native soil, and how many children of these and of living Virginians are now aiding to swell the population of other States, cannot be known; were it exhibited, it might show the prediction of Jefferson to be an approach either to prophetic accuracy or exact mathematical calculation. It may be said with some truth that the superior facility for getting prairie lands into cultivation in regions farther west has drawn emigrants over the summits and down the western slopes of the Alleghanies. The swinging of the woodman's axe and the climbing of hills may have been distasteful; and the deep river bottoms and broad alluvial plains may have had their attractions, despite the discomfort of chills and fever and the annoyance of mud and mosquitoes.

A second reason may truthfully be given in the evident fact that this region is peculiarly adapted to special enterprises, both mineral and agricultural, involving either capital or association, or both, such as coal-mining, iron-working, salt-making, oil-working, wine-making, fruit-growing, dairying, and sheep husbandry; and hence its development has been retarded.

But the most potent cause of delayed development after all, as a matter of fact which cannot be ignored or refuted, is the instinctive feeling in all unprejudiced minds that free labor is more profitable and honorable to all living upon its product than servile—yielding more comely social results and sweeter moral fruits; that it is more conducive to the general health and happiness, and more productive of true mental culture and general intelligence; and hence that its associations and consequences, in the distant future, are infinitely more desirable surroundings to that posterity for which it is the business of life to provide.

Nor are Virginians, upon this point, practically unbelieving. Whatever of prejudice, so naturally begotten, inbred and instilled by habit and education, may have swayed them, the suggestive fact remains that more of them have sought homes in the free than in the slave States. In opposition to the powerful control of habit and early association and inculcation, and ofttimes even in apparent violence to expressed opinions, humanity and self-preservation have instinctively asserted their power, as will be seen by the following figures, which designate the States in which persons born in Virginia were living in 1860:

SLAVE.		FREE.	
Alabama,	7,598	California,	5,157
Arkansas,	6,484	Connecticut,	302
Delaware,	171	Illinois,	32,978
Florida,	654	Indiana,	36,848
Georgia,	5,275	Iowa,	17,944
Kentucky,	45,310	Kansas,	3,487
Louisiana,	2,986	Maine,	116
Maryland,	7,560	Massachusetts,	1,391
Mississippi,	6,897	Michigan,	2,176
Missouri,	53,957	Minnesota,	849
North Carolina,	9,899	New Hampshire,	71
South Carolina,	1,117	New Jersey,	880
Tennessee,	36,647	New York,	3,650
Texas,	9,081	Ohio,	75,874
		Oregon,	1,273
		Pennsylvania,	11,026
		Rhode Island,	138
		Vermont,	30
		Wisconsin,	1,983
Total,	193,606	Total,	196,173

This emigration would naturally be to Kentucky and Missouri. Those States include ninety-nine thousand two hundred and sixty-seven persons from Virginia; and Ohio, Indiana, Illinois, and Iowa, extending precisely the same distance west, contain, almost exclusively in their southern portion, one hundred and sixty-three thousand six hundred and forty-four of this population. This would make the proportion, in the emigration directly westward, to free and to slave territory, as five to three.

Silently but continually, this practical expression of the superiority of voluntary labor in forming the wealth and morals of a nation has been going on, while a few ambitious votaries of wrong were maddening for a career of ruin, of which Jefferson had some premonition when he wrote as follows: "And can the liberties of a nation be thought secure when we have removed their only firm basis, a conviction in the minds of the people that these liberties are the gift of God? That they are not to be violated but with his wrath? Indeed, I tremble for my country when I reflect that God is just; that his justice cannot sleep forever; that considering numbers, nature, and natural means only, a revolution of the wheel of fortune, *an exchange of situation is among possible events — that it may become probable by supernatural interference.* The Almighty has no attribute which can take sides with us in such a contest."

Of the material composing the original population, J. H. Diss Debar, Commissioner of Immigration for West Virginia, thus writes:

"The first settlers of our territory came principally from Eastern Virginia, and they and their descendants constitute a majority of our present population. They are chiefly of English, Scotch, and Irish descent, sparsely intermixed with Pennsylvania-German blood, and, as a whole, form one of the most interesting communities of the United States. Native tact and sagacity, urbanity, hospitality, and self-esteem, are among their leading characteristics; and, although not remarkable for enterprise and public spirit, our people evince in their business transactions a degree of shrewdness and judgment, which goes far towards compensating their lack of intellectual opportunities."

The following quaint passage from a history of Virginia published in London in 1722, doubtless presents a not untruthful picture of the early settlers among those forest hills.

"They live in so happy a climate, and have so fertile a soil, that nobody is poor enough to beg, though they have abundance of people that are lazy enough to desire it. I remember the time, when five pounds was left by a charitable testator, to the poor of the parish we lived in, and it lay nine years before the executors could find one poor enough to accept of this legacy; but at last it was given to an old woman."

Simple and unostentatious as are the dwellers of these forest valleys, the course of time and surrounding influences have changed in some respects the manners of the early settlers, of the era when a fond father was fined two thousand pounds of tobacco for refusing to have his child baptised by a lawful minister; when a hog thief (for that disreputable character exists in every civilized community) was amerced to the amount of one thousand pounds (of tobacco); and when a woman, convicted of slander, was punished by ducking, as many times as the tobacco fine assessed upon her husband (and remitted if the fragrant weed was produced as an atonement) could be divided by five hundred pounds. In religious toleration the change has been equally marked, from the time when a ship master incurred the forfeit of five thousand pounds of tobacco for landing a Quaker immigrant upon Virginia shores.

The West Virginian is still a lover of the solitudes of the forest, and of the hunter's invigorating sport; he cultivates a patch of fertile Virginia soil sufficient to supply the largest physical wants of a growing household, and to leave an ample store for a rough but generous hospitality; and he lives an independent and contented life, little envious of the favors of fortune, repining not for the mere refinements of life, and enduring with little murmuring the privations of schools and the Sabbath day's journey to church.

The pure air of the hills, the long rambles in the forest for venison and turkeys, and the varied labor upon a farm just redeemed from the broken forest, give him a ruddy cheek, an elastic step, and a vigorous appetite. In the house the same evidence of health and vigor appears, not less in the rosy wife in homespun attire of her own manufacture, than in the sturdiness and strength of a bevy of boys and girls who make the cabin ring with the mirth and music of their merry activities.

Land was the inducement to western emigration, in the past as well as the present century. That which is now selling at fifty, one hundred, or two hundred dollars per acre, for its petroleum, coal, or other mineral, was obtained by the simple act of settlement. A cabin of a single room, and a cornfield just sufficient to supplement the venison and the bear meat in the larder of the family, entitled the settler to four hundred acres, with a pre-emption right to one thousand acres adjoining, to be secured by land warrant. Certificates of settlement rights, with surveyor's plot, were filed in the State land office; and if no adverse caveat was filed, a patent was issued.

Another right — the "tomahawk right" — secured

land titles by a simpler and easier mode. It consisted in deadening a few trees for a prospective clearing, and cutting the initials of the claimant upon the bark of some of them. These claims were not held to be valid, but were often bought and sold, the purchaser thus propitiating troublesome claimants. Some of the settlers, however, more resolute and bellicose, ignored the tomahawk improvement, and administered physical punishment in return for continued annoyance. So the tomahawk right yielded to the right of the strongest.

Hardships were often encountered by those early settlers. The usual course was to leave the more dependent of the family behind, while the pioneers commenced a settlement in early spring. Others, less cautious, or with smaller families, endured together the excitements and labors and discomforts of pioneer life, starting with as full a commissariat as possible. Sometimes their flour, or corn-meal more usually, was exhausted before corn could be ripened. In such cases vegetable diet was dispensed with for weeks together. Lean venison and the breast of wild turkeys then became bread, while the flesh of the bear answered for meat. The advent of roasting ears was a day of jubilee, and the coming of johnny-cakes the consummation of a summer's labor.

In surveying these allotments for farms, the division lines usually followed the tops of ridges and the course of streams of water; and the house was built on low land, to which a large portion of the farm inclined, so that the gathering in of the crops, always a grave consideration in farm economy, became more than ever a matter of *gravity*. "Everything comes to the house down the hill," they were wont to boast.

The settlers, many of whom had come from the poorer soil of lower Maryland and Virginia, placed no very high estimate of value upon their lands, supposing a few years of culture (and carelessness) would destroy their productiveness. And they were accustomed, from their previous experience, to designate a certain field as good for so many crops, and another sufficient for a certain specified number. The soil, however, was found to exceed their calculations.

Self-reliance, ingenuity, and determined resistance to obstacles, resulted from this state of society. A good degree of mechanical genius was developed. Results properly deemed astonishing, in view of the few rude tools employed, were frequently attained. Doddridge, in his notes of the early settlement of Northwestern Virginia, says that "their ploughs, harrows, with wooden teeth, and sleds, were in many instances well made. Their cooper's ware, which comprehended everything for holding milk and water, was generally pretty well executed. The cedar-ware, by having alternately a white and red stave, was then thought beautiful; many of their puncheon floors were very neat, their joints close, and the tops even and smooth. Their looms, although heavy, did very well." He further says:

"The hominy block and hand mills were in use in most of our houses. The first was made of a large block of wood about three feet long, with an excavation burned in one end, wide at the top and narrow at the bottom, so that the action of the pestle on the bottom threw the corn up to the sides towards the top of it, whence it continually fell down into the centre. In consequence of this movement, the whole mass of the grain was pretty equally subjected to the strokes of the pestle. In the fall of the year, when the Indian corn was soft, the block and pestle did very well for making meal for johnny-cake and mush, but were rather slow when the corn became hard.

"The sweep was sometimes used to lessen the toil of pounding grain into meal. * * * In the Greenbrier county, where they had a number of saltpetre coves, the first settlers made excellent gunpowder by the means of those sweeps and mortars.

"A machine still more simple than the mortar and pestle, was used for making meal, while the corn was too soft to be beaten; it was called a 'grater.' This was a half circular piece of tin, perforated with a punch from the concave side, and nailed by its edges to a block of wood. The ears of corn were rubbed on the rough edges of the holes, while the meal fell through them on the board or block to which the grater was nailed, which, being in a slanting direction, discharged the meal into a cloth or bowl placed for its reception.

"The hand-mill was better than the mortar. It was made of two circular stones, the lowest of which was called the bed stone, the upper one the runner. These were placed in a hoop, with a spout for discharging the meal. A staff was let into a hole in the upper surface of the runner, near the outer edge, and its upper end through a hole in a board fastened to a joist above, so that two persons could be employed in turning the mill at the same time. The grain was put into the opening in the runner by hand.

"Our first water-mills were of that description denominated tub-mills. It consists of a perpendicular shaft, to the lower end of which a horizontal wheel of about four or five feet in diameter is attached; the upper end passes through the bed-stone, and carries the runner after the manner of a trundlehead. These mills were built with very little expense, and many of them answered the purpose very well. Instead of bolting cloths, sifters were in general use. They were made of deerskins, in the state of parchment, stretched over a hoop and perforated with a hot wire.

"Our clothing was all of domestic manufacture. We had no other resource for clothing, and this indeed was a poor one. The crops of flax often failed, and the sheep were destroyed by the wolves. Linsey, which is made of flax and wool — the former the chain, the latter the filling — was the warmest and most substantial cloth we could make. Almost every house contained a loom, and almost every woman was a weaver.

"Every family tanned their own leather. The tan-vat was a large trough sunk to the upper edge in the ground. A quantity of bark was easily obtained every spring in clearing and fencing land. This, after drying, was brought in, and on wet days was shaved and pounded on a block of wood, with an axe or mallet. Ashes were used in place of lime, for taking off the hair. Bear's oil, hog's lard, and tallow, answered the place of fish oil. The leather, to be sure, was coarse; but it was substantially good. The operation of currying was performed with a drawing-knife, with its edge turned after the manner of a currying knife. The blacking for the leather was made of soot and hog's lard.

"Almost every family contained its own tailors and shoemakers. Those who could not make shoes, could make shoepacks. These, like moccasins, were made of a single piece of leather, with the exception of a tongue-piece on the top of the foot. This was about two inches broad, and circular at the lower end. To this the main piece of leather was sewed with a gathering stitch. The seam behind was like that of a moccasin. To the shoe-pack a sole was sometimes added. The women did the tailor work. They could all cut out and make hunting shirts, leggins and drawers."

The pioneers in the settlement of this region were primitive and rude in their manners. In the wildest portions of the State are still to be found modified representatives of those early customs. The social gatherings of those days were reaping-bees, log-rollings, cabin-building, elections, weddings, and funerals. A wedding brought out as much of character in all ages and conditions, and in both sexes, as any social meeting. The groom and attendants, starting from the house of his father, arrived at the bride's residence before noon. The gentlemen were attired in linsey hunting shirts, leggins, leather breeches, moccasins, and shoepacks; the ladies "in linsey petticoats, and linsey or linen bedgowns, coarse shoes, handkerchiefs, and buckskin gloves," with few buckles, rings, buttons, or ruffles, unless they were ancestral relics. The horses were caparisoned with pack-saddles, with a bag or blanket thrown over them, and a rope or leather string as a girth. The march, in double file, of the wedding company, was annoyed by such tricks as tying grapevines across the way, or an ambuscade and discharge of guns, followed by shrieks of the girls, a sudden spring of the horses, and occasionally a resultant accident. The preliminary race for *Black Betty*, or the whiskey bottle, by the young men, should not be omitted in the history. The story is thus told by Doddridge.

"The ceremony of the marriage preceded the dinner, which was a substantial backwoods feast of beef, pork, fowls, and sometimes venison, and bear meat, roasted and boiled with plenty of potatoes, cabbage, and other vegetables. During the dinner the greatest hilarity always prevailed; although the table might be a large slab of timber, hewed out with a broad axe, supported by four sticks, set in auger-holes; and the furniture, some old pewter dishes and plates; the rest, wooden bowls and trenchers; a few pewter spoons, much battered about the edges, were to be seen at some tables. The rest were made of horn. If knives were scarce, the deficiency was made up by the scalping knives, which were carried in sheaths, suspended to the belt of the hunting shirt. Every man carried one of them.

"After dinner the dancing commenced, and generally

lasted till the next morning. The figures of the dances were three and four handed reels, or square sets and jigs. The commencement was always a square form, which was followed by what was called jigging it off; that is, two of the four would single out for a jig, and were followed by the remaining couple. The jigs were often accompanied by what was called cutting out; that is when either of the parties became tired of the dance, on intimation, the place was supplied by some of the company, without any interruption to the dance. In this way the dance was often continued till the musician was heartily tired of his situation. Toward the latter part of the night, if any of the company, through weariness, attempted to conceal themselves for the purpose of sleeping, they were hunted up, paraded on the floor, and the fiddler ordered to play 'Hang out till to-morrow morning.'

"About nine or ten o'clock a deputation of young ladies stole off the bride and put her to bed. In doing this it frequently happened that they had to ascend a ladder, instead of a pair of stairs, leading from the dining and ball room to the loft, the floor of which was made of clap-boards, lying loose. This ascent, one might think would put the bride and attendants to the blush; but the foot of the ladder was commonly behind the door which was purposely left open for the occasion, and its rounds at the inner ends, were well hung with hunting shirts, dresses, and other articles of clothing. The candles being on the opposite side of the house, the exit of the bride was noticed but by few.

"This done a deputation of young men, in like manner, stole off the groom and placed him snugly by the side of his bride. The dance still continued, and if seats happened to be scarce, as was often the case, every young man, when not engaged in the dance, was obliged to offer his lap as a seat for one of the girls, and the offer was sure to be accepted. In the midst of the hilarity, the bride and groom were not forgotten. Pretty late in the night some one would remind the company that the new couple must stand in need of some refreshment; *black Betty*, which was the name of the bottle, was called for, and sent up the ladder; but sometimes black Betty did not go alone. I have many times seen as much bread, beef, pork, and cabbage sent along, as would afford a good meal for half a dozen hungry men. The young couple were compelled to eat and drink, more or less, of whatever was offered.

"But to return. It often happened that some neighbors or relations, not being invited to the wedding, took offense; and the mode of revenge adopted by them on such occasions, was that of cutting off the manes, foretops, and tails of the horses of the wedding company."

The people of West Virginia are departing from the wisdom of the fathers of the early days, when Sir William Berkeley, the proprietor of a large tract in Shenandoah valley, eighty years ago, wrote of the new country as follows: "I thank God there are no free schools nor printing, and I hope we shall not have these hundred years, for learning has brought disobedience and heresy and sects into the world, and printing has divulged them and libels against the best government. God keep us from both." But this departure leads in the direction of a superior wisdom, and a school system has been adopted since the organization of the State, modelled upon the best State systems in the country, the results of which will soon be manifested in general educational improvement.

Schools of a higher grade are beginning to be organized — academies and high schools, and seminaries, for young ladies — and the impetus already given to popular progress in mental culture will soon occasion a further demand for superior educational facilities.

There is awakened throughout the State a spirit of lively interest in the construction of roads and the improvement of river navigation, in new enterprises that develop its varied resources, in all measures essential to its security, and the happiness and thrift of its people, and to their mental and moral advancement.

There is a feeling of relief from an irksome and heavy burden in separation from Virginia, whose malign influence has long rested like a nightmare upon this region. It is manifested in the new impetus given to industry and enterprise, which is already beginning to stimulate immigration, to fill up the ranks decimated by war, and to swell the aggregate of population existing when the last census was taken. The following table will be found useful in future comparisons:

WEST VIRGINIA.

Population of the Counties comprising West Virginia by the Census of 1860.

Counties.	Free.	Slave.	Total.
Barbour	8,863	95	8,958
Berkeley	10,875	1,650	12,525
Boone	4,682	158	4,840
Braxton	4,888	104	4,992
Brooke	5,476	18	5,494
Cabell	7,715	305	8,020
Calhoun	2,493	9	2,502
Clay	1,766	21	1,787
Doddridge	5,169	34	5,203
Fayette	5,726	271	5,997
Gilmer	3,707	52	3,759
Greenbrier	10,686	1,525	12,211
Hampshire	12,700	1,213	13,913
Hancock	4,443	2	4,445
Hardy	8,791	1,073	9,864
Harrison	13,208	582	13,790
Jackson	8,251	55	8,306
Jefferson	10,575	3,960	14,535
Kanawha	13,966	2,184	16,150
Lewis	7,769	230	7,999
Logan	4,790	148	4,938
Marion	12,659	63	12,722
Marshall	12,968	29	12,997
Mason	8,797	376	9,173
Mercer	6,457	362	6,819
Monongalia	12,947	101	13,048
Monroe	9,643	1,114	10,757
Morgan	3,638	94	3,732
McDowell	1,535		1,535
Nicholas	4,473	154	4,627
Ohio	22,322	100	22,422
Pendleton	5,920	244	6,164
Pocahontas	3,706	252	3,958
Preston	13,245	67	13,312
Putnam	5,721	580	6,301
Pleasants	2,930	15	2,945
Raleigh	3,310	57	3,367
Randolph	4,807	183	4,990
Ritchie	6,809	38	6,847
Roane	5,309	72	5,381
Taylor	7,351	112	7,463
Tucker	1,408	20	1,428
Tyler	6,499	18	6,517
Upshur	7,080	212	7,292
Wayne	6,604	143	6,747
Webster	1,552	3	1,555
Wetzel	6,693	10	6,703
Wirt	3,728	23	3,751
Wood	10,870	176	11,046
Wyoming	2,797	64	2,861
Total	358,317	18,371	376,688

CHAPTER III.

LOCATION. — VALUE OF LANDS. — STOCK GROWING. — FERTILITY. — NO WASTE AREAS. — COMPARISON WITH MARYLAND, MINNESOTA, AND NEW HAMPSHIRE.

A MORE central and accessible location could scarcely be pointed out upon the map of the United States; not central in a continental sense, but eminently so as regards the Atlantic seaboard and the area almost encircled by the lakes, the upper Mississippi and Ohio rivers; central as regards the populous cities, the markets of the country. Harper's Ferry, on the extreme east, is but eighty-one miles from Baltimore, one hundred and twelve from Washington by railroad (scarcely half that distance in a direct line), one hundred and seventy-nine from Philadelphia, and two hundred and eighty-six from New York. Wheeling, on the northwestern border, is but one hundred and thirty-seven miles from Cleveland, and four hundred and ninety-one from Chicago. Parkersburg, the terminus on the northwestern Virginia branch of the Baltimore and Ohio railroad, is three hundred and eighty-three miles from Baltimore, five hundred and sixty-eight from New York, five hundred and twenty-two from St. Louis, five hundred and forty-four from Nashville, and two hundred from Cincinnati. It is connected with the tide-water of the Atlantic coast by railroad, eighty-one miles distant. The water communication by the bays and rivers of Maryland and Virginia, is neither appreciated nor improved as it will be in the future, having some of the deepest and largest harbors on the continent. The shore-line of Virginia alone is made fifteen hundred and seventy-one miles by the Coast Survey. The western border of West Virginia lies three hundred miles on the Ohio river, and is in immediate communication by water with the whole Mississippi valley, permitting the exchange of products with the Louisiana planter at his doors; admitting of traffic along the banks of the Missouri in the wilds of Dakota, and allowing side-wheel steamers from the Kanawha to vex the waters of the far-off tributaries of the Upper Mississippi.

The ploughs and automaton harvesters, which will hereafter garner the annual wealth of western prairies, may be transported to all those plains in vessels fabricated by the labor of West Virginia from her own oak and iron, and the metal of those implements may there be mined, the ore heated by adjacent strata of coal, the requisite flux obtained from the same hill, and all compacted into a perfect machine, with timber found growing on the surface, which has been manufactured by a perpetual water-power that leaps the crags of the summit and falls gently into the vale below, meandering towards the Ohio, quiet as the meditative ox that fattens on the sweetest of perennial herbage upon its banks.

Where, in the wide world, lies so broad a network of water communication at the very feet of a State so full of the varied treasures of the forest and of the mine? That such a country, with an elevation above

VALUE OF FARMS.

the malarias of the lowlands, and never rising above the level of corn and sorghum production; within a few hours of the sea, and its treasures and facilities for transit — a land peculiar for its green pastures flowing with milk, for its bright flowers laden with honey, and for its river slopes that promise to run with wine — should lack inhabitants, or the hum of industry, or the show of wealth, is an absurdity of the present and an impossibility of the future.

The farm lands embrace at least four-fifths of the area, amounting to ten million eight hundred and ninety-six thousand three hundred and ninety-four acres, or seventeen thousand and twenty-five square miles, and they averaged in value, by the assessment of 1860, eight dollars and three cents per acre. The State of Virginia, before division, comprised thirty-one million fourteen thousand nine hundred and fifty acres in farm lands, worth eleven dollars and ninety-one cents per acre. In view of their central location, access to eastern markets, and connection with all parts of the Mississippi Valley by river navigation, munificence of forest and field, and greater wealth of minerals beneath, this is cheaper than any lands of similar position and value in the country. With a little improvement in each county, of a character that is an earnest and guarantee of progressive and steady advancement in material development, eight dollars per acre has become twenty, and eighty-seven millions in the aggregate already more than two hundred millions. And such improvements nearly pay for themselves as they are made, leaving fully one hundred millions of dollars, in a very few months, to burden the pockets of the people, who have had the industry and enterprise to make them.

Indeed, it would be difficult to compute with accuracy, in Federal currency, the actual appreciation already attained at the present writing, since the census of 1860. It would amount to tens of millions of dollars in advanced rates at which property is held, much of which is founded upon actual cash purchases within the past year. While this advance is mainly speculative, there is energy and enterprise and skill enough, as well as capital, interested and actually engaged in the development of these valuable resources, to insure a steady and permanent progress of industrial improvement. There is some danger that speculation may drive the farmer and farm laborer to localities valuable for agriculture only, by raising the price of land above a point that can be remunerating to agricultural operations. With proper encouragement to labor, such as enlightened interest must dictate to capital, this result need be neither general nor permanent.

Stock farming has long been profitably carried on in this region. Cattle find abundant pasturage from the first of May to December, often till January; and not unfrequently they are left to shift for themselves through the whole year, coming out of the winter in good condition, if the autumn was favorable for grass, and the snow light. They are rarely, if ever, stabled in winter, but occupy woodland pastures, through which their fodder is scattered from wagons, if the herds are large. Ten, twelve, and sometimes fifteen dollars per head, as profit, rewarded the care of bullocks kept a single

STOCK GROWING.

year (before the rebellion), which were sold to go to the eastern markets, or to the stall feeders of the south branch of the Potomac, and their places made good by the young cattle from the southwestern counties. The mountain range was largely depended on, with its sweet natural grasses, the pea vine, and aromatic shrubbery.

When forest trees and wild grasses are subdued, the blue grass as naturally appears as robins follow the opening spring. Timothy and clover are the seeds sown in cultivation; but they are extirpated in four or five years by the more vigorous blue grass. Many farmers have preferred not to cultivate lands that are well set in this valuable grass, of which two acres are ample to keep a bullock in fine condition, believing it more profitable to depasture than to plough.

Ten years ago a circular was sent out by the Agricultural Division of the Patent Office, inquiring the cost of raising stock in different sections of the country. The cost of a steer three years old was reported to be twenty-five dollars in New York, twenty-four dollars in Ohio, fifteen dollars in Illinois, twelve dollars in Iowa, and but eight dollars in West Virginia. In Arkansas and Texas it was still less, with counterbalancing disadvantages in distance from the best markets. For stock growing in proximity to markets, it is unsurpassed, if not unequalled, by any other State.

The mountain regions are unexcelled as sheep-walks, and are beginning to be improved as such. Preston has nineteen thousand and eighty-four, Monroe twelve thousand two hundred and eighty-eight, Greenbrier sixteen thousand and sixty-seven, Pendleton fourteen thousand one hundred and forty-three. The whole State is waking up to the fact of its peculiar adaptation to this business. Yet it is only a beginning that has been made. The number of sheep already there (four hundred and fifty-three thousand three hundred and thirty-four in 1860) is but a moiety of the number that will at some time contribute their triple munificence of fertilization to the soil, and food and raiment to the people. The mildness of the climate and excellence of mountain pastures, are conditions favoring the production of the best quality of wool. For sweetness and flavor, the mountain mutton of Virginia is deservedly celebrated. The production of fine spring lambs, of Southdown or Cotswold blood, for the markets of eastern cities, would prove here a most profitable business.

General Washington, whose cool judgment, and rare opportunities as a surveyor, gave him the choice of desirable wild lands, early evinced an appreciation of those of the Ohio and Great Kanawha Valleys. He made selections of some of the finest locations upon those rivers, and obtained patents for thirty-two thousand three hundred and seventy-three acres — nine thousand one hundred and fifty-seven on the Ohio, and twenty-three thousand two hundred and sixteen acres on the Great Kanawha, fronting many miles upon the river. A favorite location was the vicinity of the Burning Spring, a few miles above Charleston; another superior tract was a thousand acres on Round Bottom, which he sold to Archibald McClean. As an evidence of the quality of these lands, it may be stated that George Edwards, upon similar lands in the vicinity, near Moundville, sold sufficient hay in 1863 and 1864, in addition to pasturage for his cattle, to make an average of one hundred dollars per acre for his farm — a profit equivalent to its cost.

A Mr. Shultz was reported, a few years since, to have grown, in an interior county, a crop of fine white wheat amounting to three hundred and sixty-eight bushels from eight acres, or forty-six bushels per acre. A little farm of twenty-eight acres, not in the best condition, has yielded, in a single season, four hundred bushels of corn, eighty-six of wheat, twenty-one tons of hay, fifty bushels of oats, one hundred of apples, with pasturage for three cows and a horse. A little farm of thirty acres, a few miles from Parkersburg, occupied by a plain farmer and his wife, last year rewarded its owner with a surplus of nine hundred dollars above expenses and the cost of living, from common culture of field crops and dairying. Instances could be multiplied, showing the profit derived from agriculture in West Virginia. If these statements do not convince the skeptical, let a personal examination be made at any point, and the result will add to the reputation of these mountain lands.

The following statement of a correspondent, C. S. Richardson, of Briarport Mines, in the Kanawha Valley, illustrates the character of the virgin soil:

"Comparatively unknown, and seemingly uncared for, there are extensive tracts of rich and fertile lands in the wilderness, whose capability of productiveness, when developed, would astonish the dwellers in the open country if they were made acquainted with the facts. Isolated from general view through the absence of any roads, the traveller has but little chance of making their acquaintance. The dwellers in these solitudes are not of a very communicative disposition; hence so little is known of their real value. During a series of topographical and geological surveys on the Elk and Coal Rivers, my attention was called to numerous spots that I conceived would make beautiful farms. Gentle slopes, flat-top ridges, and level dells were frequently met with. These were primitive forests, and a stranger to the woodman's axe or the saw of the lumberman. Being interested in the mining resources of Kanawha, and having in view one of its fundamental principles of development—population—I determined to try an experiment to ascertain the truth or fallacy of my ideas. With this end before me, I selected a spot scarcely ever trodden by the foot of man. It is called 'Ginseng Hollow,' and lies between the main Briar Creek (Coal River) and the Davis Creek ridges, in Kanawha. As an inducement to my first pioneer tenant, I offered to let him have fifty acres of land, rent free, for five years, and after he had got his log-house built, fields enclosed, and a road cut for a way out, he should have a lease for twenty-one years at thirty dollars a year rent. I soon found a tenant, and thus far I can report the experiment eminently successful. It has been two years in cultivation. The first year was chiefly devoted to clearing, or rather girdling the trees, fencing, breaking up the ground, and building his house and barn; but, nevertheless, several acres were cultivated, and yielded a very fair crop of corn. Last year, the ground being tolerably well cleared of roots and underbrush, the trial commenced. The summer was unusually dry; scarcely any rain fell for three months; but the soil being new, and a humid atmosphere, which always prevails in the dense woods, keeping the heated air cool, the crops grew vigorously: and when the harvest came, my tenant had the pleasing satisfaction of being able to report he possessed the *finest crop of corn in the district*. Even on our bottom lands there was nothing superior.

"I have since visited another spot, although not quite

KINDS OF TIMBER. 47

so isolated, where similar results were obtained. This small trial shows very conclusively that if immigration is judiciously encouraged, and land-owners induced to be more liberal in their concessions to the industrious laboring classes, thousands of acres of our back forest lands may be brought into a profitable state of cultivation, thus creating a new field to agricultural enterprise, increasing our population, reducing our taxation by distributing its burden over a greater number of contributors, and materially augmenting our nation's wealth, prosperity, and greatness. Many persons will be inclined to remark: 'This is all very well in theory, but in practice will it pay?' Now let us see. These lands, on an average, can be purchased for less than four dollars per acre. Fifty acres, then, cost two hundred dollars. Add five years' interest on this before any rent is received, which is sixty dollars, and forty dollars for miscellaneous expenses, making three hundred dollars. The rent on this, at thirty dollars a-year (which is about half of what is usually asked), produces ten per cent. Now these lands I speak of are mineral lands, and as soon as the country is intersected with railways (which we all hope it soon will be), then every acre in proximity to such lines will be worth from twenty-five to one hundred dollars.

"Of timber we have all the varieties common to our latitude and altitude, but the different kinds of oak, of the finest quality, predominate. Pines are rare, and spruce and hemlock are seldom met with, except near the 'Glades,' or on the borders of our small mountain streams. No country can furnish superior wild cherry; and walnut and butternut abound on our alluvial and richer soils. The magnificent flowering poplar is found in great abundance on our better class of soils, surpassing all our forest trees in magnitude, and is in great request for lumber. We have, also, hickory, ash, sugar maple, and the minor and varied species of timber in ordinary and sufficient supply.

"Our soils run through every grade of fertility, from the argillaceous to the silicious, but a generous loam, with a substratum of clay, slate, or sandstone, predominates. A light stratum of limestone is found near the surface in most sections of the county, varying in thickness from one and a half to four feet; but the great vein before spoken of ranges from forty to sixty feet in thickness, and is of superior quality. Our river bottoms, though limited in extent, are very fertile, which, with much of our higher lands, especially in the central and southern portions of the county, are well adapted to the growth of Indian corn, while every part at all susceptible of cultivation would produce abundantly all the cereals and lighter grains, if treated with fair and liberal cultivation. Even with our present wretched system of culture, our soils yield remunerative crops. Our agriculture has been slightly improved within the few past years, but it is still miserable and exhaustive. But ours is pre-eminently a grazing country, and already much success has rewarded those who have engaged in it. Dairies are springing up and yielding large returns. Sheep husbandry has already enlisted the attention of very many of our citizens, and, although in its infancy, it is probably the most remunerative pursuit of our people. This element of our wealth will undoubtedly, at no distant day, stand pre-eminently above all others, our minerals excepted."

The mountain regions of West Virginia, in the imaginations of strangers conversant with the rocks and crags and general barrenness so often associated with mountains, may seem unworthy of the attention even of farmers. It is a fallacious idea. In many localities, in which a field of level land is unknown, and all is abrupt and almost precipitous, there is no sign of a gully, or evidence of washing visible, or a swamp, or pool of stagnant water, even the bottom of the "sinks," or "devil's punch-bowls," which are hopper-like depressions, sometimes fifty to a hundred feet in depth. Such a region is that of Monroe and Greenbrier, green with luxuriant herbage or umbrageous with heavy forest, with a natural drainage

NO WASTE AREAS.   49

scarcely improvable by art, and exhibiting in a powerful light the great value of thorough drainage, in promotion of health of man and beast, and enhancement in quality and quantity of nature's products.

The absence of unproductive or waste areas is noticed by the most casual traveller through this region; and in this particular there is little difference in the several sections of West Virginia. Steep hillsides, abruptly falling from a giddy height, are smooth as a lawn, and as green. Rocks may diversify the landscape, as a rare exception, but, as an almost universal rule, they repose unseen beneath the surface, and never disfigure the view, or do violence to the economy of nature, or arouse the spleen of the ploughman. A writer in the "Farmer's Library," in 1847, simply tells the truth of a large portion of the new State, in a mention of Monroe county: "Here where not a drop of water lies anywhere on the surface for a moment after it falls, the foot, and the sides, and the tops of hills, over hundreds of acres, whether cleared or in wood — all parts seem alike fertile and verdant. At the top no less than the base does the timothy flourish until eaten out by the yet more nutritious and fattening blue grass, which takes final possession; and such seems to be the nature of all this region — with this distinction, that where the oak is the principal growth, there the land is more gravelly, throws up an undergrowth of wood, and is better adapted to *grain;* while the prevalence of the maple, the buckeye, and walnut, shows more fitness for grass, and, like the blue grass of Kentucky, is clear of undergrowth."

In comparison with the opulent and ancient State

of Maryland, the showing for West Virginia is not altogether a meagre one. The latter State, though less than half as large, has somewhat more of improved land, with a far smaller proportion of unimproved land, and an average valuation of farm lands of thirty dollars and eighteen cents per acre. Maryland produced in 1860, six million one hundred and three thousand four hundred and eighty bushels of wheat, and thirteen million four hundred and forty-four thousand nine hundred and twenty-two bushels of Indian corn; but of live stock and slaughtered animals scarcely larger figures than those of West Virginia are shown — fourteen million six hundred and sixty-seven thousand eight hundred and fifty dollars the value of the former, and two million eight hundred and twenty-one thousand five hundred and ten dollars of the latter.

The area of Minnesota is more than threefold that of West Virginia, but the occupied farm lands were, in 1860, much less, viz., five hundred and fifty-four thousand three hundred and ninety-seven acres of improved, and two million two hundred and twenty-two thousand seven hundred and thirty-four of unimproved, averaging but six dollars and eighty-six cents per acre. The amount of wheat produced was a little less than in West Virginia; there was less than half as much corn, about two-thirds as much butter, little more than one-fourth the value of live stock, and yet almost twice the amount of West Virginia's hay crop is required and produced.

The population of West Virginia is, by the last census, three hundred and seventy-six thousand six hundred and eighty-eight. It thus stands the twenty-seventh State in the order of its population, with

COMPARISON WITH NEW HAMPSHIRE. 51

nine below it namely: New Hampshire, Vermont, Rhode Island, Minnesota, Florida, Delaware, Kansas, Oregon and Nevada.

New Hampshire, the next below in point of numbers of its inhabitants, contains thirty-five to each square mile. West Virginia has sixteen, as nearly as can be calculated in the imperfect condition of her surveys. To realize more fully the present material status of this new member of the family of States, let a comparison be instituted with this older member of the family. It will be found useful, in the future, in illustration of the growth of a region blessed with marvellous resources, when relieved of the incubus of dwarfing and degrading caste, and fairly started in the race of improvement.

	New Hampshire.	West Virginia.
Population	326,073	373,321
Acres of improved land	2,367,039	2,346,137
Acres of unimproved land	1,377,591	8,550,257
Cash value of farms	$69,689,761	$87,525,087
Average value of lands per acre	$18.58	$8.03
Value of farming implements and machinery	$2,682,412	$1,973,158
Horses and mules	41,111	87,536
Cattle	264,067	310,089
Sheep	310,534	453,334
Swine	51,935	327,214
Value of live stock	$10,924,627	$12,382,680
Wool, pounds of	1,160,212	1,073,163
Potatoes, bushels of	4,137,543	746,606
Barley, bushels of	121,103	60,368
Buckwheat, bushels of	89,996	342,518
Wheat, bushels of	238,966	2,302,567
Rye, bushels of	128,248	71,263
Indian corn, bushels of	1,414,628	7,858,647
Oats, bushels of	1,329,213	1,649,090
Orchard products, value of	$557,934	$234,273
Market-garden products, value of	$76,256	$44,299
Butter, pounds of	6,956,764	4,760,779
Cheese, pounds of	2,232,092	131,585
Hay, tons of	642,741	154,136
Home manufactures, value of	$251,013	$502,671
Animals slaughtered, value of	$3,787,500	$2,124,869

Though the area of the Granite State is but forty per cent. of that of West Virginia, the improved land is equal in extent, while the unimproved farm lands are little more than one-seventh as extensive; yet the average cash value in the State so generally improved is but eighteen dollars and fifty-eight cents per acre, against eight dollars and three cents per acre in the State which has but one-fifth of its land under improvement. New Hampshire, has, of live stock, fewer horses and mules, cows and young cattle, sheep and swine, but more working oxen. Her excess of working oxen, of higher value than cows and young cattle, in part offsets the superior numbers of the horses of West Virginia, so that the proximity of the White Mountains to the fine markets of manufacturing cities, and the famed Cambridge market, is really little superior in position to the western slope of the Alleghanies, so accessible to Cincinnati and Louisville on one side, and Baltimore and Washington on the other. New Hampshire has the advantage of quite fifty per cent. in the value of animals slaughtered, but West Virginia can offset something in her sales of horses. With a smaller number of animals to feed, more than four times as much hay is used by New Hampshire farmers; and it is not altogether owing to the consumption of a greater amount of corn in feeding stock that so little hay is used by West Virginia farmers, but it is due to the comparatively short and mild winters, and the abundance of excellent pasturage. This fact adds greatly to the comparative profit of stock-keeping in the new State, and will eventually add to the market value of her broad acres.

INTRINSIC VS. NOMINAL VALUE.

The bushels of corn and wheat, and other grain, plainly point to the fertility of the soil, having been produced by imperfect and slovenly culture, the blemish and disgrace of Southern, Western, and, in fact, of American farm husbandry.

The item of a half million dollars of home manufactures is creditable to the habits of rural simplicity and to the self-reliance of the women of West Virginia.

To show how low an estimate has been made of prospective real estate values, let the valuation be placed on the basis of that of adjoining States — Pennsylvania and Ohio. In intrinsic wealth of soil and minerals combined, aside from the accidents of settlement or position, West Virginia can scarcely be said to be inferior to either. The present farm valuation is eighty-seven million five hundred and twenty-five thousand and eighty-seven dollars. At the Ohio valuation, thirty-two dollars and thirteen cents per acre, it would amount to three hundred and fifty million one hundred and one thousand one hundred and thirty-nine dollars; at the Pennsylvania valuation, thirty-eight dollars and ninety-one cents, it would be four hundred and twenty-three million nine hundred and seventy-eight thousand six hundred and ninety dollars. The impetus given to improvement by inaugurating the policy of voluntary labor, with all of its tendencies to material and moral development, is sufficient to give instantly one hundred millions of dollars additional value to the farming lands of the State.

CHAPTER IV.

CLIMATE. — ALTITUDE. — TEMPERATURE. — RAIN-FALL. — SALUBRITY. — SCENERY.

A STUDY of causes affecting the climatic condition of West Virginia will be found interesting. In its latitude, lying as it does mainly between 37° and 40° north, it is neither suggestive of hyperborean blasts in winter, nor a torrid temperature in summer; of pent-up valleys, blockaded with drifted snow and solid ice for weary months, nor sweltering plains, parching and baking under a brazen sky. It has neither the saturated and leaky canopy that overhangs old England, nor the rainless sky of a California summer, but a pleasant medium, giving a covering of snow in winter just sufficient to protect the grass and grain, a rain-fall in seed-time ample for the proper preparation of the soil, and a diminished supply in gentle showers during the later growth and ripening of vegetation. Its mountains, unlike those of Europe, or the Rocky mountains in the west, do not very materially affect the conditions of climate, except to reduce the temperature in proportion to altitude. There are local differences, to be sure, the result of peculiar position, but the interior valleys of the Alleghanies have nearly the same temperature as the broad slopes on either side, and these opposite slopes scarcely differ in their climatic peculiarities. Unlike the mountains of Europe, however, the

Alleghanies in this latitude have less rain than the plains below.

The average altitude of the highest summits is two thousand five hundred feet in this section of the Alleghany range, increasing southward. The upper valley of the Kanawha, instead of being an arid desert like the Colorado and other elevated plateaus, is luxuriant in verdure, differing comparatively little in humidity and temperature from the Atlantic coast and the Ohio valley in the same latitudes; indeed, the elevation of the Kanawha is but two thousand five hundred feet in southern Virginia near its source, descending more than one hundred miles before it bursts its Alleghanian barrier in Monroe county, West Virginia, where it ranges between eighteen hundred and thirteen hundred feet, thence rapidly falling to little more than six hundred feet at the foot of the falls near the mouth of the Gauley, whence it flows gently, with the slight descent of a few inches to the mile, to the Ohio river. The following table exhibits the elevation of the Alleghanies and their slopes in this section of that great mountain range:

Summit elevations.

Summit in latitude 37½°	2,650 feet.
Summit at crossing of Baltimore and Ohio railroad	2,620 feet.
Western plateau at White Sulphur springs	2,000 feet.
Source of Cheat and Greenbrier rivers	2,400 feet.
Blue Ridge, near Harper's Ferry	1,800 feet.

Elevation of the valley of Virginia.

Near the Potomac	800 feet.
At Covington	902 feet.
At Staunton	1,222 feet.

Elevations west of the mountains.

Cheat river, valleys of western declivity	1,375 feet.
Mouth of the Greenbrier	1,333 feet.
Tygart's valley, lowest within the mountains	1,000 feet.
Ohio river at Pennsylvania line	675 feet.
Ohio river at Kentucky line	550 feet.
Kanawha river at Charleston	600 feet.

The first of these divisions, the summit and table-lands of the Alleghanies, comprises a narrow strip of little more than the average width of the county, and extends from the Alleghanian backbone to the chain of mountains which are really a continuation of the Cumberland range, and known as Cotton Hill, Gauley, Laurel Hill, &c. The valley between these two ranges lies at a level of thirteen hundred and fifty to two thousand feet above the sea; the Greenbrier valley, for instance, for a length of one hundred and fifty miles, having an average elevation of fifteen hundred feet. Much of the cultivated land of Greenbrier county, which is one of the summit counties, lies at a height of eighteen hundred to two thousand feet, and yet ripens corn and sorghum without difficulty, and enjoys a winter climate of great mildness.

The second division includes the valley of Virginia or the Shenandoah valley, averaging, perhaps, fifty miles in width, and extending through the old State of Virginia in a southwestern and northeastern direction. Only the mouth of the valley is embraced in West Virginia. Its average elevation in this section is, perhaps, one thousand feet.

The third section, which may be said practically to represent the elevation of the State, containing at least sixteen thousand square miles, or two-thirds of its entire area, including and almost bounding on the east the great coal basin, lies between the altitudes of six hundred and fifteen hundred feet. The uplands, a few miles from the Ohio, with an elevation differing considerably at different points, may be averaged at eight hundred feet. In the Kanawha valley, below the falls, the river is little more elevated than the Ohio, from Parkersburg to Point Pleasant, but the river bluffs rise precipitously, giving the surrounding country an average of at least one thousand feet for sixty miles, with a considerable increase towards the falls. The average for the entire section is, perhaps, eleven hundred feet. By a comparison with other points in the Mississippi valley, this elevation will not be found to indicate a region particularly mountainous in its altitude:

Bellefontaine summit (highest land in Ohio), 1400 feet.
Hillsboro', Ohio, . . . 1131 feet.
Portsmouth, Ohio (Ohio river), . . 540 feet.
Columbus, Ohio, . . . 762 feet.
Northern Indiana, sources of Maumee, 850 feet.
Prairies of Illinois and Wisconsin, . 950 feet.
Blue Mounds, Southern Wisconsin, . 1640 feet.
Chicago, Illinois, . . . 590 feet.
Central Kentucky, . . 800 feet.
Louisville, Kentucky, . . . 441 feet.
St. Louis, Missouri (Upper), . 480 feet.
Knoxville, Tennessee, . . . 960 feet.
Chattanooga, Tennessee, . . 643 feet.
Huntsville, Alabama, . . . 600 feet.

Thus the greater portion of West Virginia, though appearing so mountainous from the broken character of the surface, is of less elevation than Logan and Hardin counties, in Ohio, which are so level in districts of highest elevation as to present the appearance of swamps, and suggest to the agriculturist the necessity of surface drainage, while the ascent has appeared like a continuous plain from the Ohio river.

The slope of the Alleghanies on the west is more abrupt than on the east, making a rapid descent for the rivers for a short distance, whence their flow is gentle, with grades not unlike those of rivers upon the eastern side of the Ohio, the only essential difference being the greater rapidity of the Alleghanian streams near their sources.

The mean temperature of West Virginia for the year, as may be seen by an examination of the isothermal lines, is lower than any other locality in the same latitude east of the Missouri river. It lies between the lines of fifty degrees and fifty-four degrees, which embrace the southern and central portions of Ohio, Indiana, and Illinois, with contiguous portions of Missouri and Iowa; on the Atlantic, deflecting northward to include the coast line between New York and Baltimore. The isothermal, indicating a mean temperature of fifty-five degrees, passes through Baltimore and Washington, circles round the southern boundary of West Virginia, intersects the northern border of Kentucky, and strikes St. Louis, leaving Philadelphia and Cincinnati a very little north of the line. The line of fifty-two degrees would come very near the centre of West Virginia. This would make the average temperature slightly lower than that of those two cities. The following table, prepared from the Smithsonian record, shows the highest, lowest, and mean temperatures for each month of 1859, of Philadelphia and Cincinnati, with two points on the

Kanawha, one near the top of the Alleghany range, the other nearly on a level with the Ohio river.

Month.	Kanawha county, West Virginia.			Lewisburg, West Virginia.			Philadelphia, Penn'a.			Cincinnati, Ohio.		
	Highest deg.	Lowest deg.	Mean temperature.	Highest deg.	Lowest deg.	Mean temperature.	Highest deg.	Lowest deg.	Mean temperature.	Highest deg.	Lowest deg.	Mean temperature.
January....	62	6	35.14	62	-2	32.55	54	...	30.79	60	7	36.11
February...	66	18	41.69	64	13	38.40	62	20	36.44	68	14	40.32
March......	75	30	51.58	72	30	47.68	70	22	48.12	70	31	50.19
April........	80	31	53.98	85	25	51.96	78	33	50.28	78	31	52.37
May.........	86	48	65.62	82	48	68.03	85	48	64.65	86	54	70.03
June.........	91	42	68.51	90	38	69.93	95	49	70.65	98	52	72.87
July	95	57	74.07	92	50	75.93	95	58	76.00	100	56	79.52
August......	92	52	73.38	92	60	74.33	95	55	74.53	94	54	75.64
September	84	50	65.03	79	34	61.29	81	48	66.18	86	56	68.36
October.....	80	25	50.99	69	20	48.35	80	32	52.32	80	32	54.37
November..	79	20	46.01	70	14	44.23	68	30	47.49	74	20	49.30
December..	76	17	34.97	71	5	33.33	70	11	33.00	68	2	30.18

The lowest monthly points reached average the same in Philadelphia and Kanawha county; the highest monthly temperatures average, for the year, the same in Philadelphia and Greenbrier county, while the average of the lower extremes is less in the latter locality. Kanawha county and Cincinnati show very similar extremes, the former being slightly more moderate in high temperatures, with a still greater depression in low temperatures, giving a pretty wide thermometrical range, though the mean temperature is very nearly the same as that of Cincinnati. As elsewhere in the interior or continental area, or basin of the Mississippi, the extremes are greater than on the coast of lake or ocean. Thus the table above, as might be expected, gives Philadelphia a temperature less liable to extremes.

The following table includes a record of temperature, as furnished by authorities and in periods as follows: Lewisburg, two years (Agricultural Report); Richmond, four years (Darby's U. S.); Washington, thirteen years (Army Meteorological Register); Baltimore, four years (record, Fort McHenry); Philadelphia, thirty-two years (Daily Inquirer); Cincinnati, twenty years (Ray); St. Louis, twenty-eight years (record, Jefferson Barracks).

Period.	Lewisburg, W. Va.	Richmond, Va.	Washington, D. C.	Baltimore, Md.	Philadelphia, Pa.	Cincinnati, Ohio.	St. Louis, Mo.
January	35.4	33.7	34.1	32.8	31.8	33.1	32.6
February	34.2	39.8	36.7	34.2	32.3	34.1	35.1
March	44.4	47.1	45.3	42.3	41.0	43.5	45.1
April	53.8	54.7	55.7	52.7	51.8	54.1	57.1
May	64.9	65.4	66.3	63.1	62.5	63.6	66.3
June	69.0	73.8	74.4	71.6	71.5	71.4	74.1
July	77.1	77.6	78.3	76.7	76.0	76.5	78.0
August	73.9	74.8	76.3	74.7	73.2	74.2	76.4
September	68.8	67.1	67.7	67.8	63.8	66.0	68.1
October	53.5	57.5	56.7	55.7	54.5	53.2	55.7
November	45.0	44.2	44.8	45.1	44.0	42.5	43.1
December	35.4	38.1	37.3	35.6	34.5	33.8	33.8
Spring	54.4	55.7	55.8	52.7	51.8	53.7	56.1
Summer	73.3	75.4	76.3	74.3	73.6	74.0	76.2
Autumn	55.8	56.3	56.4	56.2	54.1	53.9	55.6
Winter	35.0	37.2	36.1	34.2	32.9	33.7	33.8
Year	54.6	56.2	56.1	54.3	53.1	53.8	55.5
Altitude	1800ft.	120ft.	80ft.	10ft.	40ft.	543ft.	472ft.

The mildness of the winter and spring temperature at Lewisburg is remarkable, and must result in part, at least, from the prevalence of southerly and southwesterly winds at that season. It will be seen that the summer temperature is lower than that of any other point named. The purity of the summer air at this point modifies the effects of the heat, and relieves it of sultriness and the depressing influence of a vitiated atmosphere.

The average of the five hottest days in five years, from 1832 to 1836 inclusive, according to the record of J. H. Diss Debar, taken in Doddridge county, very near the geographical and thermal centre of the State, is ninety degrees Fahrenheit, and the average of the coldest days, for the same period, six degrees Fahrenheit.

From the extremely broken character of the surface there are sheltered localities upon which the summer sun must pour a merciless flood of fiery beams, and high plateaus, or elevated slopes, over which the wintry wind must sweep in fury. This very fact of unevenness furnishes a choice of pleasant sites for comfortable residences, of localities for vineyards and orchards, and of a general adaptation of situation to circumstances.

The distribution of rain in West Virginia is admirably calculated, in quantity and seasonableness, to insure success to husbandry and give facility to all its successive operations. The spring opens early, and with its opening come gentle and frequent showers. The summer, with less humidity than any surrounding State, is not subject to long-continued droughts. The grasses spring green and fresh upon the summits of the loftiest mountains during all the summer.

The amount of rain precipitated in West Virginia is from thirty-two to thirty-six inches only, as indicated by partial records kept in different parts of the State, and especially in the vicinity of Lewisburg and the White Sulphur Springs, where the same quantity was indicated on both sides of the Alleghanies. The mean annual rain-fall decreases to some extent southward from Pittsburg, and its minimum quantity is found in summer. No complete record of the rain-fall of localities in West Virginia for a term of years being at hand, it is fair, from partial data at different points, from general statements in Blodgett's Climatology and other works, and from expressed opinions of the most intelligent residents, to take Pittsburg, in Pennsylvania, as a basis of comparison between Western Virginia and other localities, with the balance of authority in favor of a slightly lower figure for the average throughout the State than is given in the following table for that city:

Place.	Spring.	Summer.	Autumn.	Winter.	Year.
Cambridge, Massachusetts	10.85	11.17	12.57	9.89	44.48
New York City	11.69	11.64	9.93	10.39	43.65
Philadelphia, Penn'a.	10.97	12.45	10.07	10.06	43.56
Pittsburg, Penn'a	9.38	9.87	8.23	7.48	34.96
Washington, D. C.	10.45	10.52	10.16	11.07	41.20
Cincinnati, Ohio	12.14	13.70	9.90	11.15	46.89
Hudson, Ohio	9.76	8.87	6.16	8.00	32.79
Milwaukee, Wisconsin	6.60	9.70	6.80	4.30	27.20
St. Louis, Missouri.	12.86	14.09	8.71	6.29	41.95

The only region here shown to be of like humidity is that of the lakes, of which Hudson, Ohio, is a representative. From data believed to be reliable, the Kanawha valley is characterized by a rain-fall almost precisely similar to that of the country bordering upon the Southern and Western shores of Lake Erie.

It would scarcely need the corroboration of sanitary facts to prove the healthfulness of this region. The altitude, the irregularity of surface, the absence of marshy plains, so peculiarly characteristic of West Virginia, would give, in connection with its medium temperature, assurances of health and longevity to her population. The following is an exhibit of the yearly percentage of mortality, for twenty years past, in the different sections of the country:

Place.	1850.	1860.
Mississippi Valley, proper	2.38	1.81
Southern Atlantic coast	1.45	1.34
New England	1.25	1.24
Interior areas	1.19	1.32
Alleghany region	.96	1.08
Northwestern States	1.01	.98
Pacific coast	.92	.95

Thus the sections of greatest salubrity are the Alleghanian, Northwestern, and Pacific; yet, in view of the fact that the Northwest and Pacific are virgin settlements, filled with a youthful and middle-aged population, while the Alleghany region has a homogeneous and home-staying people, we must conclude, if we accept the above percentages as an accurate basis of calculation, that the highlands of the Alleghanies are of equal, if not superior, salubrity.

This mountain range extends nine hundred miles, nearly parallel with the sea-coast, consisting of ridges fifty to one hundred miles apart, and parallel with each other, watered and wooded to their summits, with extensive and fertile valleys between. The Blue Ridge, Alleghany and Cumberland, with many other subdivisions, as North Mountain, Laurel Hill, and Greenbrier, are but parts of the great Alleghany system. That portion of this section embraced in West Virginia, abounds in many a plateau, with an elevation just sufficient to insure a pure and bracing atmosphere, and all conditions essential to vigorous and healthy growth both in animal and vegetable life.

The scenery of West Virginia is worthy of a volume, rather than the fragment of a chapter. Under the influence of so genial a climate that semi-tropical forms of vegetation are almost native to its soil, its flora may safely be presumed to equal, if not to surpass, in variety and magnificence, the wealth of nature in any other State or Continent. In its fauna it is equally distinguished. Birds, beautiful in plumage and sweet in song, give life and grace and cheerfulness to field and forest. The surface is infinite variety. Rills meet in rivulets, and rivulets swiftly swell into rivers, which leap their mountain barriers and quietly subside into the placidity of the plains below. Mountains rise like little Alps on Alps; glades, those meadows of the mountain, freshen the summer atmosphere with delicious coolness; cultivated slopes, as in Greenbrier and other of the older counties, move the imagination as by a wand of enchantment; deep, winding, fertile valleys, lie at the foot of beetling bluffs, full of the fatness of fertility. Everywhere the vision is greeted with variety and beauty. Nature has not only been partial, but prodigal; yet the hand of man is needed to direct and to use this beneficence of benefaction.

European travellers have been enraptured with the ever-varying scenery of the Cheat River region, as seen in a trip by rail; and none have been more impressed by it than those who have climbed the Alps, and viewed with awe their towering heights and darkening depths beneath. It exerts unwonted emotions thus to wind around the steep side of a mountain spur, and emerge from its shadows into a sun-lit slope that falls abruptly away, at the very edge of the car, hundreds of feet, and reveals at the bottom of a long and winding valley, a singularly dark stream, whose chocolate-colored waters contrast while harmonizing with the forest growth that reaches from the golden sunlight of the mountain top down to the river's brink. It is nothing strange that the excited Frenchman should exclaim at the prospect, as one is said to have done ; "*Magnifique! Zere is nossing like zis in France!*" The sturdiness of the forests — the hardy vigor of all vegetable life — the munificence of all visible nature, impress the traveller accustomed to see bare rocks and stinted vegetation amid mountain scenery. There is nothing of poverty suggested, and no intimation of sterility; few jutting crags are seen, unless hewn out of the mountain side in cutting the wild pathway of the railroad; and no rough rocks, piled heap upon heap, offend the eye as it sweeps the gracefully rounded knobs.

This is the general character of the mountain scenery of West Virginia. Abrupt and broken as the surface appears, there is scarcely more of waste area than there is on a western prairie. No plough indeed may vex the virgin soil; it may even be too steep for pasturage, except by the sheep or sure-footed goat; but let a tornado sweep away the kings of the forest, and in their place prolific nature will send forth rank grasses and wildwood flowers. Lonely as the vast reaches of woodland appear, and bold and varied as is the contour of the mountain-face, there is always present the suggestion that every acre is habitable—that the hand of art may heighten the beauties and soften the few asperities of the scene.

The traveller pursues his westward way down the Alleghanian slope, through scenery similar in its type, but slowly and continually modifying, till it becomes noticeable only as a hilly, fruitful country, divided into farms naturally suited to the diverse uses of meadow, pasturage, and tillage, and watered with frequent and rapid streams.

In the eastern section of the State, the lower Shenandoah valley presents views of greater beauty, with less of wildness and grandeur. More than a hundred miles, between Harper's Ferry and Cumberland, the Potomac, "a flashing thread of silver," runs out a winding boundary between Maryland and West Virginia; and the neighboring meadows, and wheat-fields, and golden-fruited orchards, and wild forests, make graceful pictures of rural realities and possibilities that touch the heart while they delight the eye.

The scenery of West Virginia is worthy of the highest efforts of the painter and the poet. Its "Hawk's Nest" mountain a thousand feet in almost perpendicular height; its "Hanging Rocks," leaning over the perpendicular, like the tower of Pisa, five hundred feet from the surface; its "Lost River," burrowing in the earth, and "revisiting the glimpses of the moon" in numerous outlets miles away; its caves, and falls, and Indian mounds;—these, and many other peculiar features of her landscape, are worthy of more accurate delineation. This scenery, said the historian Bancroft, a few years ago, "has a character of grandeur of its own; and in the wonderful varieties of forest and lawn, of river and mountain, of nature in her savage wildness and nature in her loveliest forms, presents a series of pictures which no well educated American should leave unvisited. We cross the Atlantic in quest of attractive scenes; and lo! we have at home, along side of the great central iron pathway, views that excel anything that can be seen among the mountains of Scotland, or in the passes of the Apennines;" and had the writer visited the beautiful valley of the Great Kanawha, his rapture, with no danger of abatement, might have warmed into a still brighter glow.

CHAPTER V.

TOPOGRAPHY AND STATISTICS OF COUNTIES. — THE VALLEY GROUP.

IT is proposed to take a cursory view of the several counties comprising the State, grouped in natural divisions, with a glance at the topography and statistics of each section. A few isolated, representative facts, happening together, as by accident, will answer instead of a description, which would fill a volume in itself, were a connected and complete statement of the more interesting features of each county attempted. The figures are those of the census of 1860.

The lower part of the valley of Virginia, from Harper's Ferry west to the summit of the Alleghanies, embracing the counties of Jefferson, Berkeley, Morgan, Hampshire, Hardy, and Pendleton, is included in West Virginia. For the variety and fertility of its soils, fine water-power, central position, salubrious and delightful climate, beauty and grandeur of scenery in plain and on mountain, it can literally, and with severity of truth, be said to be unsurpassed, if equalled, in the United States; or as a farming region in which to make homes of comfort, opulence, and refinement.

This district is a little more than three thousand

seven hundred square miles in extent, and is bounded on the east by the Shenandoah, and on the north and northwest by the Potomac and its north branch. The eastern front ridge of the Alleghanies is near the western boundary; Hampshire, Hardy, and Pendleton are intersected by parallel ridges and valleys of the Alleghany range; the Branch Mountain range extends in a similar direction, and the North Mountain forms the eastern boundary of Hardy County.

The valley is mainly of a limestone formation, with some sandstone and patches of red and black slate. The Opequon runs through a narrow strip of slate soil, of inferior fertility to the fine limestone region on either side of it, in Jefferson and Berkeley. These counties, it has been said, "contain a greater portion of fertile lands than any other section of the State." The surface of the mouth of the valley between the Blue Ridge and Little North Mountain was originally a broad rolling prairie, with fringes of timber on water-courses. Some portions of this district towards the mountains contain a proportion of what is termed "liver soil" by the farmers, productive in wheat and grasses. The South Branch Valley has a soil noted for its fertility, its superior wheat, and the perennial freshness and succulence of its summer verdure. The markets of Baltimore and Washington and the stock-dealers of Maryland and Virginia attest the fatness and the flavor of stock reared and fattened in this mountain valley.

The valley lands of this section, in various locations and states of improvement, have commanded from thirty to one hundred and fifty dollars per acre; highlands under cultivation, from five to fifty dollars; wild lands, from twenty-five cents to ten dollars per acre. The highlands are in high esteem as sheep farms, and have contributed much in this branch of husbandry to the wealth of this region.

Jefferson County, bordering on the Potomac, is intersected by the Shenandoah, which debouches into the Potomac at Harper's Ferry, where the united streams burst the barriers of the Blue Ridge, creating a landscape so remarkable that it was deemed by Jefferson "one of the most stupendous scenes in nature," "worth a voyage across the Atlantic." The county-seat is Charlestown, memorable as the place of execution of John Brown, of Ossawattomie. Harper's Ferry, its principal town, was the site of the United States Arsenal which was destroyed at the beginning of the war, and was alternately, for three years, a foot-ball for the National and Rebel forces. It has been nearly destroyed in the strife.

The soil of this county is of remarkable fertility, a fine limestone prairie, in a high state of improvement. More desirable farming land is scarcely to be found in the United States.

Berkeley County was formed in 1772. Its surface is much broken, but the soil is fertile, especially upon the banks of the Potomac River and Back and Opequon Creeks, which drain the county. Coal is found in the western part of the county. Martinsburg, the county-seat, has suffered severely during the rebellion by frequent changes of military masters, and by wholesale destruction and plundering by Rebel armies.

Many of the settlers of this county were Scotch-Irish Presbyterians. As early as 1754, a community of Baptists emigrated from New England and established a church at Opequon, under charge of Rev. John Gerard.

Colonel Crawford, leader of expeditions against the Indians (in one of which he was captured and barbarously burned alive, in western Ohio), emigrated from this county to Pennsylvania in 1768. Felix Grundy, of political note, was also born in this county, in a log house on Sleepy Creek.

Morgan County borders on the Potomac, and is intersected by the Cacapon River. It was organized in 1820, and named in honor of General Daniel Morgan, of revolutionary memory. It is mountainous, and possesses both coal and iron. It is the smallest of the counties of this group, and the least improved, with the exception of Pendleton. In this county, two and a half miles from St. John's Run, on the Baltimore and Ohio Railroad, and thirty-six miles from Winchester, are the Berkeley Mineral Springs, much frequented, as they have been since the days of 1777, when Generals Washington and Gates, and Charles Carroll, of Carrollton, attested their virtues, and built cottages there for summer residence. Twelve hundred gallons per minute are said to flow through the bath-rooms of the present establishment. The baths are much celebrated from their character and quantity and agreeable temperature (74°), and the scenery around is highly picturesque. The 'Maryland Gazette,' in 1784, said of it: "In Berkeley County five bathing-houses, with adjacent dressing-rooms, are nearly completed. An assembly-room and theatre are also constructed for the innocent and rational amusements of the polite who assemble there." Near these springs is a fountain of chalybeate waters, which stimulate like strong tea.

Hampshire is a large county, containing five hundred and forty-nine thousand three hundred and thirty acres of farm lands, of which one hundred and seventy-two thousand six hundred and ninety are improved. Almost four millions of dollars are represented as the total assessed valuation of farms, and a much larger sum could be obtained for them at the present time. Of all the counties of West Virginia, Hampshire heads the list for precedence in horses, cows, corn, buckwheat, butter, and farm implements.

In Hampshire County are the medicinal waters known to travellers as the Capon Springs, four miles from the Cacapon River, on the west side of the North Mountain. The Shannondale Springs, near the Shenandoah River, a few miles above Harper's Ferry, have been celebrated for their efficacy in scorbutic affections. Several ebbing and flowing springs exist in this region, and a subterranean river, an affluent of the Shenandoah, is said to furnish a winter resort for millions of the finny tribe, multitudes being caught in fall and spring as they enter and return.

Ice Mountain, in Hampshire, twenty-six miles northwest from Winchester, is another natural curiosity worthy of mention. At the western base of the mountain, which is here some seven hundred feet high and very precipitous, is an area of one hundred yards in length, and a breadth of thirty feet up the mountain side, covered with loose rocks, under which, at all seasons of the year, blocks of ice of several pounds weight may be found. Snakes passing over the rocks stiffen and die, and flies perish in the same way. Butter or fresh meats are preserved here almost indefinitely. At the base of this bed of ice flows forth a spring of intensely cold water; and yet these rocks are exposed to the rays of the sun after nine o'clock in the morning.

An explanation of this phenomenon has been given by C. B. Hayden, in 'Silliman's Journal:' "The solution I conceive is to be found in the large and unusual collection of rocks, which, from their porous homogeneous texture, are extremely poor conductors of heat. One side of the mountain consists of a massive wall many hundred feet in thickness, and heaped up against this, as an abutment, is a mass of rocks containing many thousand cubic feet. As the mountain has a general direction from northeast to southwest, the talus heap containing the ice has a northwest exposure. The cavernous nature of this heap would admit the free entrance of atmospheric waters, which during the winter would form ice in the interior of the mass. The ice thus situated would be protected from external heat by the surrounding rocks, as ice in a refrigerator is isolated and protected from the external temperature, by the non-conducting sides of the refrigerator." Thus the Ice Mountain is simply a huge sandstone refrigerator, so large that one deposit of ice suffices for the entire season.

Caudy Castle, a cone-like elevation five hundred

feet high — the retreat of an early settler fleeing from the Indians — is a bluff of the Capon River.

The Tea-Table, a few miles east of the Capon, is a solid rock, four feet in height, resembling a man's hat standing on its crown, and from its top issues a clear stream of water.

The Hanging Rocks near Romney, four hundred feet high, are notable curiosities.

Pendleton, the most southerly of these counties, is very mountainous, having a mean elevation of two thousand feet above the sea level. Its unimproved lands amount to two hundred and twenty thousand, six hundred and forty-two acres; improved, eighty-one thousand, one hundred and eighty-four acres. Of horses, it numbers two thousand five hundred and forty-three; milch cows, three thousand four hundred and twenty-three; other cattle, six thousand three hundred and eighty-three; sheep, fourteen thousand one hundred and forty-three; swine, five thousand seven hundred and forty-four; value of farm stock, three hundred and seventy-one thousand, two hundred and twenty-eight dollars; value of slaughtered animals, forty-five thousand three hundred and nineteen dollars — a fair show of stock for so small an area of improved land. To keep it during the winter, but four thousand one hundred and sixty-five tons of hay are reported, or little more than three hundred weight to each animal requiring it. This result is in part due to the mildness of the climate, which admits of winter pasturage, especially to sheep, that are always able to find their living in the forests; and may be partially attributed to the custom of buying and feeding stock from the counties during the summer months.

The natural features of Pendleton are among the most varied and striking to be noticed in any portion of West Virginia. North Mountain is on its southeastern boundary, and Jackson Mountain intersects it. The north and south forks of the south branch of the Potomac, and the south branch itself, drain this country, and afford some fine alluvial soil for corn and wheat and the most luxurious pasturage. The mountains are covered with the densest timber. Besides the north and south branches, this section is drained by the Cacapon and Lost River. The Opequon forms the southeastern boundary of Berkeley county. Lost River is one of the wonders of nature. After coursing through a fertile valley for twenty-five miles, it breaks through the Lost River Mountain and bursts the barriers of Timber Ridge, and then encounters a new obstacle in Sandy Ridge, which it passes by a curious piece of fluvial strategy, mining its way among the loose rocks of the underlying strata, but loses itself in its subterranean meanderings of three miles, coming to the light again rather in the capacity of strong springs, than as the powerful current of a river which has lost its way, to become anew the sources of a considerable stream—the Cacapon.

Hardy was detached from Hampshire, and became a separate county in 1786. It was named for Samuel Hardy, a member of Congress of that period. The surface is rugged and rough; a portion of the soil is sterile, but the valleys are granaries and depots of live stock—especially the South Branch valley.

The Regurgitory Spring is one of the natural curiosities of this county. It is on the summit of a mountain, a few miles from Petersburg; ebbs and flows every two hours; emits a noise when rising like the gurgling of liquor from a bung-hole, and falls till the water entirely disappears at the end of two hours' depression.

The Devil's Garden is a strip of ground between two ranges of mountains, rising gradually about three miles, and terminating in an isolated pile of rock five hundred feet high, on the face of which is the profile of a grim figure overlooking with frowning aspect the savage scene.

The soil of Frederick county (which may be included in West Virginia, with the consent of her voters), is productive; an area of sixty thousand to sixty-five thousand acres is limestone divided into farms of two to three hundred acres, worth in former years from thirty-five to fifty dollars per acre. It is a well watered region, almost every farm having its springs and streams, which preserve their flow with great constancy and little diminution in the lapse of time. Lime has long been applied, even to a limestone soil, with great benefit. It has, until recently, been purchased at twelve and a half cents per bushel for agricultural purposes.

STATISTICS OF THE VALLEY.

Table of farm lands and farm stock in the valley counties in 1860.

Counties.	Acres of improved lands.	Acres of unimproved lands.	Price per acre.	Value of farms.	Value of farm implements.	Number of sheep.	Value of live stock.
Jefferson...	85,735	24,348	$51.84	$5,652,143	$119,176	7,269	$466,168
Berkeley...	90,892	41,231	26.84	3,547,566	79,976	7,057	336,757
Morgan....	27,147	48,116	6.37	479,987	27,931	2,992	111,439
Hampshire	172,690	376,640	7.18	3,947,900	166,316	21,287	763,454
Hardy......	85,564	200,927	9.00	2,579,581	57,753	11,378	453,768
Pendleton	81,184	220,642	5.32	1,606,532	47,838	14,143	371,228
	543,212	911,904	$12.24	$17,813,709	$498,990	64,126	2,501,814

Table of farm products.

Counties.	Bushels of wheat.	Bushels of rye.	Bushels of oats.	Bushels of Indian corn.	Tons of hay.	Pounds of butter.	Value of slaughtered animals.
Jefferson	422,514	15,198	54,798	358,267	6.259	131,684	$110,221
Berkeley	237,576	18,672	76,176	275,525	8,031	160,069	93,555
Morgan	19,404	16,082	10,122	47,575	1,576	61,152	21,325
Hampshire ...	106,310	75,257	49,259	375,090	11,366	239,360	109,834
Hardy..........	39,946	28,043	20,200	286,618	4,688	102,603	71,698
Pendleton	11,475	11,927	16,516	122,997	4,165	101,838	45,319
	837,235	165,179	227,071	1,466,072	36,085	796,706	$451,952

This exhibit indicates what may be done for West Virginia by immigration, facilities for intercommunication, and development of her resources of forest, soil, minerals, and water-power. A portion of this territory is more precipitous and rough than the country west of the mountains; very little is richer in soil than the arable lands of the State generally; and yet the whole tract, to the summit of the Alleghanies, is valued at twelve dollars twenty-four cents per acre. Jefferson County, with an average of fifty-one dollars thirty-four cents per acre for farming lands, almost double the average for the State of Ohio, illustrates well the market value of a central position, contiguous to great markets, over the richest prairies thousands of miles away.

With two and a half millions of dollars in live stock, nearly half a million dollars yearly in butchers' meat, almost a million pounds of butter, three millions of bushels of grain of all sorts, little less than two hundred thousand pounds of wool, and other wealth of the farm in like proportion, in six small counties, let it not be said that West Virginia is a poor locality in which to find a rural home.

CHAPTER VI.

SURVEY OF COUNTIES CONTINUED.—THE MOUNTAIN GROUP.

THE mountain section proper has an elevation from thirteen hundred to two thousand five hundred feet above the sea level, including Preston, Tucker, Randolph, Hardy, Pendleton, Pocahontas, Greenbrier, and Monroe counties. Those north of Greenbrier and west of the summit of the main ridge may appropriately be considered together. They are covered with heavy timber, with isolated patches of improved land, including but two hundred and twenty-six thousand six hundred and thirty-two acres in the four counties. Springs are abundant, though comparatively scanty in summer, and fall abruptly over precipitous ledges near their sources, and expand into quiet rivers, with occasional rapids in the lower valleys, forming valuable mill-seats.

The soil is excellent for grasses, much of it containing a good admixture of clay. With indifferent culture it produces from thirty to fifty bushels per acre of corn; in some cases a much larger yield. Wheat usually gives fifteen to twenty bushels. But the greatest value exists beneath the soil, in iron and bituminous coal, and other minerals.

High among the western ridges of the Alleghanies, south of the Cheat Mountains, and between the

Alleghanian backbone on one side and the Black and Droop Mountains on the other, lies Pocahontas County, seventy-six miles in length by seventeen to twenty in breadth. The mountain springs of this elevated region contribute to swell the waters of the James, Potomac, Mengetia, Elk, and New Rivers, while the Greenbrier flows through the entire length of the county, at certain points through a beautiful valley.

In their rough mountain heights, remote from railroads and navigable rivers, dwell three thousand nine hundred and fifty-eight hardy mountaineers, occupying eight hundred and twenty-eight thousand nine hundred and twenty-one acres in farms (less than ten per cent. improved), worth two million fifty-one thousand seven hundred and eighty dollars. Sheep husbandry flourishes here (numbering ten thousand three hundred and thirty-eight animals, producing twenty-three thousand and forty-one pounds of wool), and cattle abound. The total value of live stock is three hundred and twenty-eight thousand and two dollars. The production of one hundred and twenty-one thousand three hundred and ten pounds of butter and six thousand two hundred and twenty-five pounds of cheese, in addition to liberal supplies of milk for prolific households, indicates no mean capacity for dairying. Of Indian corn the product is forty-eight thousand two hundred and twenty-nine bushels; rye, ten thousand seven hundred and seventy-eight bushels; wheat, eight thousand nine hundred and thirty-three bushels; flax fibre for the supply of the old spinning wheels, one thousand six hundred and eighty-four pounds;

and of home-made sweets, sixty-five thousand seven hundred and twenty-five pounds maple sugar, two thousand five hundred and fifty-nine gallons molasses, and eight hundred and sixty-six pounds of honey. The value of their animals slaughtered is forty-one thousand five hundred and fifty-four dollars; of their home manufactures, fourteen thousand eight hundred and forty-six dollars. These few figures are given merely to show that the Alleghany mountain tops, among the most remote and inaccessible portions of West Virginia, may and do contain the homes of comfort and plenty, and sturdy independence.

The mineral resources of Pocahontas are valuable. Iron ore is found, said to produce eighty-three per cent. of pure metal; and lead, copper, and silver exist. Coal crops out along the ranges of mountains on the western boundary, which is the eastern border of the great coal basin.

The heavy and valuable timber of this region, and abundant water-power everywhere at hand, will at some time combine to add materially to the wealth of this mountain region.

Randolph is the next county north, upon the western declivity of the Alleghanies. It is still large, though its former proportions are much reduced, having now, in farms, forty-eight thousand two hundred and forty-nine acres improved, and two hundred and seventy-eight thousand and eighty-three unimproved, with a population of a little less than five thousand. It has, of course, immense tracts of wild lands not included in farms. The soil is productive in grasses, and the few patches in cultivation support eight thousand one hundred and three cattle, and seven thousand five hundred and sixty-five sheep. The live stock is valued at two hundred and forty-four thousand eight hundred and fifty-seven dollars. Of maize. there is produced fifty-five thousand two hundred and twenty-five bushels, twenty thousand two hundred and forty-eight bushels of oats, besides wheat, rye, potatoes, &c.; of maple sugar, forty-three thousand six hundred and ninety-two pounds, and one thousand three hundred and fifty-one gallons molasses, and one thousand three hundred and seventy pounds of honey.

The headwaters of the Cheat and Tygart's Valley Rivers drain this county. The valleys produce good wheat and corn, and the mountains make fine pasturage to their summits when denuded of their heavy timber. Coal, iron, and limestone are abundant, and other minerals exist.

Tucker County lies between Randolph and Preston, south of the Baltimore and Ohio Railroad; has a small area, containing farm lands, eleven thousand one hundred and one acres improved, and forty-three thousand five hundred and fifty-nine unimproved, with but four hundred and forty-eight houses, and producing nineteen thousand nine hundred and fifty-five bushels of corn, six thousand and forty-nine of oats, four thousand three hundred and forty-six of potatoes (and even a few sweet potatoes), two thousand four hundred and eighty-three pounds of honey, and other products in proportion.

Preston, the most northern of these mountain counties, wild and mountainous as it is, and undeveloped in its vast mineral resources, still shows from slight beginnings of improvement made in the last

PRESTON COUNTY.   83

few years and the recent opening of railroad communication through its borders, what comfort and beauty and wealth will one day be added, by labor and skill and enterprise, to the wild attractions of these highlands. Let the reader compare the facts of its progress and production with the exhibit made by other mountain counties equally favored by nature.

The population is thirteen thousand three hundred and twelve. It has ninety-two thousand six hundred and sixty-three acres of improved land in farms, and one hundred and ninety-five thousand three hundred and fifty-one of unimproved, worth two million two hundred and fifty-seven thousand three hundred and fourteen dollars — nearly eight dollars per acre. Its flocks number nineteen thousand and eighty-four sheep; cattle, eleven thousand four hundred and thirty; horses and mules, three thousand three hundred and sixty-seven; animals slaughtered yearly, eighty thousand four hundred and seven dollars; wool, forty-seven thousand four hundred and ninety-three pounds; butter, three hundred and forty thousand nine hundred and eighty-eight pounds; cheese, nine thousand one hundred and forty-two pounds; and value of live stock, four hundred and sixty-one thousand one hundred and thirty-three dollars. With all these twenty-three thousand domestic animals, so mild is the winter of these mountain valleys that but five thousand three hundred and eight tons of hay are cut, and one hundred and four thousand three hundred and seventeen bushels of oats harvested. Of corn there is produced seventy-one thousand and sixty-three bushels; wheat, eight thousand nine hundred and thirty-three bushels; rye, ten thousand seven hundred and seventy-eight bushels; potatoes, forty-four thousand six hundred and fifty-five bushels; and buckwheat, ninety-five thousand three hundred and fifty-seven bushels. Flax is grown to the extent of five thousand three hundred and fifty-five pounds of lint; maple sugar, sixteen thousand seven hundred and twenty-three pounds; honey, fifteen thousand four hundred and seventy-four pounds; maple molasses, one thousand seven hundred and twenty-one gallons; and (strange as it may seem for mountain regions) sorghum syrup, five hundred and thirty-nine gallons.

With abundant water-power, there is as yet little manufacturing done. There are four small woollen factories, several shops for the manufacture of "shooks" (stuff for barrel staves), tanneries, &c.

The following extract from correspondence with H. Hagans, of Brandonville, in Preston County, well illustrates its resources:

"Preston County, geographically, lies in the right-angle formed by the Maryland and Pennsylvania lines, and is several miles west of the main Alleghany range, though east of, and bounded on the west by, Laurel Hill, the most western member of the great Apalachian chain. The county has an average width, from east to west, of twenty miles, and is traversed by Cheat River from its south end north some twenty miles to the mouth of Muddy Creek, within fifteen miles of the Pennsylvania line, where it deflects to the northwest, forcing its way through lofty hills, and Laurel Hill itself, and debouches into the Monongahela just within the limits of Pennsylvania. Sandy Creek, rising in Pennsylvania, east of Laurel Hill, takes a southerly course, and joins Cheat River before that stream passes through the mountain. Thus, Preston County is chiefly included in a basin, bounded on the west by Laurel Hill, and by a coterminous range on the east, called Briery Mountain, which mountain, however, runs several miles west of, and nearly laterally with, the Maryland line, and the space between the said line and mountain is occupied chiefly by a part of the region called the 'Yough Glades.'

"Although our county lies principally in a basin, it is for more than two-thirds of its length, from north to south, geologically more elevated than the mountains on either side, which is shown by the eastern declination of the great limestone vein which crops out on the west, at the crest of Laurel Hill, and the western declination of the same stratum cropping out at the crest of Briery Mountain on the east, other rocks and minerals conforming substantially thereto. A fine illustration and proof of this fact is afforded where Cheat River cuts its way through Laurel Hill. In the centre of this rugged passway, this great calcareous stratum is seen eight hundred feet above the troubled river, and, travelling up the struggling stream, it declines eastward at the rate of about two and a half degrees, and at a short distance below the mouth of Muddy Creek, where the river has made its course northwest, the limestone plunges under the river bed, and is seen no more until it rises and makes its eastern out-crop, as above stated. Above this great limestone seam are found nearly all our minerals —that is to say, a six, a four, an eight feet, and some minor seams of bituminous coal, all of which, however, vary in thickness, as well as in quality, in different localities. In the southern section of the county, and especially at Tunnelton and Newburg, on the Baltimore and Ohio Railroad, and its vicinity, has our mineral coal wealth been most developed, as well as its superior quality, yielding, as is proved by analysis, about ten thousand cubic feet of gas per ton of two thousand two hundred and forty pounds. The seams worked at these localities are from six to eleven feet in thickness, and the same are found to range through all these neighborhoods.

"Our whole county is underlaid by these bituminous seams, though in most parts eight feet is the heaviest vein that has yet been developed. Cannel coal has also been found, and manufactured to some extent into oil.

"Interspersed with our coal measures are corresponding veins of iron ore, of nearly all the varieties and forms of the hematite class found in the Alleghany range. These ores are diffused, more or less, through every farm in the county, and are found in many localities in strata, pure or intermingled, ranging from one to four feet in thickness, and yielding about thirty-three per cent. iron. But little attention has been hitherto bestowed upon this great and indispensable element of our wealth. The see-saw policy that has resulted from the prevalence of antagonistic parties has at one time encouraged, and at another discouraged, enterprise in the manufacture of iron, and finally ruined thousands who had engaged in it These are among the reasons why our rich iron ores have not been better developed and turned into the great channels of commerce. I believe but four blast furnaces have ever been built in the county. Two of them, many years since, near the northern section, and distant from water transportation, have fallen into dilapidation. Two others have been erected about eight years, and are now in successful operation — one near Independence, on the Baltimore and Ohio Railroad, with hot blast, producing some seventy tons per week; the other on Muddy Creek, near Cheat River, cold blast, capable of producing forty to fifty tons per week. These are moderate sized half-stacks, supplied with inexhaustible beds of rich ores, and all the elements for the manufacture of iron in close proximity. Though on a small scale, these two furnaces prove the richness of our ores, as the ore at Muddy Creek produces one ton of good foundry iron from two tons of roasted ore, and I believe the other yields nearly the same. Such establishments, and more extensive ones, might be multiplied indefinitely through the county. I have no doubt that there are some locations in other parts of our great country more favored with means of transportation or proximity to a ready market than is this, but such fortunate places are generally occupied, while we have abundance of the best elements of iron yet inviting the hand of industry and enterprise."

CHAPTER VII.

SURVEY OF COUNTIES CONTINUED.—THE "PANHANDLE."

THE little point upon the northwestern boundary, entering as a wedge between the Keystone and Buckeye States, is regarded with wonder by casual map observers, who cannot account for so strange a freak in surveying, yet it is easily accounted for when it is recollected that Virginia once owned the territory west of Pennsylvania and north of the Ohio River, and that that river became the line between Virginia and Ohio, leaving the four small counties, Marshall, Ohio, Brooke, and Hancock, between Pennsylvania and Ohio. They comprise little more than the area of an average county, and contain one hundred and sixty-nine thousand six hundred and twenty-six acres of improved land, and one hundred and eleven thousand five hundred and thirteen unimproved, or two hundred and eighty-one thousand one hundred and thirty-nine in farm lands, valued at nine million eighty-eight thousand and seventy-seven dollars, or thirty-two dollars fourteen cents per acre. Marshall, the largest, averages twenty dollars forty-six cents; Ohio, forty-four dollars seventeen cents; Brooke, forty-four dollars eleven cents; and Hancock, thirty-four dollars twelve cents.

From these figures it may be seen that this region, so broken and irregular in surface, may become, through the agency of intelligent and persistent labor, a blooming and fruitful garden.

Marshall County, named in honor of Chief Justice Marshall, has a river front of thirty miles, and an eastern border of twenty miles on the Pennsylvania line. With the Ohio bottoms, and those upon small local tributaries, Fishing and Grave Creeks, the county has a fair share of alluvial soil, much of which is very productive, yielding eighty to one hundred bushels of corn under judicious and careful culture. It was here that William Alexander, a few years since, produced two hundred and eighty-eight bushels of corn upon two acres, for which he received a premium. One field to which the attention of the writer has been directed, has been in cultivation in corn for sixty consecutive years, without manuring, and the yield has been reduced to twenty bushels by the gradual depletion of the soil. One of the old-line farmers here gives as the accustomed system of husbandry, a twenty-one years' course, namely, twenty years in corn, and a *rest* of one year in wheat, to be followed by twenty years in corn again.

The uplands, which are slopes of hills and small valleys, with comparatively little of level land, are very rich, as is indicated by an abundant production of cereals and grasses, and exports of stock, corn, wheat, and fruit, especially apples. Good crops of potatoes are usually secured, variable in quality, with soil, season, and culture, from fifty bushels upwards, a yield of eight hundred bushels per acre having been known, and even one thousand bushels of the large reds.

Excellent crops of wheat are usually obtained.

James Burley, State Senator, has secured forty bushels per acre, and others have had similar success, while the usual average is about the same as for the State of Ohio, scarcely more than a third of that quantity. Oats and barley do very well, and good meadows produce from two to three tons of dry hay per acre.

Farmers formerly threw their manure into the river; they are now learning something of its value, and are beginning to husband carefully their resources of fertilization. As a means of enhancing fertility, the value of sheep is beginning to be appreciated. An instance may be given of an old field grown up in briers, which, with no other manure than the droppings of sheep, aided a little by the folding of mules, gave a return of one hundred bushels per acre.

This county forms the junction of the "Panhandle" with the great Virginian pan itself, and partakes largely of its characteristics, a diversified surface, slopes sometimes gentle and sometimes abrupt, alluvial formations in valleys, and a soil of more than average general fertility, whether in valley or upland.

The mammoth Indian mound at Moundsville, twelve miles below Wheeling, near the mouth of Grave Creek is one of the most interesting of the monuments which a former race has left to perpetuate the fact of their existence. It is sixty-nine feet high, and nine hundred in circumference at its base, surmounted by a flat surface of fifty feet in diameter. An oak, seventy feet high, within the past generation, died of old age upon its summit, one hundred years old. A Mr. Tomlinson, in 1838, pierced the mound horizontally one hundred and eleven feet, and discovered a vault twelve feet long, eight feet wide, and seven feet high, in which were found two skeletons. A second vault was discovered above the first, in which were numerous ivory beads, copper bracelets, and another skeleton. The interior of the mound appeared to be composed of earth mingled with burnt bones. The mound is upon the second bench of land, seventy-five feet above the present level of the river. Many interesting aboriginal relics have been found in this vicinity.

Ohio County, in which Wheeling is situated, is in a high state of cultivation, supporting from thirty-seven thousand four hundred and eighty-seven acres of improved land, amounting to less than two townships of the government surveys, one thousand four hundred and forty-one horses and mules, one thousand four hundred and eight milch cows, two hundred and forty-six working cattle, one thousand three hundred and eighty other cattle, forty thousand and fifty sheep, three thousand two hundred and forty-four swine, worth altogether two hundred and fifty-three thousand and ninety dollars; and producing twenty thousand and forty-eight bushels of wheat, five thousand six hundred and thirty-nine of rye, one hundred and thirty-eight thousand four hundred and thirty of corn, eighty-two thousand one hundred and one of oats, twenty-two thousand and seventy-two of barley, four thousand three hundred and seventy-two of buckwheat, twenty-one thousand four hundred and forty-nine of Irish potatoes, eight hundred and twenty-three of sweet potatoes, one hundred and twenty-eight thousand four hundred and forty-eight pounds of butter, one hundred and two thousand and thirty-two pounds of wool, six thousand four hundred and seventy-nine tons of hay, besides the value of fourteen thousand four hundred and twenty dollars in garden products, ten thousand one hundred and seventy-four dollars in fruits, twenty-six thousand nine hundred and thirty dollars in slaughtered animals, and a variety of other productions.

The vine has been cultivated with uniform and gratifying success in the vicinity of Wheeling, both on the hill slopes, at the top, or near the bottom, and also on the islands of the river. Low lands, especially islands, have been avoided in other localities as sites for vineyards, but a look at the islands of this vicinity will suffice to solve the mystery of their adaptedness. If subject to overflow, it is only at rare intervals of winter or spring floods, the water soon subsiding, and settling through the gravelly substratum with a rapidity almost coincident with the subsidence of the river itself. If the vine were potted by a skilful gardener, the drainage would scarcely be superior. In such a soil a great expense for trenching is an entirely unnecessary part of the labor of preparing ground for a vineyard. The island at Wheeling, known as Zane's island, and owned by descendants of the original owner and pioneer of that name, has a large vineyard, which gives annually a yield greater than the average yield of American vineyards. When new vines are added, the ground is broken thoroughly sixteen inches deep, with three horses, then furrowed, and holes dug one foot deep in the furrows for the reception of the vines. C. L.

Zane, one of the proprietors, claims an average product of five hundred gallons of wine per acre.

A fine vineyard of J. B. Ford, and others, a few miles below Wheeling, on the breast of one of those heavy slopes, is a good illustration of the capabilities of the bluff lands for grapes. Being covered with a heavy forest growth, the expense of starting the vineyard was much higher than it otherwise would have been. The timber felled, and the stumps dug out, a furrow of twenty inches deep was cut with a mammoth plough, and roots so effectually eradicated that no sprouts have ever appeared. The soil was a clayey loam, with an admixture of shale. The vineyard comprises fourteen and a half acres, and with enclosures and building improvements cost about five hundred dollars per acre exclusive of the land, which overlies a coal mine. The product of the fourth year from planting was two thousand gallons of wine, mainly Catawba; the fifth year (1863) yielded four thousand gallons, or nearly three hundred per acre. In 1864 the product was six thousand gallons.

Few localities in the country can claim so large and sure results of vine culture during ten years past as are shown in this county. It is an interest rapidly growing here, and evidently destined to continue in prosperity.

Other fruits succeed here admirably. Among pears, the Bartlett, Seckel, and Duchess d'Angouleme seem to be favorites, and some, when asked to name six most desirable varieties, would duplicate the three already given. The Winter Nelis gives high satisfaction as a winter pear.

The favorite apples are the Yellow Bellflower, Rambo, Putnam, Russet, Rome Beauty, and Northern Spy. The Rambo is the most productive on the bottom lands. For early marketing, the Yellow June-eating is highly regarded, being a heavy bearer every year.

The fertility of the soil is plainly shown by the size of forest trees, and the rapidity of their growth. The writer has noticed in the grounds of L. Lunsford, a tree twelve years old, which is twenty-two inches in diameter. From the ashes of log heaps spring up locusts with great rapidity. A sedate and truthful man alleges that they have been known to grow to the height of one foot before the log heap had done burning. An opening in the woods, with the least exposure of the surface to the sun, is immediately covered with a carpet of green. Vegetation is everywhere luxuriant as the farmer could desire.

As early as 1769, a settlement was made of the site now occupied by the city of Wheeling, by Colonel Ebenezer, Silas, and Jonathan Zane, and others, from the south branch of the Potomac. The American Pioneer ascribed the name given to the place to the Indians, who are said to have placed the head of one of their white victims on a pole with the face to the river, from which the name *weeling*, the *place of a head*, designated the locality. A Directory of Wheeling, for 1839, assumes that the name was derived from a Catholic priest, from Europe, who once occupied the place temporarily as an Indian missionary station.

Wheeling is memorable in the history of our border warfare, for the siege of Fort Henry, situated just above the mouth of Wheeling Creek, which was saved by the courage and heroic determination of a small band of settlers, fighting thirty times their number, led by the notorious Simon Girty. It was here that female heroism was so memorably illustrated by Elizabeth Zane, who replenished their exhausted supplies of powder, from an outside magazine, in the face of the savage enemy, who were astounded by the sublime audacity of the movement.

Wheeling is at present the capital of West Virginia, as it is the commercial metropolis of the State. Geographically its position is near its northwestern extremity, yet it is in the direct line of trade and travel between Baltimore and all the prominent cities of the West. It is ninety-five miles from Pittsburgh by the river, and three hundred and sixty-five miles by water from Cincinnati. Its railroad communications are furnished by the Baltimore and Ohio, the Central Ohio, the Cleveland and Pittsburg, and the Hempfield Railroads. It has thus naturally become the focus of a trade embracing a wide scope of country, which is steadily increasing with the development of the agricultural and mineral resources for which the region is distinguished. The National Road, the great artery of Western travel before the era of railroads, and proud monument of the wisdom of Henry Clay, the statesman of the West, crosses the Ohio River at this point, by a wire suspension-bridge of one thousand and ten feet span.

The site of the city is a narrow alluvial tract extending three miles along the river, of varying width, shut in by high hills. The facile pen of N. P. Willis thus sportively described the town and its location on his visit there in 1859:

"Wheeling, as a town, confesses to the one little drawback of too *coal'd* an atmosphere for the lovers of clean linen — the idlest inhabitant being under the necessity of two clean shirts a day (too much 'coke upon littletown')— but its suburban capabilities are unequalled. Close behind the town, divided from it only by the high hills which form the bank of the Ohio, is a deep-down mountain-girt, well-wooded valley, inlaid with a most beautiful tributary stream, and giving hundreds of such sites for gentlemen's villas as no landscape artist could better contrive. It quite made my blood tingle to stand on the hill-top, overlooking the town on one side and this glorious vale on the other, and imagine what it would be when Wheeling shall be suburbanized like Boston — the original Wheeling a thousand times more picturesquely beautiful than the original Boston!"

Wheeling derives its chief reputation and a large portion of its business and wealth from its manufactures of iron, glass, paper, &c.; which occupy the labor and attention of a large per centage of its population.

There are now in operation four mills, producing annually forty thousand tons of nails and spikes, whose quality and finish challenge comparison with any manufactured elsewhere. Two railroad iron works claim an annual production of fifteen thousand tons. Three mills for making bar, sheet and plate-iron, produce annually twelve thousand tons. The total value of the annual products of these mills exceeds five million dollars. Seven foundries produce yearly one thousand tons of stove, and one thousand five hundred tons of other castings.

Four shops for the manufacture and repair of

steam-engines and machinery, in addition to the repair-shops of the Baltimore and Ohio and Hempfield Railroads, turn out work amounting to three hundred and fifty thousand dollars annually.

The product of five glass works amounts to five hundred thousand dollars yearly.

Ten breweries annually produce forty-five thousand barrels of fermented liquors, of which thirty thousand are ale.

Six tanneries produce the value of three hundred thousand dollars.

Three paper-mills produce printing and wrapping paper and bonnet-boards one hundred thousand dollars' worth yearly.

Two oil distilleries yield an annual product of ten thousand barrels of refined oil.

Steamboat-building is a prominent branch of industry. Seven boats were built throughout during the past year, and as many more were furnished with cabins and engines.

It was formerly a great depot for wagon-building, mainly for the Southern market. The same manufacture is now diverted to the furnishing of ambulances and army-wagons to the government.

A very superior common cigar, known as the "Wheeling Stogy," is made here, the demand for which is so increased that seventeen shops are engaged in the manufacture. There were made fifteen million of these cigars last year, valued at one hundred and fifty thousand dollars.

The manufacture of candy has become an important item, amounting to one hundred thousand pounds per annum.

In addition to this enumeration, there are four steam saw-mills, three planing-mills, three sash and blind-factories, one of cotton and one of woollen-goods, with shops for the manufacture of copper-ware, furniture, clothing, harness and trunks, lead-pipe, and many other articles of general and local necessity.

For manufactures requiring large motive power or large quantities of fuel, Wheeling will always be a desirable point. The vast beds of coal which under-lie all the adjacent hills, and which are often of such easy access, that the coal can be wheeled from the mines to the furnace without intermediate handling, will always afford an inexhaustible supply of fuel at the very lowest price. At the same time the manu-facturer has easy access by river and railroad to all the markets of the country.

The city is well supplied with water from the Ohio River, by powerful and well-arranged water-works, and lighted with gas, which is furnished at the lowest price; the business streets and wharves are well paved; while the moral and mental welfare of its inhabitants are well provided for by twenty-two churches representing all the leading Christian de-nominations in the country; by several public halls and assembly-rooms, a public library, two high-schools for boys, two seminaries for young ladies, a public school-house in each ward, and a thorough and efficient common-school system, which will com-pare favorably with that of any Western city.

Brooke County was formed in 1797 from Ohio County, is the most northern portion of the State, averaging scarcely more than six miles in width — a wedge entering between Ohio and Pennsylvania. The Ohio River washes its western border, its surface uneven, soil quite fertile, and its hills full of bituminous coal. It has been said of it, years ago, if it cannot strictly be said now, that for a considerable period neither a distillery nor a criminal prosecution was known within its limits. Wellsburg, the county-site, was laid out in 1789, and first called Charlestown, afterwards named for Alexander Wells, who built the first flouring-mill on the Ohio. The first settlers were from New England, and among the fathers of the settlement were the able and eminent Philip and Joseph Doddridge, one a Congressman, the other author of a history of the Indian wars of Northwestern Virginia. Bethany, eight miles from Wellsburg, is the site of the college founded by Rev. Alexander Campbell, who was also the founder of the sect known as "Campbellites." It was in this county that "Rice's Fort" was defended, when summoned—"Give up—too many Indian—Indian too big—no kill!" when the defiant reply was: "Come on, you cowards! we are ready for you. Show us your yellow hides and we will make holes in them for you."

Of the peculiar adaptation of the mountain slopes and valleys of Virginia to sheep husbandry, there is abundant evidence. Where circumstances have favored population, this interest, by inevitable gravitation, has settled down into a permanent and prominent place in farm industry. The "Panhandle" furnishes a notable illustration:

SHEEP HUSBANDRY.

Counties.	Acres of Farm lands.	No. of sheep.	Lbs. wool.
Hancock	49,132	21,402	60,214
Brooke	55,488	40,620	112,774
Ohio	54,840	40,050	102,032
Marshall	121,679	10,022	27,385
Total	281,139	112,094	302,405

The area of a country of average size, little more than five hundred square miles, with two hundred and eighty-one thousand, one hundred and thirty-nine acres in farm lands, supports one hundred and twelve thousand, ninety-four sheep — one for every three acres of the entire tract, inclusive of wild or waste lands; one for every two and a half acres of the actual farming lands; and in the three counties above Wheeling, one for every acre and a half. In fact, for one hundred and ten thousand, four hundred and ten acres of improved land in Hancock, Brooke, and Ohio, those counties have one hundred and two thousand, seventy-two sheep — almost an acre to each sheep, rivalling England itself in numbers compared with area, and far distancing Ohio, whose productive acres are more populous with sheep than any State in the Union, having eight acres to each sheep in 1860, with a great increase since.

This would look like giving up pasture and field to sheep, and leaving no place for cattle or grain; but, no — there is undoubtedly more of these products than if the sheep were absent, the flocks of the farm adding more to its fertility than they subtract from it. The following table shows that sheep husbandry tends to no diminution in price of lands, or extent or variety of farm products:

Counties.	Value of farms.	Price per acre.	Value of live stock.	Bushels of wheat.	Bushels of Ind. corn.
Hancock	$1,676,745	$34 12	$182,746	16,423	61,346
Brooke	2,447,903	44 11	282,439	23,490	142,122
Ohio	2,423,520	44 17	253,090	20,048	138,430
Marshall	2,489,909	20 46	280,860	74,759	241,911
Total	9,038,077	32 14	999,135	134,720	583,809

It is a curious fact, that lands of Brooke and Ohio (one with a large city, the other having no towns) are almost precisely alike in price, in exact proportion to the number of sheep kept; while those of Hancock, with flocks forty per cent. less numerous, are ten dollars less per acre; and those of Marshall, with one-fourth the number of sheep in twice the area, have less than half the value, or twenty dollars per acre.

It cannot be said here that sparseness of population accounts for diminished values and products. Hancock has a population of forty-four hundred and forty-five, and Marshall of twelve thousand nine hundred and ninety-seven, giving a slight advantage to Marshall; Brooke has fifty-four hundred and ninety-four, and Ohio twenty-two thousand four hundred and forty-two; yet the price of their lands is the same. It would seem that the population of Wheeling has less influence than the flocks of the neighboring farms in raising the price of lands of the county!

CHAPTER VIII.

SURVEY OF COUNTIES CONTINUED.— THE RIVER DISTRICT.

THE river counties, excepting those of the "Panhandle," and those south of the Kanawha, are Wetzel, Tyler, Pleasants, Wood, and Jackson. They contain a great variety of soil, from light silicious to deep alluvial of the river bottoms, with hill-tops of decomposed shales in a large admixture of humus, and slopes with a sufficiency of lime and clay for certain and heavy crops of cereals. Some of the bottoms have a sandy, others a clayey subsoil. In some localities the uplands along the Ohio river have a sandy loam, admirably adapted to fruit and market garden culture, seemingly quite light, but of a fine and silty texture, richly intermixed with vegetable mould. It is a quick soil and highly productive, and is easily worked, but free, becoming exhausted rapidly, yet easily kept "in heart" by annual dressings of manure, green manuring, or other modes of fertilization. It is a soil that richly repays the labor of the skilful and industrious husbandman. There is a fine body of such soil in Wood County, above Parkersburg.

Unlike the "Panhandle," this section has a much larger amount of unimproved than improved farm lands. In Wetzel the acres of each stand relatively: one hundred and twenty-four thousand eight hundred and twenty-one to thirty-one thousand three hundred and thirty-two; in Tyler, thirty-nine thousand seven hundred and ninety-four to ninety-seven thousand nine hundred and twenty-two; in Pleasants, fifteen thousand eight hundred and nine to thirty-six thousand seven hundred and ninety-eight; in Wood, forty-six thousand one hundred and ninety-nine to ninety-four thousand two hundred and twenty-nine; in Jackson, thirty-six thousand four hundred and fifty-seven to one hundred and two thousand eight hundred and eighty-one. This difference in improvement, with perhaps a little difference in quality, occasions a great diminution of the average value, as is shown by the following table of values and products:

Counties.	Value of farms.	Av. price per acre.	Bushels of wheat.	Bushels of corn.	Pounds of tobacco.
Wetzel	$1,176,511	$7 53	31,652	180,150	84,989
Tyler	1,500,003	10 89	43,729	182,239	11,225
Pleasants	649,220	12 36	22,785	102,172	27,930
Wood	1,673,864	11 92	27,488	115,046	166,365
Jackson	1,355,201	9 72	88,338	219,377	74,691
Total	6,354,799	10 14	213,992	798,984	365,200

Considering the proportion of unoccupied lands, the proximity to the Ohio River, and the sparseness of population, this section must speedily receive the benefit of progressive and high development, and its land owners the advantage of corresponding enhancement of prices. It is a successful tobacco region, producing (in 1860) three hundred and sixty-five thousand pounds of tobacco. Nor has the troubled state of the country prevented its culture during the war, as is shown by the fact that the tax on what has been manufactured in Parkersburg during thirteen months, amounted to fifteen thousand eight hundred and eighty-one dollars.

An examination of the census returns shows a good variety of products, and a yield indicating a quick and fertile soil. In noting the quantity, it should be remembered that the population of the five counties is but thirty-five thousand five hundred and seventeen, divided as follows: Wetzel, sixty-seven hundred and three; Tyler, sixty-five hundred and seventeen; Pleasants, twenty-nine hundred and forty-five; Wood, eleven thousand and forty-six, and Jackson eighty-three hundred and six. Comparatively a wilderness, it is one which flows with milk and honey, yielding four hundred and nine thousand and fifty pounds of butter after feeding the population, and giving sixteen thousand and seventy-seven pounds of honey, in addition to forty-four thousand two hundred and sixty-six gallons of sorghum syrup. A profitable trade in grain and in fruit, principally apples, is carried on by means of the river — a trade which has extended even to New Orleans, a distance of eighteen hundred miles, and which has been conducted with scarcely more expense than for one hundred miles by railroad. The variety of apples producing best and most saleable, have been the Roxbury and Golden Russets, and the Yellow Bellflower. Tobacco is a lucrative crop here. The soil is well adapted to the growth of a superior quality. Corn and grass are the principal crops. There is a tendency to a greater prominence in sheep husbandry. Five hundred sheep have recently been introduced from Brooke County, notwithstanding the unsettled state of the country, and the exposure to loss from guerillas. A beginning has been made in grape-growing, which promises to be successful.

Nor has live-stock been neglected. A fair proportion of sheep and wool have been produced, and horned cattle are profitably grown and fattened. A few of these products are given in the following table:

Counties.	Gallons of Sorghum.	Pounds of honey.	Pounds of butter.	Bushels of potatoes.	Products of orchards.	Value of slaughter'd animals.
Wetzel...............	6,270	5,507	124,342	14,430	$7,510	$28,182
Tyler................	11,900	6,014	130,527	23,733	11,997	35,150
Pleasants...........	4,514	1,711	30,500	7,747	5,868	15,284
Wood................	7,266	690	12,175	33,166	2,460	51,682
Jackson.............	14,316	2,155	111,506	32,630	9,281	40,260
Total...........	44,266	16,077	409,050	111,706	37,116	170,558

The price of lands in this section has advanced wonderfully of late. One year ago, before the oil excitement, farms on the Ohio River, mostly improved, with timber for fuel skirting the adjacent hills, an orchard in bearing, and comfortable farm buildings, brought from fifty to one hundred dollars per acre. The upland, nearly all susceptible of cultivation, with a surface undulating, rolling, or hilly, in some places with ridges marking a very sharp outline, if brought under good cultivation, in favorable localities, sold at twenty-five or thirty dollars per acre. Less improved, further from railroad or river, or rougher or poorer, could be bought for ten and fifteen, and some even for five dollars.

The Ohio bottom lands produce corn, as do the best prairie and bottom lands in the country, more according to culture than to difference in quality, at the rate of fifty to one hundred bushels per acre. The average of wheat, which is grown on the hills, more generally in loam than upon aluminous soils, among stumps and roots, and sometimes rocks, and greatly exposed to the raids of innumerable inhabitants of adjacent forests, is about the same as in Ohio, perhaps fourteen bushels per acre, while occasional fields produce two or three times that amount.

Wood county has a great variety of soils. The northern portion is a sandy loam, productive, excellent for fruit and vegetables, easily kept in condition with light dressings of manure and judicious culture. On the Little Kanawha the soil is pretty stiff with clay, and in the southern portion of the county a limestone soil is found. A fair crop of corn here is about fifty bushels per acre.

The surface of Jackson County is rolling. Many of the hills have a limestone soil; some localities are characterized by heavy clay. Some of the bottom lands are clay, and others alluvion based on sand or gravel.

Pleasants is a small county, with good lands considerably improved, averaging a higher value in 1860, than those of any other county in the group, not excepting Wood. St. Mary's is the capital and principal town. Middle Island, French, Cow, and Calf Creeks, already famous throughout all the borders of Petrolia, are in this county.

The counties of Tyler and Wetzel, lying between Marshall and Pleasants, are possessed of fertile hill lands, with a small proportion of bottoms. Alluvial soil of great fertility, upon the Ohio river, is highly valued. The streams are small and unimportant. A very small percentage of waste land exists. Still there remains much unimproved land to be utilitized.

Parkersburg, the second city in the State, is situated in Wood County, at the junction of the Little Kanawha and Ohio Rivers. It takes its name from Mr. Adam Parker, who owned the site at the beginning of the present century. The county was established in 1800; the town was not laid out till 1817; incorporated in 1820, and obtained a city charter in 1860. It is estimated to contain six thousand inhabitants, twice its number when West Virginia was organized as a State.

The growth of Parkersburg is at present a marvel of rapidity. Many hundred dwellings have been built within two years, and the demand is more urgent than ever. Its position in the new State, its commercial importance, healthfulness, picturesque surroundings, and quick and fertile soil, would have stimulated rapid and continuous improvement, without extraneous or extraordinary influences; but the petroleum excitement, of which it is the business head and geographical centre, has lent wings to progress, and almost realized the fables of oriental dreamers in actual life. Not that the city, by any means, is finished, or has attained its maximum size; on the contrary, it is evidently but fairly, though rapidly, started on its career.

On the Ohio, its location is midway between the north and south line of the State, as Wheeling is midway between this point and Pittsburg, one hundred and eighty-four miles distant. It is also but forty-five miles north of a point midway between Cincinnati and

Pittsburg; and, in view of the greater difficulty, at certain seasons, in navigating the Upper Ohio, it is fair to consider it a half-way station between the Iron and Queen Cities. To this place, the river is always navigable with ease and safety. The shortest railroad line from Baltimore or Philadelphia to Cincinnati and the West, is through Parkersburg. The distance from Baltimore is three hundred and eighty-two miles; from Cincinnati, one hundred and ninety-five miles by the Marietta and Cincinnati Railroad, and two hundred and seventy-seven miles by the river. This line is a saving of about sixty miles, over any other, from Baltimore to Cincinnati; and more than half as much between Philadelphia and Cincinnati.

The site could scarcely be surpassed. Its area embraces three square miles, two miles on the Little Kanawha, and one and a half on the Ohio, covering two plateaus, one forty, the other sixty feet above low-water, looking upon scenery lovely as any the Hudson can boast, and as beautiful naturally, if not as strongly marked, as any upon the famous Rhine. For many miles, the Ohio, like a broad silver ribbon, gleams brightly in the sunlight; and wide prairies stretch out to kiss the feet of the circling hills, dark with the shadows of a thousand forest kings. Romantic Blennerhassett, classic with the story of intrigue and treason, sleeps in deserted beauty in the rays of a setting sun. On the opposite bank of the Kanawha, before the very heart of the city, rises an almost perpendicular wall of ragged rock, several hundred feet in height, surmounted now by a fort, its crest pierced for frowning guns, and the starry flag floating high above all in the thin air.

The soil of contiguous lands, north and east, is a rich sandy loam, of exceeding fineness and perfect drainage, unsurpassed for flowers and fruits, and garden vegetables; south and west across the Little Kanawha, a soil of clay is found, cultivated with less facility, but productive when properly managed, and very durable. The variety of surface, riverward slope, and predominent character of soil, forbid the accumulation of water to stagnate and breed miasma, and explain the prevalent healthfulness of the whole region, and its especial exemption from malarious diseases.

The streets are regularly laid out, sixty feet wide, in squares of three hundred and forty feet, with few exceptions, graded and gravelled. Two rivers afford ample wharfage for the rapidly accumulating transportation business. The south branch of the Baltimore and Ohio Railroad opens rapid communication through the State, and turnpikes lead towards Winchester, Staunton, Charleston, Elizabeth, and St. Mary's.

Six fine houses of worship accommodate the religious exercises of the Methodist Episcopal, Methodist Episcopal South, Protestant Episcopal, Catholic, Presbyterian, and Baptist Churches. The United Brethren contemplate the immediate erection of another.

Facilities for education have not hitherto been adequate to the wants of the town. A fine Catholic school-building, now filled with pupils and teachers, is accomplishing something; and the new school-law, modelled after the best of the free-school system, will in time furnish facilities for a thorough common education of all the children.

A stock company, with a capital of fifty thousand dollars, is preparing to supply the city with gas; and another with a similar capital, is organized for machine-shop and foundry operations. Steamboat-building is contemplated, and expected to be ultimately undertaken upon an extensive scale. Lumber is certainly destined to be a great element in the trade and manufacture of the city. The Little Kanawha and its affluents drain a country unsurpassed for the variety and excellence of its timber. It would be an excellent point for the manufacture of agricultural implements, and must become an important manufacturing place when the railroad to the southwestern interior shall give cheap and easy access to the rich coal mines of the adjoining counties.

But it is to petroleum that the present flourishing condition of Parkersburg is indebted, and to which much of its progress in the immediate future is to be accorded. Hundreds of wells are already in construction or operation within twenty-five miles; and derricks are multiplying far out into the interior by every river and run. Barrels come literally "booming" down the stream, floating with oily facility upon the surface. Boats bring forward in "bulk" their slippery burden. The ingenuity and economy of shrewd men is taxed for its cheapest transportation. The product is rapidly augmenting, and will continue to increase, to what extent it is impossible to say, and almost useless to conjecture. That it will add immensely to the business of the city, there cannot be a reasonable doubt.

The following statement of the trade of Parkersburg is furnished by J. E. Wharton (as are many of the facts above), in his sketch of the city:

"The trade and business of the city during the last year has been as follows: Sales of groceries and liquors, eight hundred and fifty thousand dollars; of dry-goods, three hundred thousand dollars; of clothing, three hundred thousand dollars; of boots and shoes, two hundred and fifty thousand dollars; iron, hardware and tin, two hundred thousand dollars; of jewelry and notions, one hundred thousand dollars; of furniture, sixty thousand dollars; drugs, twenty-five thousand dollars.

"The products of manufactures and labor have been as follows: Milling, three hundred thousand dollars; lumber, doors, sash, &c., two hundred and sixty thousand dollars; ten steamboats built, one hundred thousand dollars; wagons, &c., thirty thousand dollars; tanneries, one hundred and twenty-five thousand dollars; machinery, seventy thousand dollars. The oil refined in four refineries amounts to eight hundred thousand dollars; while there is not far from two million dollars worth of crude oil handled here annually, and the amount will be largely increased during the coming year. The breweries yield five thousand dollars; saddleries and harness, three thousand dollars; manufactures of measures, five thousand dollars; bandboxes, three thousand dollars; sundries, twenty-five thousand dollars. The whole manufactures employing about twelve hundred persons, besides those employed in mechanics and common labor.

"The machine, blacksmith and carpenter shops of the Baltimore and Ohio Railroad Company, employ about sixty hands, and their works are being enlarged and improved.

"The packing of pork and beef here was only commenced the last season, but it amounts to about forty-five thousand dollars, and will be increased, as this is on the direct route to the Eastern market from the best hog and cattle-growing portions of Ohio; while the growth of hogs in this immediate section of our own State is largely increasing, which will make this one of the best pork markets east of Cincinnati.

"Tobacco is grown extensively in this vicinity, and the machinery for manufacture in this city is equal to the product of an article worth one hundred and twenty-five thousand dollars, but the manufactures have been quiet for a few months past to await the action of Congress in the imposition of taxes.

"Coopering and the manufacture of oil and flour barrels is extensively carried on in the city and vicinity, the product of which, as near as we can gather is one hundred and thirty thousand dollars per year.

"There are three banks, two National and one local, with an aggregate capital of two hundred and fifty thousand dollars, and current deposits at the present time, not less than one and a half millions."

CHAPTER IX.

SURVEY OF COUNTIES CONTINUED.—THE KANAWHA VALLEY.

THERE are few localities promising more attractions to industrial enterprise, or higher rewards to free labor, than the Kanawha Valley of West Virginia. Climate, soil, timber, fuel (wood above and coal below), minerals in variety, water-power, navigation two thousand miles to the Gulf of Mexico, and to all the tributaries of the Mississippi, conspire to render this valley, even now animated with the earlier sights and sounds of developing industries, the future home of mechanical skill and intelligent labor, and consequent refinement, wealth, contentment, virtue, and happiness.

Its climate is mild and agreeable, with heat less intense in summer than at Washington or Baltimore, and a winter temperature comparing favorably in mildness with that of Louisville and St. Louis.

The distribution of rain through the different seasons is remarkably uniform, being not far from eight inches rain-fall in each of the seasons—spring, summer, and autumn—and scarcely more than ten during the winter, or about thirty-six inches for the year.

The centre of the lower valley, or basin of the Great Kanawha, is in latitude 38°. The extreme length of the river (considering the "New River" a part of the Kanawha, as it is in all but the name), is about four hundred miles. It rises in Ashe County, in North Carolina, and traverses or forms the boundary of six counties in Virginia and eight counties in West Virginia, viz: Mercer, Monroe, Greenbrier, Raleigh, Fayette, Kanawha, Putnam, and Mason. It first flows between the Blue Ridge and Iron Mountain, and in the northern part of Grayson County, Virginia, it bursts the barriers of the Iron Mountain and continues in a northeastern direction through Carroll, Wythe, and Pulaski counties, where it turns abruptly to the northwest, winding through several ridges of the Alleghanies, as if instinctively seeking association with the future of "*la belle riviere,*" Ohio, and the great "Father of Waters." After crossing the Greenbrier range, and passing through Fayette County, West Virginia, it receives the Gauley River from the right, spreads into a broad expanse of five hundred yards, and assumes the dignity of the Great Kanawha. Here, two miles below the junction, and more than a hundred miles from the Ohio, the stream is precipitated twenty-two feet over a ledge of rocks, with a total descent of fifty feet, including rapids and perpendicular falls, placing a limit to steamboat navigation, and also furnishing one of the best water powers in the world.

The area drained by this noble river is stated to be more than ten thousand square miles—a territory a little larger than the State of Massachusetts.

A correspondent of the Department of Agriculture, in this valley, a manufacturer previous to the war of the rebellion, asserts that, so abundant was the coal in his vicinity (on Coal River, a branch of the Kanawha), that it could be mined and placed in his factory at a cost of *forty-five cents per ton*. Of this coal there are "four seams above water level, within a vertical distance of two hundred and forty feet, giving an aggregate thickness of seventeen feet, or twenty-five thousand tons of coal to the acre, consisting of gray splint, rich bituminous, block splint, birdseye cannel, steam and smiths' coal." This is within ten miles of Charleston, on Navigation.

With such mines of undeveloped wealth, above and below the soil, and in water-power, and in facilities for a highly developed agriculture, a great impetus will be given to enterprise when industry resumes its wonted channels, under the new State organization. The salt and iron, coal and petroleum, which exist in almost fabulous abundance, will occupy the ready capital and willing labor of tens of thousands of thriving citizens; and manufactures will flourish, and agriculture advance, and the wilderness of the past, full of floral beauty, and lavish with wild profusion as it has been, will blossom with a sweeter fragrance and a richer magnificence under the magic touches of the hand of free and intelligent labor. With coal at forty-five cents per ton, or whatever the cost of mining may prove under advanced prices, and iron in almost equal cheapness, the best of timber for the cutting and hauling, oil defying facilities for cooperage, abundant harvests from fertile soils, and a magnificent river to float the products of industry to market — what a region in which to manufacture the sugar mills and reapers and other implements of western agriculture!

THE KANAWHA VALLEY. 115

Mercer County, perched upon the slope of the Alleghanies, is drained by the New or Kanawha River and several small tributaries. Great Flat-top Mountain extends along the northwest border. Excellent pasturage exists wherever forests are girdled or felled. But one-sixth of its farms are improved, yet its yearly exhibit of animals slaughtered is fifty-eight thousand one hundred and thirty-two dollars, and its corn amounts to one hundred and thirty-one thousand six hundred and fifty-four bushels; wheat, forty-three thousand one hundred and thirty-one bushels; and oats, fifty-five thousand eight hundred and forty-three bushels. Its capital is Princeton. The soil is mainly limestone, unsurpassed for pasturage, and yielding fine crops of wheat.

Monroe, next to Kanawha and Greenbrier, is the most populous of this group. South of Greenbrier, rising to the Alleghanian summit on the east, it has a very similar soil and climate, a like variety of mineral springs, and enjoys a like celebrity as a cool and healthful mountain region, with good water, a bracing atmosphere, beautiful scenery, and rural plenty universally enjoyed. The New or Upper Kanawha and the Greenbrier Rivers furnish its drainage. Union is the county-town.

Greenbrier County was settled during the revolutionary war, in 1777. It is a mountainous region, yet possessing a mild climate; is fertile, and a portion of its lands highly improved, especially in the valley of the Greenbrier.

Lewisburg, the county-seat, is the site of an old frontier fort, and was named for General Lewis, being the place of rendezvous for his army before the battle of Point Pleasant, at the mouth of the Kanawha, on the Ohio. It is a fine location for a town—a beautiful and fertile prairie, originally called "the Savanna."

The famous White Sulphur Spring is situated a few miles west of the height of the Alleghany, in a beautiful valley of half a mile in breadth, gradually widening in graceful undulations westward. This was the great pleasure-resort of the South before the war, swarming with visitors, the many in search of amusement, some courting the goddess Hygeia, pledging her often in full bumpers dashed with "sulphate of lime, sulphate of magnesia, sulphate of soda, carbonate of lime, carbonate of magnesia, chloride of magnesium, chloride of sodium, chloride of calcium, peroxide of iron, phosphate of lime, sulphate and hydrate of sodium, precipitated sulphur, iodine," and flavored with various gases. It is not strange that dyspepsia, scrofula, rheumatism, and neuralgia should flee at the approach of a drug depository in epitome.

The Blue Sulphur Spring has been a popular resort. It is a bold spring, flowing a half gallon per minute.

This county occupies a depression of the Alleghany range, the mountain summits scarcely more than two thousand feet high, and the mean elevation of the arable lands of the county fifteen hundred. The soil is, much of it, strongly impregnated with lime, and consists mainly of a rich, black, friable loam. Such soils, in the southern slopes of hills and in the valley of the Greenbrier, produce abundant crops of maize, ordinarily from thirty to fifty bushels per acre, with careless culture, and seventy-five to one hundred bushels on the best locations, with skilful management. The soil and climate peculiarly adapt this region to the purposes of the grazier. If a ray of sunlight can reach a spot in the densest forest, that surface soon becomes green with the blue-grass sod. Thousands of cattle yearly depasture these mountain plains and slopes.

It is not alone to its mineral waters that the attractions of this region are due. The balmy breath of spring invades the atmosphere of summer; pleasurable exhilaration tempers the sultriest of July days; the blue-grass maintains its rank luxuriance through the dryest season; and scenes of rural beauty, outspread upon those elevated plains and mountain slopes, fill the eye with their unpretending magnificence. Thousands in each summer season gather here from the poisoned atmosphere of cities.

Raleigh, with one hundred and sixteen thousand nine hundred and forty-five acres in farms, has but eleven thousand six hundred and thirty-two acres which are improved; consequently the average value is reduced to three dollars and fifty-four cents. Its cereals make a proportionally small exhibit. Quite a prominent place is given to tobacco, of which thirty-four thousand eight hundred and twenty-seven pounds are cured. Of flax, two thousand and two pounds are prepared. It is drained by the head streams of Coal River, and bounded on the east by New River, and slopes toward the northwest. This county was named for Sir Walter Raleigh, and was formed from a part of Fayette.

Fayette lies next to Raleigh, upon the river, and above Kanawha. Its county-seat is Fayetteville.

The Gauley makes its junction here with the New River. The famous Falls of the Gauley occur a little below the junction. Its mineral and agricultural advantages are attracting the attention of capitalists abroad, and will secure immigration and rapid improvement.

Kanawha, the first of the three counties below the Falls, has an area of eleven hundred and seventy-six square miles, beautifully diversified with mountains, hills, and fertile valleys; the highlands inexhaustible with coal, and the valleys salt with abundant saline springs. This area is intersected by the Elk, Coal, and Pocotalico Rivers, which afford enlarged facilities for manufacturing and transportation of the mineral treasures beneath the soil, the products of its cultivation, and the timber which towers above it. Its population was nearly sixteen thousand one hundred and fifty in 1860, and its assessed valuation about three and a half millions.

This county is as old as the United States Government, having been formed from Greenbrier and Montgomery in 1789. The first settlement was made some twenty miles above Charleston, at a stream now known as Kelly's Creek. Kanawha is said to be, in Indian dialect, the "River of the Woods," its tributary Pocotalico signifying "Plenty of Fat Doe." It was, and is, a country of magnificent forests, and abounded in bear, buffalo, deer, raccoons, and other game, upon which the early settlers mainly subsisted.

Charleston, the principal town, is situated upon the north bank of the Kanawha, about three hundred miles from Richmond, and less than fifty from the Ohio River. The river at this point is a broad and beautiful stream, little less than a thousand feet in breadth, affording navigation from the falls to the Ohio in all except the dryest season of the year. Beautiful vistas are opened to the delighted vision in many portions of this valley; sweet scenes of rural beauty captivate the traveller's eye at many points, and unfold a panorama of industry and thrift, in which flocks and herds give motion and variety to the broad expanse of field and forest, aspiring hill, and lowly valley.

Some six miles above Charleston was the Big Lick, frequented for its salt, both by the wild beasts and wilder Indians. Remains of pottery, evidently used for evaporating the brine, have often been discovered. The first salt well sunk here was in 1809. From one to three millions of bushels of salt annually have for a long period been manufactured in this vicinity, of which mention is made in another chapter.

Putnam has a fine location between Kanawha and Mason, being the second county from the river. It is intersected centrally by the Great Kanawha, which flows here in a northwesterly direction. Its soil is fertile, the bottom lands very productive, and the hills combine superior advantages for the growth of grapes or other fruits. Its location, soil and minerals, render its real estate highly eligible for investment.

Mason County was formed in 1804, from Kanawha. It is bounded on the south by the Kanawha River, and on the west by the Ohio. The junction of these streams is historical ground, being the battle-ground of the famous contest of Point Pleasant, between the pioneers and the Indians in 1774. The forces of the whites, numbering eleven hundred, were led by Gen.

Andrew Lewis. The Indians, led by the noted warrior Cornstalk, included the braves of the Shawnee, Delaware, Mingo, and Wyandotte tribes. It was a sanguinary fight, in which Indians and whites, by turns, charged with dauntless impetuosity, and retreated bravely, confronting desperate and overpowering assaults, and in which the Indians, almost victors, were flanked and compelled to flee from their strong line on Crooked Creek, extending almost across from the Ohio to the Kanawha. Col. Charles Lewis and Col. Field were killed, and several captains and lieutenants — in all seventy-five killed and one hundred and forty wounded.

This county has about fifty miles of bottom lands on the Ohio, and more than thirty on the Kanawha River, with other low-lying or alluvial lands, together constituting an area of good farming lands, perhaps unsurpassed by any other county. The coal and salt of this region are attracting much attention, from the fact that no other section of the Ohio River, from Wheeling to Cincinnati, possesses so valuable coal property in convenient proximity to the river. Opposite, upon the Ohio shore, coal mining has been extensively and profitably prosecuted. Several new companies, owning large tracts of coal lands, are already organized in this county and vicinity, and are preparing to prosecute the enterprise with vigor. The salt at Hartford City and New Haven, has long been a source of revenue, and a provision of profitable industry. New coal banks have recently been opened near West Columbia, at which point increased activity is manifested in the old mines.

The four lower counties of the valley, immediately

connected with the river, have a population of nearly forty thousand, of whom little more than three thousand were slaves in 1860. As this section of West Virginia contained a large portion of all the slaves embraced within the limits of the new State, it may be well, as a relic of the old regime, to include this element in the population, which was as follows, in 1860:

Counties.	Whites.	Increase of free population since 1850.	Slaves.	Aggregate population.
Mercer	6,428	2,410	362	6,819
Monroe	9,536	464	1,114	10,757
Greenbrier	10,500	1,950	1,525	12,211
Raleigh	3,291	1,562	57	3,367
Fayette	5,716	1,936	271	5,997
Kanawha	13,785	1,786	2,184	16,150
Putnam	5,708	1,015	580	6,301
Mason*	8,750		376	9,173
Total	63,714	11,034	6,469	70,775

The following is a statement of the agricultural statistics of the Kanawha Valley of West Virginia, comprising the above eight counties:

Area in square miles 4,746
Acres of improved land . . . 426,235
Acres of unimproved land . . . 1,352,802
Acres of unassessed or waste lands . 1,256,403
Value of farms. $16,093,679
Average value of farm lands per acre . $9 03
Value of farm implements . . . $334,455
Number of horses 14,220
Number of cattle 55,588
Number of sheep 65,589

---

* Decrease in free population, 89.

Number of swine	70,350
Value of live stock	$2,303,280
Bushels of wheat	476,286
Bushels of rye	33,852
Bushels of buckwheat	30,659
Bushels of Indian corn	1,487,828
Bushels of oats	335,556
Pounds of flax	26,866
Pounds of tobacco	1,247,365
Pounds of wool	134,416
Bushels of Irish potatoes	95,442
Bushels of sweet potatoes	12,112
Pounds of butter	658,562
Pounds of cheese	20,144
Tons of hay	19,529
Gallons of wine	478
Pounds of maple sugar	153,362
Gallons of maple molasses	14,730
Gallons of sorghum molasses	7,902
Pounds of honey	74,896
Value of orchard products	$28,404
Value of home manufactures	$139,481
Value of slaughtered animals	$477,589

It appears from the above that scarcely half the area is included in farms, and about one-seventh in actual cultivation. A great variety of products is shown, embracing almost everything cultivated in temperate latitudes. It seems literally a land of milk and honey, wine and oil.

CHAPTER X.

SURVEY OF COUNTIES CONTINUED.—THE SOUTHERN GROUP.

THE counties south of the Kanawha — Boone, Cabell, Wayne, Logan, Wyoming, and McDowell — are mountainous, covered in great part with original forests heavily timbered, well watered by the Guyandotte, Sandy, and other rivers, and exceedingly rich in iron, coal, and other minerals. The minerals will at some not distant day be valuable, and the soils available for the production of fruit, wool, and butcher's meat. It is intersected by mountains in continuation of the Cumberland range, and nearly all of it included in the great coal measures of the Ohio Valley.

The Guyandotte River region abounds in bituminous coal, some of which, upon analysis, is shown to contain but one and a half per cent. of refuse or ash — rivalling the best Lancashire for illuminating purposes. Cannel coal of excellent quality exists here in the hills, and in the river bed, at different altitudes. Professor Rogers once called the attention of the board of public works of Virginia to the extraordinary mineral wealth of this region. Other explorers have made equally favorable reports, making the principal coal vein ten feet in thickness, lying above the water level, and cropping out on the banks of the river.

All the counties of the southern group are rich in coal of various qualities, including the best cannel.

The coal of this region, as will be seen from samples described is remarkable for the amount of oil which it contains.

Not only coal, but iron, lead, arsenic, sulphur, salt, gypsum, and even silver, are claimed as a part of the resources of this group. Rough as the surface seems, a large population will one day be sustained, engaged in mining, manufactures, and the various branches of agriculture, especially in pastoral pursuits.

The soil of the narrow "bottoms," partly alluvial, is generally strongly impregnated with lime, sometimes pretty stiff with clay, and quite productive. It is a durable soil, and in some localities has been thoroughly tested by many years of defective culture. The upland soil is almost equal to that of the valleys, and the mountains preserve their fertility to the summits, affording excellent pastures of natural blue grass wherever the smallest space is cleared for it, and a gleam of sunlight can fall upon it. Here, as elsewhere in the State, the soil of the north sides of the mountains is a rich loose loam, while on the south the surface seems to have been denuded of its humus, leaving the underlying stratum, a clay loam, or mixture of clay and shale, with more or less of lime. This peculiarity has been attributed by some to the effect of the sun's rays striking vertically upon the south hill sides.

Boone County is drained by Coal and Little Rivers and Laurel Creek. It was named in honor of Daniel Boone, and is yet to a great extent as wild a forest as that adventurous pioneer could desire. Yet it has fifteen thousand and fifty-four improved acres, and two hundred and eighteen thousand eight hundred and seventy-three unimproved in farms, valued at two dollars twenty-two cents per acre. Its live stock is valued at one hundred and twenty thousand five hundred and eighty-nine dollars; its corn yields one hundred and forty-three thousand eight hundred and eight bushels, about ten bushels to every acre of improved land, in addition to a variety of other farm products, including hay and some pasturage, although woods and pastures are adequate to a fair support of stock in summer, and a partial supply of winter feed. A good idea of the dependence placed upon winter pasturage and corn fodder may be had from the fact that only seventy-four tons of hay are cured for the use of eighty-nine hundred and ninety-four farm animals — a surfeit of sixteen pounds to each animal for the winter! This certainly does not indicate a poverty of pasturage, or extreme severity of weather or depth of snows. Again, there is produced thirty thousand eight hundred and seventy-nine dollars from slaughtered animals, about two dollars per acre for the entire area of improved lands, exclusive of forests, in addition to other farm products.

Wayne County occupies the southwest corner of the State, and is separated from Kentucky by Sandy River. The surface is much broken, well covered with valuable timber, affording some excellent soil; and the earth beneath is rich with a variety of coals, including cannel. It is here that the enterprise of Eli Thayer was inaugurated, at Ceredo, which terminated in failure from causes having no connection with the intrinsic value of the resources there ready for development.

Cabell County, on the Ohio River, is intersected by

the Guyandotte River, and has more improved lands than Boone; this degree of improvement, small as it is, with somewhat better facilities for transportation, makes the assessed value of farms about ten dollars per acre. It has some fertile lands; is a fine region for fruit, and already derives some revenue from orchards; grows sorghum finely, sweet potatoes, &c. This county is also very rich in minerals. Cabell was organized as a county in 1809, and was taken from Kanawha. It took its name from Governor William H. Cabell. Barboursville, the county-seat, is about seven miles from the Ohio, upon the Guyandotte River. The first settlement was made in 1796 at Green Bottom. Upon these beautiful plains remain the vestiges of an ancient race, indicative of a civilization far superior to that of the most advanced of known Indian races. In Howe's Historical Collections is this description: "The traces of a regular, compact, and populous city, with streets running parallel with the Ohio River, and crossing and intersecting each other at right angles, covering a space of nearly half a mile, as well as the superficial dimensions of many of the houses, are apparent, and well defined. Axes and saws of a unique form — the former of iron, the latter of copper — as well as other implements of the mechanic arts have been found."

Logan, Wyoming, and McDowell are drained by the tributaries of the Sandy, and by the Guyandotte, and occupy the extreme south of West Virginia. This region is rough, but fertile, rich in woods and mines, scarcely available or valuable at present for want of water or other cheap transportation. It is immediately valuable, however, for wool-growing.

Lying between the latitude of 37° and 38°, on the same parallel with the southern point of Illinois, and yet elevated above miasmatic influences — a country of genial sunshine and bracing air, of trout-brooks and running streams — it is eminently a fit and healthful locality for sheep. Ample pasturage for extensive flocks is afforded in the openings of the forest, in which nutricious grasses spring up spontaneously, and grow vigorously. A commencement has been made, and this district, of eight counties, unsettled as it is, and comparatively unpeopled, had, in 1860, thirty-six thousand nine hundred and eighty-three sheep, producing sixty-five thousand one hundred and eighty-three pounds of wool. This does not fairly exhibit the wool-producing ability of the region, as the sheep, roaming in the forests, are little cared for, and lose much of their wool upon bushes and briars when warm weather comes, and the proper shearing time is neglected or delayed. It is acknowledged by all acquainted with this section that the cost of keeping sheep here is merely nominal, and their growth and condition as favorable to profit as could be desired.

CHAPTER XI.

SURVEY OF COUNTIES CONTINUED.—THE CENTRAL GROUP.

HAVING traversed the borders of the State, let the reader glance at the broad area embraced in the interior counties, which are drained by the Monongahela and its branches, the Little Kanawha, the Elk, and the Gauley, with numerous smaller streams, which mingle with the waters of the Ohio or the Kanawha. It is here that the prices of lands are yet reasonable; that general agriculture promises to be most remunerative; that improvement is rife; and here, too, abundance of coal and iron and petroleum is found in addition to the wealth of the surface. The capital of the State may be located here; the Baltimore and Ohio Railroad cuts this section in two directions, and a road cutting the State longitudinally is already contemplated, and its commencement and completion cannot be far in the future.

The surface of this section is varied. Like most of the State it is uneven, hilly, broken, and declivitous in different localities, with a small per centage of level bottom lands, and smaller still of level uplands. The soil is good, coming naturally into grass, and yielding all farm products well. The northern slopes of the hills contain more of humus than the southern, and produce most of the corn, while the southern slopes are stiffer and more tenacious, as though partially denuded of vegetable mould by washing, by some old-time abrasion, or other cause, and therefore suited best to wheat culture.

Some items relative to this section have been kindly furnished by J. H. Diss Debar, of St. Clara Colony, Doddridge County, Commissioner of Emigration for West Virginia, who has enjoyed the advantages of years of close and intelligent observation and experience. This colony is itself an illustration of the remunerative character of agricultural effort and industry expended upon these lands. In a few years a few straggling pioneers have given place to fifty thriving families; and Irish and German immigrants, with means to procure a plough and a single cow, have been able to stock and pay for their farms, and live in peace and plenty. The following extracts show the price and character of farm lands in this district, prior to the recent upward movement of prices in consequence of oil operations:

"The main valleys of the west fork of Tygart's Valley River, both being branches of the Monongahela, and to some extent the valleys of both Kanawhas, contain bottom lands equal in quality, though not in breadth, to those of the Ohio, and on the former stream, in the counties of Lewis, Barbour, Upshur, Harrison, Taylor, Marion, and Monongalia, the hills in many instances rise from the valleys in more gentle slopes, and present a greater and superior arable surface than those along the Ohio River. Farms in those counties, with about one-third timbered land, range from twenty-five to fifty dollars per acre, and are amply worth it.

"On the smaller valleys of tributary streams the price of farms in the above named counties, similarly proportioned as to cleared and unimproved land, vary from fifteen to twenty-five dollars per acre; and further towards the heads of streams, and more remote from thoroughfares, from ten to fifteen dollars per acre.

"Many farms, chiefly hill-land, but all fit for grazing and sufficiently watered, with primitive home improvements, can yet be had at from five to ten dollars per acre, with twenty to twenty-five acres in a hundred, more or less, prepared for cultivation.

"Large tracts of wild land are not found in any of the above named counties, except in Upshur and Lewis, where timbered mountains, containing some table land fit for small grains and grass, can be bought at from two to four dollars per acre. In the other counties very little timbered land, fit in part for the plough, can be bought for less than five or six dollars per acre, and some of it not under ten to twelve dollars.

"The counties of Wirt, Ritchie, Doddridge, Roane, Calhoun, Gilmer, and Braxton, are not watered by streams presenting extensive bottoms, but contain very little land absolutely worthless. The surface of these counties varies from undulating or rolling to hilly, and the proportion of bottom to hill may be safely set down as from five to fifteen per cent. As a general rule, lands of the same quality are rated lower in the latter than in the first named counties, on account of their inferior state of improvement.

"Farms with about thirty per cent. cleared can be bought here for six to ten dollars per acre, according to quality or proximity to market or roads. Wild lands, in lots to suit purchasers, from two to eight dollars per acre. Lands near the Northwestern Branch Railroad bring comparatively high prices, in part from the value of the timber, which is generally of superior growth and quality. Mineral lands are higher.

"A correct statement of the average amount of grain produced per acre, in any given county of the State, would not give an accurate estimate of the producing capacity of our soil, because on all recently cleared land, stumps, roots, and loose stones on the surface, and also the vermin of the adjacent forest, materially contribute to diminish the yield to be expected from the quality of the soil; while, on the other hand, there is a wide difference in professional skill and industry among our farmers. We have still among us a goodly number of the old hunter pioneers, or of their immediate descendants, who are content to live almost from hand to mouth, and never used any other plough but the one-horse shovel.

"The bottoms of rivers, with few exceptions, yield, under good cultivation, from fifty to one hundred bushels of corn, and an average of about twenty bushels of wheat, from twenty to thirty-five of rye and oats, one hundred and fifty to two hundred bushels potatoes, and from two to two and a half tons of timothy hay. Turnips sown on fresh cleared land, barely scarred by the shovel-plough, have been known to produce near eight hundred per acre. Tobacco, on new-made land, also proves to be very remunerative, and certainly grows most luxuriantly, though I have not at hand the figures under this head to show cash results.

"Hillside lands of the same quality of those bottoms, except in depth, must naturally yield less on account of their unadaptedness to the same thorough cultivation, and also because of the diminished number of plants growing on declivities, yet a great portion of those lands, when lying towards the sun, produce for many years in succession from fifty to sixty bushels of corn, and other grain in proportion. In the yield of grass, this difference is not so sensible, and rolling or steep lands are generally sown in grass after two or three grain crops, and devoted to grazing.

"The yield of wheat, which does not average over thirteen or fifteen bushels per acre in the rougher portions of the State, would be greater if its cultivation was confined to limestone land or to dry upland or table land. As it is, wheat is sown there on rich porous soil, in order to get in sod, the grass seed being generally sown with it, and on such soil, particularly on hill-sides, and when put in late after cutting up the corn, wheat is exposed to freeze out during a severe winter.

"When devoted to grazing and in good sod, more or less mixed with blue grass, which comes up spontaneously on limestone land and old grazed pastures, from two and one-half to three acres are allowed for the fattening of a three-year-old steer per season, say from 1st of April to middle or end of August, and the weight thus gained by the animal is estimated at the minimum of ten dollars, ranging from that to fifteen dollars, while the latter figure is realized on many cattle grazed from March till June only, when properly cared for during the preceding winter."

The grain produced is uniformly consumed upon the farms, with few exceptions, in localities favored by river transportation with good facilities for reaching good markets and high prices. Feeding surplus grain to stock is wisely preferred to selling it, not only because it thus transports itself to the railroad and a market almost without trouble or expense, but because a large percentage of its value is returned to the soil as manure, furnishing one of the surest, most feasible, and valuable modes of fertilization known. This mode of manuring must ever commend itself to West Virginia, with its uneven surface and liability to wash, which will tend to increase with increasing thoroughness in pulverization. It is fair to say, however, that the excessive liability to wash existing in some soils does not characterize those under consideration. The rearing and fattening of stock is destined to be the principal business of the farmer, as it is the most profitable everywhere — a fact attested by the dependence placed upon it in England for paying the high rents of that country. The yield of the cereals is equal to the average throughout the west, but they are less remunerative than hay and grass, except in very rare instances of accidental fluctuations in price.

Mr. Debar refers to numerous instances in his knowledge in which the fertility of the soil has been tested by annual products for fifteen years of fifty to seventy-five bushels of corn per acre, without manure;

THE CENTRAL GROUP. 133

then, after clover two or three years, and ploughing ten or twelve inches deep, and one good crop of wheat, it has yielded from two to two and a half tons of hay per acre. This whole region, and indeed West Virginia generally, though particularly adapted to meat and wool producing, dairying and fruit-growing, is suited to the production of almost every product natural to the temperate zone, while, in certain glades and mountain heights, buckwheat, oats, potatoes, and grass, are the main reliance; yet throughout almost the entire area the soil is well adapted to corn, wheat, oats, buckwheat, potatoes, roots, hemp, flax, tobacco, sugar-cane, fruits, and grasses.

Monongalia County lies upon the Pennsylvania line. Laurel Ridge rises on its eastern border, and the Monongahela and Cheat Rivers intersect it. The county-seat is Morgantown. Among its exports are cattle, lumber, flour, and iron, which are transported both by railroad and steamboat. It is an enterprising, productive, and improving section of the State.

Marion, the next county south, is also drained by the Monongahela, formed here by the confluence of Tygart's Valley and West Fork Rivers. It is a small county, rich in coal and iron, with abundant water-power, magnificent forests, and fine pasturage. Fairmount, a pleasant village on both railroad and river, is its capital.

Taylor is a very small county, embracing an area less than that of four townships of Government surveys, and formed from Harrison, Barbour, and Marion. It is prominent as the point at which the Baltimore and Ohio Railroad bifurcates to Wheeling and Parkersburg. To the traveller its surroundings are picturesque, but very forbidding in the eye of the prairie farmer wandering eastward. It has a population of only seven thousand four hundred and sixty-three, yet its railway facilities have given to land valuation something like its intrinsic worth, the average of farms being already sixteen dollars and one cent per acre. Among these mountains grow yearly seventy-eight thousand and one bushels of corn, eighty thousand three hundred and fifty-seven pounds of butter are produced, and three thousand one hundred and sixty tons of hay are made, and animals are slaughtered to the value of twenty-two thousand three hundred and eighty-three dollars. Grafton, the point of intersection of the Parkersburg branch with the main stem of the Baltimore and Ohio Railroad, is in this county.

Barbour County lies further up Tygart's Valley River, and is also drained by Buckhannon River and Elk Creek. Philippa, famed as the opening scene of the war of the rebellion in the State of Virginia, is the county-seat. Its assessed valuation averages scarcely half as much as that of Taylor, simply because it is less favored in facilities for transportation. The fertility of its soil is well attested by one hundred and ninety-seven thousand four hundred and fifty bushels of corn, and three hundred and seventy-seven thousand six hundred and ninety-three dollars value of live stock, fifty-three thousand four hundred and fifty-two dollars value of slaughtered animals, and large figures generally for farm products, considered with reference to its population of only eight thousand nine hundred and fifty-eight.

This county is claimed to be the scene of the first

permanent settlement of Northwestern Virginia. Two brothers, John and Samuel Pringle, deserters from Fort Pitt, went up Tygart's Valley River, ascended its right fork, or Buckhannon River, and sought a home in a hollow sycamore at the mouth of Turkey Run. Here, exposed to the tomahawk of the Indians, and fearing to approach the bounds of civilization at the risk of arrest as deserters, they lived for several years, surrounded by herds of buffalo and deer, their ears pierced by the shrieks of panthers and the howling of wolves, if not attuned to the melodies of nature. When assured of the return of peace, they turned their backs upon their forest home, but returned in 1768, from the South Branch of the Potomac, accompanied by friends, who eventually established themselves in this now growing settlement.

The county was formed in 1843, from Harrison, Lewis, and Randolph.

Taking the west fork of the Monongahela, the reader will come to Harrison County, of which Clarksburg is the principal town, situated upon the Northwestern Virginia Railroad, a branch of the Baltimore and Ohio. It possesses a limestone soil, fertile and durable. It is perhaps the most improved of the inland counties, and has a farm valuation of four million six hundred and forty-two thousand seven hundred and ninety-four dollars, exceeded only by that of Greenbrier and Jefferson. The value of its live stock is six hundred and forty-four thousand three hundred and twenty-five dollars, exceeded only by Hampshire and Greenbrier. With such figures, the value of slaughtered animals, seventy-five thousand eight hundred and eighty-three dollars, will not be deemed extraordinary. In corn, of which the product is three hundred and twenty thousand nine hundred and forty-six bushels, it is exceeded only by Hampshire and Jackson. Clarksburg is the seat of a fine trade in coal. It also contains valuable iron ore. It was named in honor of a former Governor of Virginia.

Lewis is directly south of Harrison, higher up on the same stream; produces four thousand four hundred and sixteen tons of hay, considerable quantities of grain; possesses excellent pasturage, and many good and productive farms. It derives its name from Colonel Charles Lewis, who fell in the fight with the Indians at Point Pleasant. Weston is the capital.

Doddridge is another railroad county west of Harrison. Its staples are also corn and grass. Cattle thrive for six months of the year with no other pasturage than the range of the forests. Nutritious grasses spring naturally wherever the surface is denuded of timber. Its proportion of improved to unimproved land is twenty-five thousand one hundred and fourteen acres to two hundred and seventeen thousand five hundred and forty-three; its average valuation, by the census of 1860, four dollars and fourteen cents. It is drained by Middle Island Creek, which flows into the Ohio River, and the North Fork of Hughes River, which is a tributary of the Little Kanawha. Both of these streams have gained celebrity during the petroleum excitement; and the present prices of lands here bear little proportion to the assessed valuation of former days. West Union is the county-seat.

Ritchie County, next east of Jackson, upon the

railroad, has a variety of surface, which is broken into very abrupt ridges in places, exhibiting in dislocated strata the effects of violent upheaval; the soil, too, is variable, but generally productive. It was named in honor of Thomas Ritchie, editor of the Richmond Enquirer. It is drained by the Hughes River. But a small portion of farm lands are as yet improved. It is in the midst of the oil formation, which extends south from western Pennsylvania to the Kanawha. The famous lubricating oil, used by the Baltimore and Ohio Railroad, is pumped from shallow wells near Petroleum, twenty-two miles from Parkersburg.

Wirt County, south and west of Ritchie, is in the second tier of counties from the Ohio, upon the Little Kanawha. It is also declivitous and oil-yielding, and is the location of the oldest and most extensive system of oil wells to be found in the State. Their discovery was attended with much excitement; the proprietors of the soil are deriving immense revenues as rental, and the operators are variously meeting with returns ranging from the fullest success to the most decided failure. Some wells are improving, and others failing, after temporary suspension, are again worked. A singular geological phenomenon of the oil region has attracted attention in this vicinity. A large portion of its land is unimproved, but naturally productive; its assessed value averages five dollars and eleven cents. Its crop statistics show an average yield of farm products.

Calhoun is a small county, also intersected by the Little Kanawha, containing farms of average fertility, assessed at nearly the same value as those of Wirt, and occupied mainly for the rearing of live stock. It has of late shared in the general advance of prices, caused by the production of petroleum in the adjoining county of Wirt, and the prospect of similar results, in some degree, throughout the region drained by the Little Kanawha and its branches.

Gilmer adjoins Calhoun on the east, has fine forest ranges for cattle, and a comparatively small area of improved land. Its principal water-courses are the Little Kanawha River, and Lick, Leading and Steer Creeks. Its minerals are iron, coal, salt and petroleum. It was named in honor of Thomas W. Gilmer, a member of Congress for Virginia.

Roane, south of Calhoun, abounds in steep hills and grassy valleys, through which flow the waters of the Pocotalico and other streams, tributaries of the Great Kanawha. It is a fine region for sheep, and unwillingly furnished ten thousand dollars' worth of horses for the cavalry of the Rebels. The number of sheep was rapidly increasing in 1862; but the raiders having a taste for good mutton, it is presumed that losses and gains have left the flocks as they were in 1860. Tobacco does well in this as in the adjoining counties, yielding a product that commands a fine price for its excellent flavor. In one instance last season, twenty-one acres, with indifferent culture, brought two thousand dollars. When such results call be attained with so little labor on lands which average but a few dollars per acre, it should not be said that the soil here is unproductive or farming unprofitable. Fruit is usually abundant. Good peach crops have been enjoyed for a succession of years past. The fruit is often sold at twenty-five cents per bushel.

In evidence of the adaptation of this soil to tobacco, a statement of a correspondent may be referred to relative to the crop of a neighbor, Martin W. Kidd, of this county. The land was in forest, and cost, to clear twenty acres and cultivate the crop, eleven hundred dollars, and one hundred and fifty dollars more to get it to market. Though he lost considerable of it for want of sheds sufficient to cure it properly, he sold thirteen thousand five hundred pounds for two thousand six hundred and seventy-four dollars. This gave a profit of fourteen hundred and twenty-one dollars, or seventy-one dollars and five cents per acre — amply sufficient to buy a large farm of unimproved land.

Braxton County is more nearly than any other the geographical centre of the State. It is intersected by the Elk and Little Kanawha, and their tributaries. It is well-watered, has a very productive soil, heavy seams of valuable coal, and other mineral wealth, as iron, salt, and petroleum. It is comparatively uncultivated; little more than an eighth of the farm lands is improved. The average assessed valuation of all farm lands in 1860, was but four dollars and twenty-eight cents, a sum by no means representing their real or prospective value. They are now held at far higher rates. This county is midway between Clarksburg and Charleston, and on the proposed Central Railroad route. It was formed in 1836, from Lewis, Kanawha, and Nicholas, and received its name in honor of Carter Braxton, a signer of the Declaration of Independence. Bulltown, a locality of some prominence, is so named from Captain Bull, a chief, who resided here at the head of a small band of Indians.

Upshur County is centrally situated, south of Barbour, and gives rise to the West Fork of the Monongahela. It has a fertile soil, and is rich in a great variety of minerals. It is sparsely settled, and has but a small percentage of farm lands in actual cultivation. It contains some enterprising farmers, who have made valuable improvements, which show the capabilities of the soil. Like most of the interior lands of this State, their average value in the market has been very low, notwithstanding their intrinsic worth for agricultural and mining purposes. Buckhannon is the principal town. This county was the main theatre of war in the opening campaign of West Virginia. Here the battle of Rich Mountain was fought, and hence the defeated Rebels fled, and essayed to cross the mountains into East Virginia.

Webster, drained by the headwaters of the Elk and Gauley Rivers, a new county with resources very little developed, and lands cheap — averaging one dollar and sixty-one cents per acre, in 1860. Its mineral resources are equally abundant with those of neighboring counties, and will, in the future, be valuable. Its lands are admirably adapted to pasturage.

Nicholas, upon the south, intersected by the Gauley, has a promising future. It contains one million four hundred and sixty thousand two hundred and twenty-eight acres of farm lands, of which but thirty-four thousand nine hundred and forty-one are improved; average valuation two dollars and fifty-one cents per acre. It has clear running streams, filled with the speckled trout, and fine forest pastures and grassy glades. Though only two and a half per cent. of its farm lands are improved, its live stock is valued at three hundred thirty-four thousand eight hundred and twenty dollars; its flocks of sheep numbering nine thousand and ninety-three; and while it lies well up towards the mountains, there is required for the winter support of twenty thousand five hundred and twenty-six farm animals, but two thousand and thirty-five tons of hay. Winters cannot be very severe if one hundred pounds of hay will suffice for each animal.

Clay County lies south of Braxton, upon the Elk River. It is a small county, with but five thousand five hundred and sixty-five acres of improved land. Its location is eligible, and much of its land productive. The proposed central line of railroad must intersect it. Were the road completed, few counties could boast a more eligible position, or better prospects.

There is material enough in the mineral, agricultural and natural features of this central portion of the State for a volume. In this partial (perhaps preliminary) record of some of its striking and obvious points, only a glimpse of its natural magnificence can be enjoyed. Were a more extended view included in the present design, the disturbed condition of the country, and the topographical and geological labor necessary to a thorough survey, would materially interfere to mar the success of the work. It is believed, however, that new light will be thrown upon the resources of this remarkable country, and a truer impression of its real feature be given to people of other States.

CHAPTER XII.

STATISTICS OF PRODUCTION.

A STATEMENT of the farm products of West Virginia* will not indicate an extraordinary production in proportion to population, nor will it show so meagre a result as most people in other States would have predicted. In view of the fact that a large element of the population has been that of the forerunner of civilization, the pioneer, who desires nothing more than elbow-room and a wide forest range for game, and is content to lead a primitive life, knowing few wants and those easily supplied, these figures prove incontestably a fertile soil.

A Statement of the farm products, etc., of West Virginia, compiled from the census returns for 1860, by permission of Commissioner Kennedy.

Acres of improved land	2,346,137
Acres of unimproved land	8,550,257
Cash value of farms	$87,525,087
Value of farming implements and machinery	$1,973,158
Horses	85,862
Asses and mules	1,674
Milch cows	100,154
Working oxen	18,696

---

* The statement in this chapter, as well as those interspersed in descriptions of the several counties, is based upon the census returns of 1860. Returns made to the State Auditor, if they could be made complete, would show advancement in many of the counties even during a civil war.

STATISTICS OF PRODUCTION. 143

Other cattle	191,239
Sheep	453,334
Swine	327,214
Value of live stock	$12,382,680
Wheat, bushels of	2,302,567
Rye, bushels of	71,263
Indian corn, bushels of	7,858,647
Oats, bushels of	1,649,090
Rice, pounds of	1,163
Tobacco, pounds of	2,180,316
Ginned cotton, bales of, 400 pounds each	125
Wool, pounds of	1,073,163
Peas and beans, bushels of	31,332
Irish potatoes, bushels of	746,606
Sweet potatoes, bushels of	68,081
Barley, bushels of	60,368
Buckwheat, bushels of	342,518
Value of orchard products	$234,273
Wine, gallons of	2,368
Value of produce of market gardens	$44,299
Butter, pounds of	4,760,779
Cheese, pounds of	131,585
Hay, tons of	154,136
Clover-seed, bushels of	7,230
Grass-seeds, bushels of	10,571
Hops, pounds of	3,018
Hemp, dew-rotted, tons of	407
Hemp, water-rotted, tons of	1,020
Other prepared hemp	1,599
Flax, pounds of	183,498
Flax-seed, bushels of	8,430
Silk cocoons, pounds of	69
Maple sugar, pounds of	667,178
Maple molasses, gallons of	71,425
Sorghum molasses, gallons of	174,318
Beeswax, pounds of	30,459
Honey, pounds of	423,359
Value of home-made manufactures	$502,671
Value of animals slaughtered	$2,124,869

The value of live stock is twelve million three hundred and eighty-two thousand six hundred and eighty dollars, a sum exceeding the value of the same interest in New Hampshire, Connecticut, Delaware, Florida, Kansas, Minnesota, and other States, and exceeded in Massachusetts by only three hundred and fifty-five thousand and sixty-four dollars.

The value of slaughtered animals, two million one hundred and twenty-four thousand eight hundred and sixty-nine dollars, exceeds the income from the same source in Delaware, Florida, Kansas, Louisiana, Mississippi, Rhode Island, and Oregon. It is exceeded slightly in Maine (two million seven hundred and eighty thousand one hundred and seventy-nine dollars), Maryland (two million eight hundred and twenty-one thousand five hundred and ten dollars), Massachusetts (two million nine hundred and fifteen thousand and forty-five dollars), and Vermont (two million five hundred and forty-nine thousand and one dollars).

The product of butter exceeds that of eleven States, among them California, Kansas, the Carolinas, Mississippi, and Louisiana. Maryland makes but four hundred and ninety-four thousand five hundred and sixteen pounds more.

In flax, greater results are shown than in any of the States, with the exception of Kentucky, New York, Pennsylvania, North Carolina, and Virginia proper, the last of which is far exceeded by West Virginia in proportion either to population or area.

More of maple sugar is found than in a score of the States, and this product could be increased more than ten-fold. Sorghum is also a growing interest.

The following is the order of precedence of the counties in the several items indicated: In farm implements, Hampshire, Barbour, Jefferson. In value of farm lands per acre, Jefferson, Brooke, Ohio, Hancock. In horses, Hampshire, Harrison, Monongalia. In cows, Hampshire, Preston, Marion. In working oxen, Wayne, Kanawha. In sheep, Brooke, Ohio, Hancock, Hampshire, Preston. In swine, Jefferson, Hampshire, Berkeley, Harrison, Greenbrier. In corn, Hampshire, Jefferson, Harrison. In wheat, Jefferson, Berkeley, Mason, Hampshire. In oats, Marshall, Monongalia, Greenbrier, Preston. In barley, Ohio, Brooke, Hancock. In buckwheat, Hampshire, Pendleton, Marshall. In butter, Pocahontas, Hampshire, Marion, Monongalia, Berkeley. In hay, Hardy, Hampshire, Berkeley, Barbour, Monongalia, Jefferson, Marion. In tobacco, Putnam, Kanawha, Mercer, Wood, Monroe, Fayette. In flax, Nicholas, Upshur, Mercer, Barbour, Logan, Marion. In cheese, Harrison, Upshur, Preston, Barbour, Monroe, Marion. In potatoes, Marshall, Preston, Hampshire, Wood, Jackson, Jefferson.

Statement of the number and value of different kinds of live stock, according to the United States Census of 1860.

Counties.	Horses.	Asses and mules.	Milch cows.	Working oxen.	Other cattle.	Sheep.	Swine.	Value of live stock.
Barbour.....	3,059	81	3,726	418	7,715	11,673	9.916	$377,693
Berkeley ...	3,510	19	2,728	12	3,687	7,057	13,469	335,757
Boone........	787	9	1,444	428	3,078	3,248	7,653	120,589
Braxton.....	976	19	1,395	197	1,826	6,108	5,040	109,456
Brooke......	1,399	18	1,319	169	1,513	40,620	3,309	282,439
Cabell	1,350	66	1,475	856	3,780	5,764	8,408	195,674
Calhoun	484	10	741	242	1,491	2,412	2,956	74,651
Clay..........	286	10	538	150	637	1,603	2,412	41,824
Doddridge..	1,182	2	1,664	232	3,147	5,377	4,332	142,269
Fayette......	1,266	20	1,767	471	2,467	6,998	7,723	177,440
Gilmer	815	8	1,197	205	2,392	3,967	3,864	113,722
Greenbrier.	3,714	128	3,984	686	8,103	16,067	10,971	676,298
Hampshire	5,222	57	5,522	6	11,355	21,287	14,619	763,454
Hancock ...	1,109	4	1,127	140	1,057	21,402	2,465	182,746
Hardy	2,526	54	2,561	142	8,244	11,378	7,032	453,768
Harrison ..	4,404	35	4,501	681	12,163	13,202	11,496	644,325
Jackson.....	1,330	23	1,541	504	2,513	6,615	6,538	173,354
Jefferson ..	3,421	128	2,316	135	4,071	7,269	15,044	406,168
Kanawha ..	1,402	153	1,889	1,047	3,282	4,936	10,135	197,224
Lewis..	1,617	12	1,902	364	5,452	8,250	4,554	225,500
Logan	885	23	1,595	827	3,513	4,673	9,197	161,490
Marion	3,762	54	4,629	654	5,680	9,029	9,985	406,254
Marshall....	2,413	2	2,501	573	3,113	10,022	8,447	280,860
Mason	1,355	75	1,254	616	3,266	5,582	8,294	252,063
Mercer.......	1,552	37	2,218	199	4,128	10,225	11,308	244,954
Monongalia	3,904	32	3,881	680	7,090	10,945	8,028	454,070
Monroe	3,216	47	3,058	407	9,161	12,288	10,172	500,268
Morgan......	972	6	1,036	18	1,709	2,992	3,300	111,439
McDowell...	222	8	573	25	785	860	2,463	33,785
Nicholas ...	1,358	52	1,728	505	4,523	9,093	12,390	334,820
Ohio..........	1,441	3	1,408	246	1,380	40,050	3,244	253,090
Pendleton .	2,543	1	3,423	11	6,372	14,143	5,744	371,228
Pocahontas	1.688	53	2,447	246	5,471	10,338	5,099	328,002
Preston......	3,326	41	4,993	591	5,846	19,084	8,854	461,133
Putnam	1,229	114	1,507	924	2,891	5,924	8,084	185,995
Pleasants...	646	1	725	211	1,300	2,837	2,386	84,275
Raleigh	466	5	794	128	1,311	3,569	3,663	69,038
Randolph ..	1,189	17	1,700	237	6,106	7,565	3,267	244,857
Ritchie	1,724	36	2,117	392	3,409	7,925	7,891	213,147
Roane........	783	26	1,011	247	1,625	6,190	4,380	86,180
Taylor	1,137	30	1,347	219	2,721	4,788	3,710	162,864
Tucker......	448	6	536	78	1,337	2,651	1,291	58,850
Tyler	1,484	20	1,644	476	2,829	8,748	5,942	202,707
Upshur	1,055	5	2,508	305	4,690	9,821	5,078	271,523
Wayne	1,240	113	1,524	1,297	2,642	7,405	8,898	175,008
Webster.....	356	2	693	89	972	2,474	1,691	44,304
Wetzel	1,502	4	1,806	365	3,056	6,244	6,293	169,639
Wirt	874	14	1,086	310	1,589	5,032	4,188	110,417
Wood........	1,899	6	2,197	638	2,706	7,360	7,258	214,077
Wyoming ..	414	15	868	99	2,365	1,233	4,733	81,992
	85,862	1,674	100,154	18,696	191,239	453,334	427,214	12,382,680

The writer has endeavored to procure more recent returns from the office of the State Auditor of West

Virginia, and has succeeded in obtaining a partial record of the condition of live stock; but the southern and southwestern, and some of the mountain counties have been so infested with guerillas, and in so unsettled a condition that the statement would be too partial and incomplete to be satisfactory.

In some counties great losses have been incurred in live stock from marauding, particularly in horses. Yet the State returns for 1862 give an increase in horses, over 1860, in the counties of Barbour, Brooke, Cabell, Doddridge, Harrison, Hancock, Jackson, Kanawha, Lewis, Monongalia, Marshall, Ohio, Preston, and several others. In some cases this increase is extraordinary, as in Kanawha, from fourteen hundred and two to five thousand two hundred and twenty-two, doubtless due to a great influx from Fayette and Greenbrier, on the great highway to rebeldom, and from which there is no report. The same disturbing causes have affected other stock to some extent. Sheep had already increased, in 1862, in Brooke, from forty thousand six hundred and twenty to forty-six thousand two hundred; in Hancock, from twenty-one thousand four hundred and two to twenty-nine thousand nine hundred and thirty-two; in Harrison, from thirteen thousand two hundred and two to seventeen thousand nine hundred and ninety-one; in Monongalia, from ten thousand nine hundred and forty-five to seventeen thousand five hundred and ninety-four; in Marshall, from sixteen thousand and twenty-two to twenty-two thousand one hundred and ninety-seven; in Preston, from nineteen thousand and eighty-four to twenty-five thousand nine hundred and eighty. Since that date there has been a still heavier increase.

Statement exhibiting the quantity and value of some of the principal items of farm produce according to the Census of 1860.

Counties.	Wheat.	Rye.	Indian corn.	Oats.	Tobacco.	Irish potatoes	Butter.	Slaughtered animals.
	Bushels.	Bushels.	Bushels.	Bushels.	Pounds.	Bushels.	Pounds.	Value.
Barbour.....	37,835	4,794	197,460	29,680	596	17,256	161,027	$53,452
Berkeley...	237,576	18,672	275,525	76,176	....	18,962	160,069	93,555
Boone........	15.278	1,118	143,808	7,994	18,729	10,620	59,262	30,879
Braxton.....	22,366	604	122,749	17,695	15,534	8,300	43,772	20,327
Brooke.......	23,490	3,506	142,122	64,984	....	20,488	140,326	36,763
Cabell.......	65,715	356	248,210	18,717	68,578	11,119	45,230	49,736
Calhoun.....	10,734	56	69,847	6,423	7,882	6,088	61,050	13,455
Clay	4,433	410	44,310	6,150	26,229	4,269	27,868	12,507
Doddridge..	16,514	569	124,133	6,765	7,025	13,724	66,554	24,848
Fayette	25,693	2,403	131,425	28,433	127,713	10,223	82.082	44,107
Gilmer......	18,609	168	126,944	11,800	61,104	7,836	77,274	21,167
Greenbrier	52,017	10,610	231,479	112,055	3,000	24,858	151,156	114,265
Hampshire.	106,310	75,257	375,000	49,259	75	41,773	239,360	109,834
Hancock...	16,423	5,117	61,346	46,716	....	26,002	125,446	26,396
Hardy.......	39,946	28,043	286,618	20,200	1,450	18,534	102,603	71,698
Harrison...	55,411	936	320,946	37,501	11,715	15,357	155,419	75,883
Jackson.....	68,338	228	219,377	11,878	74,691	32,630	111,500	40,260
Jefferson...	422,514	15,198	358,267	54,798	6,700	31,876	131,684	110,221
Kanawha..	76,305	198	274,943	45,430	338,264	12,352	59,196	56,345
Lewis........	27,191	579	136,677	12,418	62,910	9,822	66,230	28,817
Logan........	11,025	530	199,385	11,067	13,545	9,794	48,247	30,559
Marion	50,894	1,159	214,706	86,409	25,012	12,618	226,852	55,990
Marshall ...	74,759	2,830	241,911	133,617	10,590	46.634	146,715	44,944
Mason	108,839	330	264,813	6,402	21,936	11,873	67,337	55,706
Mercer	43,131	5,021	131,654	55,843	182,554	10,533	81,454	58,132
Monongalia	49,124	4,999	239,024	126,198	1,380	10,586	171,876	46,934
Monroe	84,806	13,422	216,513	59,265	132,019	12,692	112,753	78,506
Morgan	19,404	16,082	47,575	10,122	2,234	7,806	61,152	21,323
McDowell..	1,041	285	20,445	2,215	1,275	1,410	6,407	8,138
Nicholas ...	12,894	6,128	103,193	26,613	14,470	16,528	110,453	64,227
Ohio	20,048	5,639	138,430	82,101	....	21,449	128,448	26,930
Pendleton .	11,475	11,927	122,907	16,516	2,073	13,366	101,838	45,319
Pocahontas	8,774	9,787	48,229	26,612	190	12,090	121,310	41,554
Preston	8,933	10,778	71,063	104,317	185	44,655	340,988	80,407
Putnam......	78,796	43	197,700	16,355	406,992	9,192	81,940	57,165
Pleasants...	22.785	319	102,172	7,395	27,930	7,747	30,500	15,284
Raleigh	6,700	1,825	39,301	11,713	34,827	3,719	22,644	13,363
Randolph ..	7,675	2,126	56,225	20,248	1,117	8,349	57,332	24,583
Ritchie.....	27,582	369	147,785	14,978	18,606	19,490	92,337	35,763
Roane	21,897	705	100,074	8,743	10,268	6,593	44,116	20,571
Taylor	20,811	898	76,001	25,610	3,139	4,294	80,357	22,383
Tucker......	1,103	1,147	19,955	6,049	710	4,346	17,057	7,721
Tyler	43,727	283	182,239	28,512	11,225	23,733	130,527	35,150
Upshur	27,765	1,719	149,496	20,337	50,900	13,639	126,350	35,217
Wayne	35,319	362	224,044	13,077	55,628	8,898	71,514	40,241
Webster	1,586	791	25,602	3,100	....	2,194	11,587	6,439
Wetzel......	31,652	1,529	180,150	26,775	84,989	14.430	124,342	28,182
Wirt	27,488	202	115,046	5,096	44,074	8,769	41,602	22,749
Wood	74,236	244	227,223	19,158	166,365	33,166	12,175	51,682
Wyoming..	5,601	962	62,420	9,515	4,778	4,024	22,855	14,740
	2,302,567	71,263	7,858,647	1,649,090	2,180,316	746,606	4,760,779	2,124,849

CHAPTER XIII.

INTERNAL IMPROVEMENTS. — ROADS AND TURNPIKES. — SLACKWATER NAVIGATION. — OHIO AND CHESAPEAKE CANAL. — BALTIMORE AND OHIO RAILROAD. — OTHER RAILROADS.

THE State of Virginia has undertaken many enterprises, and expended much money, obtained by general taxation, for the construction of roads and the improvement of rivers; but that portion of the State now constituting West Virginia has shared little in those benefits. Her interests have been ignored, her mineral treasures left inaccessible, her farm products isolated from market. Some State improvements in this quarter were, at times, feebly essayed, to silence the rising murmurs of popular discontent, and partially completed or wholly abandoned at the caprice of the State oligarchy.

The neighborhood roads, in a sparsely-settled and hilly country, cannot, of course, be in a high state of improvement; yet much labor has been expended upon them, and many of them are, in favorable seasons, quite passable thoroughfares, and some are in excellent condition. Since the existence of the new State organization, a thorough and stringent law has been enacted relative to the construction and working of roads, which is expected to answer all the requirments of a most effective system, and secure convenient means of local communication.

Numerous turnpikes add to the facilities for travel in all the more densely-settled portions of the State. Parkersburg has long been connected with Staunton, and also with Winchester, in the Valley east of the Alleghanies, by turnpike routes; and there has also been maintained a daily stage line between Guyandotte, at the mouth of the river of that name, and Covington, *via* Charleston and the White Sulphur Springs. These are all long lines, and involve considerable capital and enterprise in their management and maintenance.

Other lines, of less extent, afford facilities for trade and travel. That from Sutton to Fairmount, down the West Fork of the Monongahela, has been a prominent thoroughfare. Inaccessible as the country seems, in the interior and mountain counties, there are numerous roads chartered as turnpikes; for example, in Preston, among precipitous mountains, the "Northwestern Turnpike" passes through the south end of the county; the "Maryland and Fishing Creek Turnpike" crosses the northern end; the "Brandonville, Kingwood, and Evansville Turnpike" runs centrally north and south; the "Morgantown, Kingwood, and West Union" road divides the county in the opposite direction; the "Ice's Ferry and Tunnelton;" and the "Brandonville and Cranberry Summit," leading to the top of the mountain. Other counties are similarly provided. Yet the roads, many of them at least, are in bad condition, compared with those of older and richer settlements. By acts of the Legislature, provision has been made for the better supervision and more careful working of highways. Internal improvements will receive their proper share of attention from the Legislature in the future; and facilities for neighborhood travel will speedily be enlarged.

Steamboat navigation is confined to a very few streams, as might be expected in a mountainous country.

The Monongahela is navigated by steamboats in a good stage of water to Fairmont, in Marion County. Slackwater improvements have been made upon it at intervals through its entire course to Pittsburg. It has proved of immense benefit to the adjacent population in affording facilities for transportation of iron from the furnaces in the vicinity of the river, coal from its banks, the produce of the farmers, and supplies of the merchants.

The Great Kanawha is navigable to the falls near the mouth of Gauley river, a distance of nearly one hundred miles. Millions of bushels of salt, immense quantities of coal, and large quantities of merchandise, have thus found a market, and a large passenger trade has been accommodated. Like the upper Ohio, this river sometimes has its navigation obstructed; in the summer only steamers of light draught can ply; but with a little deepening and clearing of the channel, it may be made entirely navigable at all seasons. Some dredging has been occasionally done, and slight improvements in its navigation effected, but reliance has generally been placed on the ordinary natural facilities afforded by the stream itself. The fact that through this avenue cannel and other coals, in unlimited quantities, can be obtained for the markets down the river with one hundred miles less of transportation than from Pittsburg, should stimulate improvement in this direction, and aid in developing the magnificent coal interests of the Great Kanawha. The capital recently enlisted in coal and petroleum enterprises in this valley, will ensure a speedy improvement in the navigation of the river.

The Guyandotte river has enjoyed slackwater navigation to a certain extent. Dams were built, but no very substantial or permanent works constructed. They have fallen into neglect, especially since the commencement of the war, and are now nearly if not entirely useless. Action is already initiated looking towards the rebuilding of these works.

The Little Kanawha could easily be made navigable for a distance sufficient to add considerably to the convenience and wealth of the communities in proximity to it, and the wants of the oil region will soon, without doubt, accomplish successfully the improvement. In a good stage of water the oil is now either boated down in bulk, or floated in barrels, in large quantities, to Parkersburg. Large rafts of barrels filled with oil, present a novel and peculiar aspect of river transportation. Oil capitalists promise a speedy construction of works for facilitating the navigation of the river. The interests involved must accomplish the result at an early day.

The Ohio and Chesapeake Canal connects Cumberland, in Maryland, with Georgetown, D. C. It follows the course of the Potomac river, and for near a hundred miles of its length in West Virginia.

The Baltimore and Ohio railroad, with its branches,

furnishes the only railway facilities enjoyed by West Virginia, with one small exception. It is to the enterprise and invincible determination of this company, and not to aid from the State of Virginia, that the now partial development of the resources of the northern counties of the new State is due.

The construction of this road was commenced on the fourth of July, 1828; it was opened to Ellicott's Mills, twelve miles from Baltimore, May 22, 1830; its opening to Washington was celebrated in August, 1834. Westward its construction was pushed for many weary years, through and over mountains, across yawning abysses and over wide rivers, moving now with celerity on the surface of level glades, and then with a progress labored and slow, boring through the solid rock, until at last the waters of the Ohio and of the Chesapeake were united, the Alleghanies were surmounted, and shrill pæans to the triumph of steam in intercontinental transportation were screamed by a thousand iron throats from the seaboard to the mountain summits, and from the vine-clad banks of the Ohio to the cane-fields on the alluvial plains of Louisiana.

It was one of the first railroad enterprises undertaken in the United States, and it is one of the most extensive. The length of the main stem, from Baltimore to Wheeling, is three hundred and seventy-nine miles; that of the Washington branch, thirty-one miles. Other branches increase its total length to five hundred and twenty miles. Of sidings and second main track, there are built nearly three hundred miles more. The original cost of the entire work was thirty-one millions of dollars.

Its heaviest permanent grade on the eastern declivity of the Alleghanies, is one hundred and sixteen feet per mile for seventeen miles; its greatest altitude, two thousand six hundred and twenty feet. It has twelve repair stations, thirty-three repair shops, ninety-eight water stations, thirty telegraph stations and three lines of wires, fourteen tunnels, twelve thousand six hundred and ninety-four feet of tunnelling, one hundred and eighty-six bridges on the main stem, fifteen thousand and eighty-eight feet of bridging, about four thousand cars, and nearly two hundred and thirty-eight engines, and gives occupation to five thousand officers and employees. Its annual income, in good times, has been five millions of dollars, and since the war would have been doubled if in full operation.

The road-bed is probably superior to any line of considerable length in America. It is rock-ballasted, and laid with heavy rail strongly secured. The first rail used weighed fifty-five pounds per lineal yard, for which rail of seventy-five and eighty-five pounds was substituted.

Astonishing activity has characterized the repair of portions of the line damaged by raids during the war, and remarkable exemption from accident is noticed, as, during the entire existence of the road, it has suffered but one serious accident, and that was due to an unavoidable circumstance when the road was new.

Several years ago it was estimated by an officer of the road, that an army of ten thousand men could be transported over it in thirty hours. The prediction is more than verified in the following, received from W. P. Smith, the well-known and appreciated master of transportation of the road:

"The heaviest movement that we have made, or that has been made by any railway in the country, was of the twenty-three thousand men of Hooker's two corps, in September last, from Washington to Chattanooga. This great body of men, with all their artillery, equipage, wagons, and effects, including the cavalry horses, occupied about one thousand cars, and were carried from Washington to Benwood, on the Ohio river (four hundred miles), in about forty hours."

The greatest movement of troops on record — the most gigantic enterprise in transportation ever undertaken — has more recently been accomplished by the management of this road. It involved the moving of portions of our armies to the number of one hundred and seventy thousand men, four thousand horses, with three million pounds of baggage or effects. In the first eight days seventy thousand of the number were started from Washington. Seventy-four thousand, including the army of General Logan, took the Parkersburg route, and embarked on steamboats for Louisville—saving nearly one hundred miles of river transportation over the Wheeling route, and nearly two hundred over that *via* Pittsburg. Negotiations for this movement were made by President Garrett, and its practical details were supervised by the master of transportation, Wm. Prescott Smith. The Washington agent, George S. Koontz, executed with equal assiduity and fidelity the important trust devolved upon him.

The scenery of West Virginia along the line of this road, has been the astonishment and admiration of travellers from all quarters of the globe.

From Harper's Ferry, where the road has broken a rough passage through the frowning mountains of the Blue Ridge, to the crossing of the Potomac again before Cumberland, a distance of ninety-eight miles, the road passes through the eastern section of Western Virginia, a mingled scene of rough ravines, river rapids, widening plains, and mountain barriers, which push forth encroachingly upon the river, compelling a detour not made by the stream without a noisy yet unavailing murmur.

After a run through Maryland of little more than twenty miles, a corner of Hampshire County, in West Virginia, is struck at New Creek and Piedmont, the terminus of the first division of the road, and site of extensive machine shops. From this point a rise of about nineteen hundred feet is accomplished in seventeen miles, the steepest railroad grade in the country. Passing the glade lands of the summit, which are in Maryland, the traveller is again introduced into West Virginia, just as he commences the western descent of the Alleghanies, and views a beautiful panorama of mountain peaks piled upon receding mountains. Soon the most sublime of railroad scenery is in view; the passage of the Cheat River, the winding along the almost perpendicular sides of the mountain, with the chocolate-colored stream far down at its base, and a similar range on the opposite side, presenting to a distant observer a scene aptly represented by a walk furrowed around the spire of a towering steeple. Cheat River is crossed by a viaduct based upon abutments and a pier of solid freestone. A mile further westward, Kyer's Run, seventy-six feet deep, is crossed by an embankment of solid masonry; then Buckeye Hollow is bridged by works one hundred and eight feet in depth; and last, but not least, the famous Tray Run is crossed, at the height of one hundred and fifty feet, by a viaduct six hundred feet long, a huge net-work of iron upon a massive base of masonry. At the west end of the viaduct, from a broad ledge overhanging the precipice, an impressive view of the great chasm of the Cheat River is obtained, with the stream itself three hundred feet below, winding northward and disappearing among the mountains.

Soon another barrier is reached. Projecting spurs have been circumvented, deep ravines overleaped, aspiring knobs bisected, and the height thus perseveringly overcome; but here confronts the road a peak two hundred and twenty feet higher still, and nearly a mile in breadth, of solid earth and rock. The work of tunnelling progressed three years; a year and a half more was consumed in arching it with brick and stone, and it was finished — the Kingwood tunnel, four thousand one hundred feet in length, costing one million dollars — a monument of engineering skill and a triumph of patient labor.

Grafton, nineteen miles further on, is the point of intersection for the Parkersburg branch, which is one hundred and four miles long, while Wheeling is one hundred miles distant by the main stem. Near Fairmont, just below the junction of the Tygart's Valley and West Fork Rivers, forming the Monongahela, is an iron bridge six hundred and fifty feet in length, which has been destroyed during the rebellion and since rebuilt.

The Hempfield Railway is completed and running from Wheeling, east, to Washington, Pennsylvania, thirty-five miles. It is to be continued to West Newton, fifty-six miles from Wheeling, on the Pittsburg and Connellsville road, and thence to Greensburg, on the Pennsylvania Central road, seventy-six miles. In the route to Philadelphia, this will save the distance from Greensburg and twenty miles additional — in fact, nearly half the present distance between Wheeling and Greensburg. It will also shorten the route from Ohio, especially eastern Ohio, to Philadelphia.

These are the only railways at present in operation. Others are in contemplation, and will undoubtedly be built at an early day. One has been organized and partially constructed.

The Covington and Ohio Railroad, designed to connect Richmond with the Ohio River, was completed in 1860 from Covington to the White Sulphur Springs. The work upon the road was continued, and a large sum of money expended in grading, tunnelling, and piers for bridges. The tunnels between the Springs and the Gauley were approaching completion, and from Charleston to the Ohio the road was in a state of forwardness. It was designed to connect at Catlettsburg, on the Kentucky line, with the road thence to Lexington, which was graded and intended to be promptly finished as a section of a through line to the west and southwest. A road through the Kanawha valley, without reference to through business, was recognized as a necessity in the development of the interests of this inexhaustible depository of natural wealth, and credited as a paying investment. In a normal condition of affairs the road would, at the present time, have been completed and in receipt of a heavy trade. It must eventually be built; when, it would scarcely be safe just now to predict.

Another, and under present circumstances more important line, may first be built — a line intended to intersect the State centrally and longitudinally, to connect the Ohio River and Kanawha Valley with the Baltimore and Ohio Railroad, and eventually with roads connecting with Philadelphia and New York. A charter has been granted by the Legislature to the "West Virginia Central Railroad Company," for a road from the Pennsylvania and Kentucky line, at the mouth of the Big Sandy River. All the intermediate points are not definitely fixed, but Charleston, Sutton, and Brandonville indicate the general direction of the route. The crossing of the Baltimore and Ohio road will be at Grafton, or a short distance east of that point. The resources of the central counties, in many respects the most desirable and valuable portion of the State, can scarcely be developed without it — certainly not to the fullest extent — and an early and energetic effort will be made to build it.

A railroad is under construction from the Parkersburg branch of the Baltimore and Ohio Railroad to the McFarland's Run asphaltum lode. Another is projected from Parkersburg towards the headwaters of the Little Kanawha. Railroad improvements, undertaken in the petroleum region, will be promptly carried forward and completed.

CHAPTER XIV.

MINERAL WEALTH. — COAL.

WHATEVER may be said of the capacity of this new mountain State for general agricultural industry, or for the special rural enterprises of so much promise as fruit-growing, wine-making, dairying, or wool production, it cannot be denied that untold wealth is awaiting development in the hillsides, upon the river banks, and in their beds, and deep in the bowels of the earth. Among the minerals may be named coal, iron, lead, copper, silver, antimony, nickel, borax, soda, alum, salt, lime, petroleum, and fire-clay. The denuding of the surface by water or other agencies, and its excavation in deep and sometimes precipitous ravines, through which its drainage is secured, lays bare the several strata of rocks and minerals, brings to view the hidden treasures of the earth, and renders mining easy, and facilitates the removal and distant transportation of the precious deposits sought.

The fact of the existence of these treasures has always been known to the settlers, but their worth has never been appreciated. Of coal every man could have a bank of his own, in many a wide section; and if his house stood near an outcropping of this ready-made fuel, it was used; and if the forest growth had not been cut away from the vicinity of the rude homestead, the black diamonds remained in the hillside unappropriated. The hills were high, the valleys winding and tangled with thickets, with few and poor roads traversing them; transportation of coal to distant markets was therefore a discarded proposition. On the banks of the principal rivers, as the Great Kanawha and some of its lower tributaries, coal mining became feasible, and attracted the attention of capitalists from various portions of this country and from Europe. With slackwater improvements, the extent and profit of such operations might be greatly increased; and such hydraulic engineering was organized and prosecuted with some success. The Baltimore and Ohio Railroad opened another avenue for coal, and stimulated its shipment over the mountains to the cities of the sea.

A new era is now dawning. The capitalist has discovered, with keen vision, the abundant coal, iron, petroleum, and other wealth thus hidden, and the central location of the lands containing them; he has planted his money in these hills, and is determined to gather a golden harvest. Present facilities for developing these resources will be improved, and new ones created. New lines of railroads are already projected, and will be built; and the navigation of all rivers that are at any time navigable, will be perfected. The most energetic men of our principal cities are among those interested in these improvements; and professional men, editors, government officials, and Congressmen, have interests in these mineral lands.

While extensive purchases of coal lands have recently been made by individuals and companies from different States, foreign capitalists have been busy, and valuable property has been secured by them.

Of the coal measures of West Virginia, and the peculiarities of their varied deposits, the limits of the present volume and the absence of any complete and reliable data from geological surveys, prevent an attempt at scientific description. They embrace nearly the entire surface of the State, but are not available in the central portions towards the river, except to a limited extent, from the fact that this is the centre of the basin, and the principal seams are far beneath the surface. In other sections some of the heavier seams are everywhere found in available locations. Coal is found in immense beds in the Panhandle; it crops out at different elevations on the banks of the Monongahela and its numerous branches, away up among their sources; the hills of the Cheat River region are black with seams that are in some cases ten to twelve feet thick of solid coal. The coal fields of the Kanawha valley are scarcely excelled, and perhaps not equalled, in variety and quantity, upon the continent; while in the eastern slope of the mountains, among the head waters of the Potomac, great deposits of bituminous and semi-bituminous are successfully worked.

The following items relative to coal, from the geological report of Professor Rogers, made long since and previous to the opening of many successful mines, will give a hint merely of the great wealth of these Alleghanian coal-fields:

"At Clarksburg and northward down the valley of the

Monongahela, there exists one of the richest coal deposits in the State. One of the seams in some places in the neighborhood of this town is from ten to twelve feet in thickness, below which, and separated chiefly by a heavy bed of sandstone, there lies a thinner stratum of a more highly bituminous character. * * * * We may form some idea of the vast extent of these coal seams from the fact, that from some distance above Clarksburg they may be followed with scarcely any interruptions throughout the whole length of the valley of the Monongahela down to Pittsburg.

"On the Great Kanawha the exposure of coal is one of the most extensive and valuable anywhere in the United States.

"In Hampshire county, upon a stratum of valuable iron ore not less than fifteen feet in thickness, there rests a bed of sandstone, upon which reposes a coal seam three feet thick; above this another bed of sandstone, then a two-feet vein of coal, then sandstone, then another coal seam of four feet; again a stratum of sandstone, and over it a seven-feet vein of coal; over this a heavy bed of iron ore; and crowning the series, an enormous coal seam of from fifteen to twenty feet in thickness."

In his geological report of the survey of Kentucky, David Dale Owen, after reference to the abundant coal west of the Big Sandy, the dividing line between West Virginia and Kentucky, says, "that the coal beds increase in thickness and number east of the Big Sandy; and as far as can be seen in unwrought outcrop, the coal appears to be of excellent quality."

Professor Rogers gives analyses of the following coals among many other bituminous coals of West Virginia: From Little Sewell Mountain, near the top, carbon 80.24 per cent., volatile matter 17.48, ash 2.28; from the east side of Big Sewell, composed chiefly of shining jet black laminæ, carbon 75.88, volatile matter 22.32, ash 1.80; from the flank of Big Sewell, carbon 67.84, volatile matter 30.08, ash 2.08; from Mill Creek, Fayette county, carbon 71.88, volatile matter 26.20, ash 1.92; from Stockton's Mine, near Mill (Kanawha valley), carbon 74.55, volatile matter 21.13, ash 4.32; from L. Ruffner's, Campbell's Creek, carbon 55.76, volatile matter 32.44, ash 11.80; from Cox and Hannah's (third seam), carbon 51.41, volatile matter 42.55, ash 6.04; from Daniel Ruffner's (upper seam), carbon 49.84, volatile matter 35.04, ash 8.56. It will be seen that the coal near Charleston, in Kanawha County, is exceedingly prolific in volatile elements or oil. From the Kingwood basin, in Preston county, carbon 65.32, volatile matter 31.75, ash 6.91; from R. Forman's, carbon 73.68, volatile matter 21.00, ash 5.32; from Hagan's, Kingwood basin, carbon 68.32, volatile matter 26.48, ash 5.20; from main seam at Clarksburg (cannel in middle of seam), carbon 49.21, volatile matter 45.43, ash 5.36; coal from main seam at Morgantown, carbon 60.54, volatile matter 37.30, ash 2.14; from the Hampshire and Hardy basins, coal from the lower seam at Brantburg, carbon 72.40, volatile matter 16.72, ash 7.88; from Oliver's tract, twelve-foot seam, carbon 79.08, volatile matter 16.28, ash 4.64; from falls of Stony River, Hardy county, carbon 79.16, volatile matter 15.52, ash 5.32; from near Abraham's Creek, carbon 72.40, volatile matter 15.20, ash 12.40; from Stony River, north of turnpike, carbon 83.36, volatile matter 13.28, ash 3.36. The bituminous coals, as at Clarksburg, so rich in volatile matter, are extensively mined, and sent over the mountains hundreds of miles, to be used for gas-making in the Eastern cities.

Benjamin H. Smith, United States District Attorney, resident at Charleston, writes upon this subject:

"Four-fifths of West Virginia lie on the western slope of the Cumberland range, and nearly all the country west of it abounds in coal; but in that part of the State on the Great Kanawha and its tributaries, Elk and Coal Rivers, and on Guyandotte River, coal is found on a magnificent scale. It exists in numerous strata of different thicknesses, rising from the base of the hills to their tops, all nearly horizontal and slightly dipping to the north. This place is sixty miles above the mouth of the river. Here the hills become lofty, and increase in elevation to Cotton Hill or Gauley Mountain. Ascending the river a distance of thirty-six miles, coal of all varieties, except the anthracite, is found of superior quality—the cannel, splint, bituminous, and all varieties of each. Geologists and others report, in those thirty-six miles at different points, workable strata of good coals, amounting in all to from sixty to one hundred feet in thickness, aggregating the several strata. These strata are severally from three to fourteen feet thick. They extend over the whole country for miles, running from creek to creek, and river to river. They are readily made accessible to the Great Kanawha, Guyandotte, or Big Sandy Rivers.. * * * The amount of coal on the Kanawha and its tributaries, Elk and Coal Rivers, is incredible. There is nothing equal to it anywhere."

C. S. Richardson, of the Briarport mines, writes thus of the coal in the vicinity of Charleston:

"In the vicinity of Charleston, to the northeast and northwest, the strata is nearly level, the rise and dip being mere gentle undulations; they consist of gray, brown, red, and white sandstone, the latter being highly fossiliferous, narrow bands of blue clay slate, beds of clay and sandy shales, thin seams of iron ore, and isolated patches of limestone. Above the slates are found thin seams of very rich hematite, many stones of which I have found that will assay up to sixty per cent. in metallic iron; but the prevailing ore is the carbonate of iron found in the kidney or nodular form, in uneven segregated beds in a strong ferruginous sandstone. At Davis's Creek, about midway between Coal and Kanawha Rivers, are two seams of coal, one of cannel, two of iron and two of limestone, all within three hundred feet above water level. The general contour of the country presents a series of narrow mountain ridges and ravines, varying from three to five hundred feet in height; in these, and all above the water levels, are five workable seams of coal, one a very rich bituminous, somewhat friable, two of compact splint, and two of cannel, the latter being the uppermost of the series. The bituminous, or square-jointed seam, is three feet six inches thick, of rich quality. One splint seam, called the 'twin seam,' is divided into two parts by a parting argillaceous sandstone, eighteen inches thick; the entire stratification, or bed, is from twelve to fifteen feet; it gives seven feet of working coal. In some places both these beds are merged into one, where the coal is found from five to six feet thick. The next splint seam is four feet, and in working gives about three feet of merchantable coal. The upper cannel seam is four feet, and contains about two feet six inches of pure cannel; it is of a slaty, or partially laminated structure; it is not very good for domestic fuel, but excellent for gas and oil-making purposes, as also for steamboat uses, as it burns entirely away in flame. The second cannel seam varies in thickness from four to six feet, and gives from two to four feet of fine cannel; it is not always found uniform in character, but where perfect it is a hard coal, conchoidal in fracture, very dense, black and clean, burns with a bright white flame, is very rich in oil, makes an excellent domestic fuel, particularly that part of it called the 'birdseye cannel.' When this coal is used no other light in the room is needed, as candles or oil-lamps look dim in the glare given off in its combustion. This seam is, however, a very unreliable one; in some estates it is found changed entirely, or nearly so, into bituminous coal; in others half cannel and half bituminous. It appears best, or more regular, when imbedded in shales or laminated argillaceous sandstone, and is much easier wrought. In some mines it is between two hard rocks, without any vein of clay or shale for 'bearing in,' which makes it difficult to mine; in this case it is excessively hard, and breaks before the pick like a piece of black flint; but the coal is very fine, and sells at a high price. I believe it is undergoing a state of transition, and eventually would bear the same relation to common cannel as anthracite does to splint coal. If we take an average yield of the cannel seams, we may compute them safely at four thousand tons to the acre; but in some places they are giving over nine thousand tons, in others less than three thousand. The bituminous coal will average sixteen thousand tons to the acre over about two-thirds of the surface base of the mountain lands. Cannel coal is now selling on the Ohio at four dollars and fifty cents per ton, and the best bituminous at two dollars and fifty cents per ton. The mining cost may be put down at one dollar and fifty cents per ton, average; but that would be materially reduced if the mining companies could be persuaded to adopt modern improvements in the more of working the mines. The time, however, has not arrived when such can be done, although we have great hopes another year will not pass without some example being set, which when once done efficiently, others will speedily follow. Coal and cannel selling at the above prices, a good estate, properly wrought, will realize fifty-eight thousand dollars per acre, one-half nearly being profit."

This description was prepared several years ago for the "Mining Journal," in London. The cannel coal is now worth twelve dollars in Ohio, and the bituminous from five to seven dollars. The cost of mining is also largely increased.

CHAPTER XV.

IRON.—SALT.—LIMESTONE.—OTHER MINERALS.

THE iron ores of West Virginia are destined to prove prolific sources of wealth when capital shall organize labor for their reduction, and avenues of communication to commercial centres are somewhat increased. Furnaces exist in the valley and in Preston county, and possibly other sections of the State. The ores are hematites of various aspects, many of them yielding a high percentage of metal of the finest character.

The ores of Laurel Hill have long been worked. They occur in two groups on the western slope (according to Rogers), the upper one above the second seam of coal resting upon a lead-colored sandstone, and overlaid by silicious slates. The ore occurs in large nodules, variable in size, sometimes fine-grained, but generally coarse, and much resembling sandstone, giving indications of its existence only after burning. Underlying the lowest coal seam are two bands of ore, each about a foot in thickness, separated by shales and consisting chiefly of the per-oxide of a shaly texture. Next below comes a layer of white sandstone; then a bed of ore six or eight inches thick, undecomposed, a compact proto-carbonate; and lower still among the shales lies another thin

IRON ORES. 169

band of ore, underlaid with limestone, from which the flux is obtained for iron furnaces.

Furnaces have recently been erected in Preston County, which are producing from ore bearing a high percentage of pure metal, large quantities of iron of a superior quality. In the Kanawha coal fields there is an inexhaustible deposit of iron ore of good quality.

The iron of West Virginia is almost co-extensive with its coal, and may be said to exist literally throughout the State, and may be worked to advantage at least throughout the mountain districts.

Specimens of ore from the north branch of the Potomac have yielded some sixty-eight and some seventy-eight per cent.; in Monogahela several specimens from sixty to ninety-three per cent.; in Preston County, sixty-five, sixty-nine, seventy-one, and eighty-two per cent.

The following references to samples of ore in different localities will serve to illustrate the quality of a mineral that is widely diffused throughout the State. From Keller's Creek, Kanawha, nodular ore, dull reddish grey, fracture somewhat conchoidal, 82.55 per cent. carbonate of iron. From Nicholas, ore occurring in the hills in rounded masses, texture brittle, color chestnut brown, 80.75 per cent. oxide of iron. From Dividing Ridge between Eighteen Mile Creek and Kanawha River, structure massive, color brown, with micaceous points, 83 per cent. peroxide of iron. From Capon Mountain, structure cellular, cells lined with hematate, color chestnut brown, 84.80 per cent. peroxide of iron. Ores equally rich are found in Preston County, and thence south along the western slopes of the parallel mountain ranges, throughout the Kanawha Valley, and in the southern group of counties drained by the Guyandotte and Big Sandy Rivers and their tributaries. It occurs in various forms and combinations. Comparatively little has been done, thus far, towards the development of this branch of the mineral resources of the State. A beginning has been made in Preston County, a few small furnaces having produced iron of superior excellence. Persevering and systematic enterprise will eventually yield valuable results along the lines of railroad and river communication. Young, energetic men will yet occupy this field, open these ores, provide employment for many willing hands, and eventually amass fortunes for themselves.

The saline formation has been little explored, except in Mason and Kanawha counties. It is associated with the vast strata of sandstone that underlies the whole of this section and the southwestern counties of Virginia, in some of which large quantities of salt have of late been manufactured in the interest of the rebellion. The inference has been deemed reasonable, from the western dip of the white sandstone from which the Kanawha brine is obtained, that salt might be reached in the mountains up the river much nearer the surface; and salt has actually been manufactured upon New and Greenbrier Rivers, but with comparatively little success as yet.

The works on the Kanawha, a few miles above Charleston, are extensive and productive. The wells are several hundred feet in depth, yielding a brine of remarkable purity, almost absolutely free from sulphate of lime or gypsum, and therefore evaporated and crystallized with fewer difficulties than usual, and brought to market as muriate of soda of nearly absolute chemical purity. A specimen received from General Lewis Ruffner, of the Kanawha salines, may be seen at the Department of Agriculture. Experience has demonstrated the superiority of this salt over any other manufactured in the country. Meat cured with it has kept, while that put up with foreign and other American salts, under similar circumstances, has spoiled.

Extensive salt works exist in Mason County, making a product of excellent quality. The total manufacture of 1863 is stated as follows: Mason County Mining and Manufacturing Company, eight million eighty-one thousand and three hundred pounds; Mason City Salt Company, eight million six hundred and thirteen thousand six hundred pounds; Union Salt Company, four million five hundred and fifty-three thousand and fifty pounds. Total, twenty-one million two hundred and forty-seven thousand nine hundred and fifty pounds, or nearly a half million bushels. The product was large in 1864.

Immense quantities of coal have been used in salt-boiling, and millions of bushels of salt produced. The Kanawha works have been much interrupted, since 1861, by rebel incursions and dearth of labor, but last year produced a million of bushels.

Limestone is generally diffused throughout the State. The valley counties are largely of a limestone formation, interspersed with layers of slate. The Mountain Pass at Greenbrier exhibits everywhere limestone, interspersed with slate and shales. Throughout the mountain region, and everywhere among the iron and coal deposits, abundance of limestone is found. In the lower Kanawha, below Charleston, arenaceous and argillaceous rocks are presented, with thin layers of limestone of different degrees of purity, in some cases containing sufficient alumina to give it a hydraulic character. Interposed between seams of coal, thick beds of limestone occur on the Ohio River at Wheeling and vicinity. Associated with the coals of the Monongahela and Tygart's Valley and other branches are beds of limestone and sandstone, both increasing in thickness as the coal diminishes. There is little lack of this material, so valuable to agriculture, iron-working, and the building arts.

Specimens from Patterson's Creek, in Hampshire, are of grayish drab color, compact texture, moderately fine grain, structure slaty, bearing ninety-three per cent. of carbonate of lime. From Muddy Creek Mountain, near the Blue Sulphur Spring, of a light gray color and fine grain, containing ninety-eight per cent. From east side of Laurel Hill, in Monongalia County, of a light yellow and gray color, partially sub-crystalline, ninety per cent. From the Cheat River, in Preston County, light-gray, with blue stripes, sixty-eight per cent. From Red Creek, in Randolph County, of light gray color and compact texture, eighty-two per cent. From Morgantown, in Monongalia, dove-colored and sub-crystalline, and very hydraulic, fifty-seven per cent. carbonate of lime, nineteen per cent. magnesia, and nine per cent. alumina. A great variety exists in quality, color, and texture. Hydraulic limestone is very abundant in Ohio, Harrison, Preston, Monongalia, Hampshire, and other counties, and in the Kanawha Valley.

In Jefferson County, and in all portions of the valley to a greater or less extent, exists a deposit of marl, in beds of considerable thickness. It is found in the beds of nearly all the streams, being formed by a precipitation of calcareous matter from the limestone waters. It is known to geologists as travertine. From it a very pure lime is obtained, commanding a high price in the market, and its value to agriculture, from its general diffusion and attainment without the labor of quarrying, is not liable to undue appreciation. Much of it is obtained in a state so friable that it may be applied, as it is in Europe, directly to the soil, like marl, obviating the expense of burning. Calcareous manures have proved of incalculable benefit to Eastern Virginia, and have been applied with benefit to the calcareous soils of the valley. Each section of country, in all the States, has natural elements of fertility which, with skilled husbandry, in co-operation with the ameliorations resulting from stock-growing, are ample for all the demands of high culture. This chalky deposit is only one of many elements of fertility existing in Virginia.

Lead has been discovered in the petroleum region, in recent prospecting for oil, and has long been known to exist in other sections of the State. The lead mines of southwestern Virginia, which are not included, however, within the limits of West Virginia, were worked by white men nearly a century since; were noticed by Jefferson in 1781, and were known to the Indians long previously.

Copper, and a long list of other minerals, are claimed among the resources of the State, the value of which the future must decide. Of petroleum extended notice will be taken in another portion of this volume.

Mineral waters, in remarkable variety, exist in all portions of the Shenandoah Valley, and others still more noted and valuable are scattered among the mountain glades of Greenbrier County. These, with those in Berkeley, are in West Virginia. There are thermal, saline, carbonated, and sulpuretted waters, acidulous water, impregnated with carbonic acid, in some instances combining gas equal to one-half of the amount of the water itself. Sulphur, iron, lime, magnesia, and other elements, variously mingled, give these waters their peculiar characteristics of color, taste, and medicinal effect. Professor Rogers thus refers to them: "Viewed singly, in relation to the number, variety, and high reputation of its mineral waters, this region is well entitled to be proud of the vast resources of which it is possessed. Grouped, as these springs are, at moderate distances apart, presenting within the same district a variety of medicinal character, for which, in other countries, regions remote from each other require to be visited in succession, placed at a point equally accessible to the inhabitants of the seaboard and the great Valley of the West, and situated in a region of grateful summer temperature, of salubrious climate, and of picturesque and diversified natural beauties, they are now rapidly attaining a celebrity for powerful and varied remedial qualities, as well as for the refined social enjoyments which are annually gathered around them, destined ere long to eclipse the older reputation of the famed fountains of the Northern States, and to vie even with the long-established character of the most noted of the watering-places of the Old World."

CHAPTER XVI.

PETROLEUM. — ITS WIDE DISTRIBUTION. — DISCOVERY IN WEST VIRGINIA.

THE astonishing magnitude into which the subject of petroleum has arisen within ten years past, and the important part which West Virginia is destined to play in the development of this interest, now so prominent before the world, require more than a single chapter in the present exhibit of the resources of the State. Long before the permanent settlement of the region, the rock oil was known, collected, and used by the Indians; but it elicited scarcely more attention from the early settlers than one of the many mineral springs for which Virginia is noted. Discovery and invention had not as yet transmuted its oily flow into a stream of wealth. When "the dollar" was made manifest in it, a fractional currency of petroleum was visible in every mountain ravine, and glistened on the surface of many a run and river. Speculation gleamed in every eye; even the staid farmer and wild woodsman caught the infection; every scene was painted in roseate tints in oil colors; the whole course of business was lubricated, and men of all trades and professions naturally slipped into the alluring channel. Crude countrymen, refined citizens, even the double-

PETROLEUM. 177

distilled exquisites of the beau monde, unwilling to let "well enough alone," sought the favors of Dame Fortune, fickle now no longer. Sought—and found. And the search is not over. How will it result? Before essaying an answer, a broad field must be glanced over; it must be seen what petroleum is, where found, and in what relation to the great subject stands West Virginia.

The existence of rock oil is no new thing under the sun. Job, in his adversity, alluded to it as one of the sources of his former prosperity—"when the rock poured me out rivers of oil." Its record has been a part of the history of Greece. Alexander visited the oil springs of the Euphrates, which are flowing still; and Trajan and Julian were attracted by their wonders to that Eastern land. The spring mentioned by Herodotus at Zante, before the Christian era, is now visited by oil hunters, and will doubtless soon be found in companionship with the derrick and drill. Tacitus, Pliny, Vitruvius, and others, testified of petroleum. A very pure white naphtha is found in Persia; and a very dark petroleum, of high value, flows from a mountain there. It exists in modern Parma, Florence, Sicily, the Caspian shores, Derbyshire in England, and in France. Just east of Yaynangheaum, or Oil Creek, on the Irrawaddy, in Burmah, are said to be more than five hundred square curbed wells, three feet in diameter, and two hundred to three hundred feet deep, at the bottom of which the petroleum boils up, and whence it is taken up and stored in earthen pots, in quantities sufficient to fill four hundred thousand hogsheads per year.

In Southern Russia it is gathered in shallow pits, scarce twenty feet in depth, as it flows from beneath the neighboring hills. A live Yankee, Colonel Gowan, is said to have organized an oil company to develop the oils of the coast of Azof, and bought an oil spring on the island of Samos, that was known B.C. 450. The economical Chinese have turned to use, for heating purposes, the carburetted hydrogen gas from time immemorial. Dr. Livingston discovered rock oil in the central recesses of Africa.

In Cuba petroleum runs from the rents of the serpentine formation. The well known lake of bitumen in Trinidad, is familiar to the tyro in oil. Oil springs exist in the sea — a notable one rising through the water south of Vesuvius, and others near the volcanoes near Cape Verde.

In South America the oily treasure abounds. It floats upon the waters of Maracaibo lake, and illumines the night with phosphoric fires from the vapors of an asphalt mine upon its margin. The naturalist Bousingault alludes to great basins of it upon the Magdalena River, on the northern shores of New Granada, in Venezuela, and in Peru; while the traveller Humboldt confirms its abundant existence in South America and in the West Indies. Yet it is reserved for the United States to show the most marvelous results in this department of nature's laboratory, all along the western slope of the Alleghanies and in portions of the great central valley. Canada is also rich in this mineral wealth.

The oil springs of West Virginia were known to the earliest visitors of that region, even before the hardiest pioneers had attempted a settlement.

The Connecticut Gazette, published at New London, Connecticut, of the date of June 2, 1786, gives "accounts of several remarkable springs in Pennsylvania and Virginia, extracted from a letter from Benjamin Lincoln to President Willard, published in the first volume of 'Memoirs of the American Academy of Arts and Sciences.'" The spring at Oil Creek is described, and one "in the western part of Virginia, as extrordinary in its kind as the one just mentioned, called Burning Spring. It was known a long time to the hunters. A party arriving late one night, after making a fire, sought the spring, taking a fire brand to light their way, and were astonished to see the whole surface of the spring take fire and blaze high in the air." This was probably not the Burning Spring on the Little Kanawha, where oil operations have recently been so successful, but the more accessible spring on the Great Kanawha, of which Jefferson thus wrote in 1781:—

"In the lower grounds of the Great Kanawha, seven miles above the mouth of the Elk River, and sixty-seven above that of the Kanawha itself, is a hole in the earth of the capacity of thirty or forty gallons, from which issues a bituminous vapor in so strong a current as to give to the sand about its orifice the motion which it has in a boiling spring. On presenting a lighted candle or torch within eighteen inches of the hole it flames up in a column of eighteen inches diameter, and of four or five feet in height, which sometimes burns out within twenty minutes, and at other times has been known to continue three days, and then has been still left burning. The flame is unsteady, of the density of that of burning spirits, and smells like burning pit coal."

This "spring," so called because it contains water

after a rain, was in existence until its source was recently tapped by a neighboring well. It is on land entered by General Washington, one acre of which is reserved by his will for the use of the public. The flame resembled that of burning whiskey. It was sometimes turned to useful account in clothes-washing, the water boiling till evaporated, and the gas, which bubbled through small orifices in the sand, continued to burn till extinguished by wind or other agency.

Twenty years ago, or more, in boring in this vicinity to the depth of nine hundred feet for salt, similar streams of gas were struck, which poured forth a dense volume, and were employed in a salt furnace for heating purposes, being equivalent to eight hundred bushels of coal. These have ceased to flow, but two others are still used, supporting combustion in a salt furnace equal to two hundred bushels of coal.

The numerous salt wells of this vicinity have evolved enormous volumes of gas, and from some of them have flowed large quantities of petroleum. The following description of the "Gas Wells of Kanawha," is from the Lexington Gazette:

"They are in fact a new thing under the sun; for in all the history of the world, it does not appear that a fountain of strong brine was ever before known to be mingled with a fountain of inflammable gas, sufficient to pump it out in a constant stream, and then, by its combustion, to evaporate the whole into salt of the best quality.

"The country is mountainous, and the low grounds along the river are altogether alluvial, of about a mile in width, having been at some time the bed of the river. The rocks are chiefly sandstone of various qualities, lying in beds or strata, from two inches to several feet in thickness. These strata are nearly horizontal, but dipping a little, as in other parts of the country, towards the northwest. At the salt works they have somehow been heaved up into a swell above the line of general direction, so as to raise the deep strata nigher to the surface, and thus to bring those in which the salt water is found within striking distance.

"At first the borings did not exceed two hundred feet in depth, but the upper strata of water being exhausted, the wells were gradually deepened, the water in the lower strata being generally stronger than the upper had ever been. Until the last year (1842) none of the wells exceeded six or seven hundred feet in depth. Mr. Tompkins, an enterprising salt-maker, was the first to extend his borings to a thousand feet or more. His experiment was attended with a most unexpected result. He had somewhat exceeded a thousand feet, when he struck *a crevice in the rock*, and forth gushed a powerful stream of mingled gas and salt water.

"When Mr. Tompkins inserted his tube, the water gushed out so forcibly, that instead of applying the pump, he only lengthened his tube above the well. The stream followed it with undiminished velocity to his water-cistern, sixty feet above the level of the river. In the next place, he inserted the end of the spout from which the water and gas flowed, into a large hogshead, making a hole in the bottom to let out the water into the cistern. Thus the light gas was caught in the upper part of the hogshead, and thence conducted by pipes to the furnace, where it mingled with the blaze of the coal-fire. It so increased the heat as to make very little coal necessary; and if the furnace were adapted to the economical use of this gaseous fuel, it would evaporate all the water of the well, though the water is sufficient to make five hundred bushels of salt per day.

A description of other wells in the vicinity, which had struck gaseous fountains, is further given, in one of which the flow is intermittent, at intervals of two or three hours. At another it was found impossible to force down a tube, which was bent by the violence of its action. If the gas was struck before the heavy brine was reached, the well was deemed worthless, unless the pressure of the gas could be "tubed off." Occasionally a well was bored to a similar depth without striking the gas — the theory of the writer being, that "the well borer's auger must find it in one of the narrow routes of its upward passage, or penetrate to its native coal bed, before it will burst forth by the artificial vent." He attributed the gas to coal, and declared it "the same that is manufactured out of coal for illuminating our cities." He says further:

"It is a mixture of carburetted and sulphuretted hydrogen. Philosophers tell us that bituminous coal becomes anthracite by the conversion of its bitumen and sulphur into this gas, and that water acts as a necessary part of this process. Whether the presence of salt water causes a more rapid evolution of the gas, the present writer will not undertake to say; but somehow, the quantity generated in the salt region of the Kanawha is extraordinary.

"It finds in this region *innumerable small natural vents*. It is seen in many place bubbling up through the sand in the bottom of the river, and probably brings up salt water with it, as in the gas wells, but in small quantity. The celebrated Burning Spring is the only one of its natural vents apparent on dry land. This stream of gas, unaccompanied with water, has found its way from the rocks below, through seventy or eighty feet of alluvial ground, and within eighty yards of the river bank. It is near this Burning Spring where the principal gas wells have been found. But, twenty-five years ago, or more, a gas fountain was struck in a well two hundred feet deep, near Charleston, seven miles below the burning spring. This blew up, by fits, a jet of weak salt water, twenty or thirty feet high. On a torch being applied to it one night, brilliant *flames played and flashed about the watery volume in the most wonderful manner."*

Oil was obtained by boring in 1819, upon the Little Muskingum, in sinking a salt well. It was at that time tested as an illuminator, and the suggestion of its utility in lighting cities made public in the newspapers. In 1845, oil was struck in a similar manner in Pennsylvania. In 1854, a company was organized for boring upon Oil Creek, but no energetic effort was put forth until 1858. In Canada it was first obtained in 1857.

As early as 1825 oil was procured in West Virginia, after the manner of operations near the Caspian Sea, by digging sand-pits to the depth of a dozen feet or more. It was thus procured on Hughes' River, about a mile below the junction of the north and south forks, on the north side. Opposite, on the south side, some twenty years ago, wells were bored, from which petroleum flowed in small quantities for years. In fact one of them is yet flowing daily a small quantity of valuable oil. This Hughes' River oil was used mainly as a liniment for burns, cuts, and bruises, for man and beast, and was especially valued for horses. A very small quantity was obtained in these sand diggings — simply by pouring in water, stirring the sand with hoes, and allowing the oil to accumulate on the surface — until 1850 to 1857, when the yearly product reached nearly seventy-five barrels.

In 1842, while boring for salt, oil was discovered near Burning Spring, on the Little Kanawha, twenty-seven miles from Parkersburg. The Rathbone Farm, on which the well was sunk, has since become famous for the production of oil. Boring specifically for oil was first attempted in this vicinity in the fall of 1859, after the first successes in oil in Pennsylvania had attracted the attention of the world; although Dr. Hildreth, of Ohio, as early as 1836, alluded to the abundance of petroleum on the Little Kanawha.

CHAPTER XVII.

HOW ORIGINATED.—POPULAR AND UNPOPULAR THEORIES.

THE origin of petroleum has elicited the attention of the scientific and the unlettered alike, and if both have not been at times equally visionary and absurd, each has been equally at variance with other individuals of his own class. There are doubtless fewer opinions than persons in the debate; and as data for comparison shall be accumulated and the truth systematized and made clear, the scientific, the professors of geology, will have the advantage of the well borer; but at present the professors appear to be almost as much in the mud as the delvers are in the mire. An examination of the prominent theories of the production of petroleum, will be found interesting and suggestive; and if the reader is of a speculative turn, he may amuse or improve himself by constructing others, equally plausible if not equally sound. The difficulty is, though petroleum is not new, its geology is, as well as its chemistry; and its originating cause is by no means indicated by the harmonious agreement of a scientific convention. Rapid progress has been made in acquiring facts, which may at an early day reveal the truths which shall be crystalized into science.

Professor E. B. Andrews, of Marietta College, in

the centre of the great oil basin, after years of examination of the philosophy of oil generation, assumes it to be a product of the distillation of bitumen at low temperatures, in opposition to the old theory that oil was produced at the original bitumenization of animal or vegetable matter. Oil is not found with bituminous coal, as might be expected in view of the latter theory, but in fissures of the rocks underlying bituminous strata, which have been opened since the coal strata was bitumenized.

The theory has been maintained by some geologists, that petroleum is the result of pressure upon coal, as oil is expressed from the olive. It supposes a vegetable origin for coal, a submerged condition, and a destructive distillation, but not so high a temperature as to cake the coal, evolving hydrocarbons. On this theory, greater pressure and higher heat resulted in the production of anthracite coal, the hydrocarbons becoming volatilized, and ages since disappearing from the surface, washed away by the floods of time, and floating off on the bosom of the primeval ocean.

Professor Eli Bowen, of Pennsylvania, holds a different opinion. During the early Devonian era, in his view, the entire Alleghanian system was submerged; it consisted of connecting basins, similar to those of our existing northwestern lakes, with adjacent prairies producing the rankest of vegetation, and resembling in character the St. Clair flats. At a sufficiently early date, before the recession of the open sea in what is now the Mississippi Valley, these basins, at least the lowest of them, were salt or brackish, as is evidenced by marine as well as fresh water fossils existing on the western slope of the Alleghanies. The resinous secretions of coal plants — largely comprising various species of coniferous trees, growing with astonishing luxuriance in the moist, misty atmosphere of that era — were strewn upon the earth, drained into these lakes, forming a tarry crust upon the surface, which was suddenly submerged beneath an inundation of sedimentary matter, burying the vegetable oils beneath the rubbish of the forests and the sand and mud which they held in suspension. When the waters drained off, another crop of vegetation furnished supplies for another stratum of liquid bitumen, which was again submerged by the rush of waters bursting accumulated barriers, and other strata of sand and mud deposited, forming another mass of sandstone, or the shales that overlie it. Over all was finally deposited a seam of clay, which effectually imprisoned the oil, except along the margins or in the crevice of a seam.

The veins producing coal were made in the same way, but at a period when there was not so much evaporation, because the atmosphere was not then adapted to its absorption; but there was ample time to allow the mass to solidify. The oil was imprisoned suddenly; the veins of coal were accumulated slowly, from more resinous material, not so rich in liquid oils.

Such is the theory of Mr. Bowen, very briefly but fairly stated, very nearly in his own words. He says further, of the more southern slopes: "On the Kanawha, in Virginia; on the Big Sandy, in Kentucky, and generally on the headwaters of the Monongahela, we find richer and more fatty oils than we find on the Alleghany, the Clarion, or on Oil Creek. And why is this? Because the coals themselves are richer in oils, and because a species of vegetation flourished in those points which secreted more oils than those of Pennsylvania."

Professor Erni, Chemist of the Department of Agriculture, author of a new work upon the subject,* says:

"Petroleum is doubtless a product of chemical decomposition, derived from organic remains, plants, and animals, whole generations of which perished and accumulated during many destructive revolutions at the various ages or epochs of our planet. As to the manner in which these oily hydrocarbons were originally produced, scientific men are still divided in opinion. Some believe that they resulted, like the artificial oils we dwelt upon, from a dry distillation — *i.e.*, the effects upon vegetable tissue of heat, such as hot gases or steam generated by volcanic action, untold ages before our solid earth had acquired its present thickness and stability of surface."

After canvassing at length the prominent theories of oil production, he is inclined to believe that the oils of Canada, and perhaps of Michigan and Kentucky, found in sub-carboniferous strata, or the Devonian rocks, are of animal origin, from animals of a low order, such as crinoids, brachiopods, and trilobites, successive generations of which must have been buried in the waters and covered with earthy

---

* "Coal Oil and Petroleum; their Origin, History, Geology, and Chemistry, with a view of their importance in their bearing upon national industry. By HENRY ERNI, A.M., M.D., Chief Chemist Department of Agriculture." Published by Henry Carey Baird. 406 Walnut Street, Philadelphia.

ORIGIN OF PETROLEUM. 189

and mineral deposits, when, removed from atmospheric action, as in a closed retort, the carbon and hydrogen, existing greatly in excess of oxygen, would enter into such combinations as are found in petroleum and the various hydrocarbon gases.

Of that produced from the vegetables of the carboniferous period, he shows, from its chemical qualities, that it must have been produced by a process analogous to the dry distillation of peat — that it is composed mainly of volatile hydrocarbon oils, yielding, with nitric acid, less of nitro-bensole, and of analine dyes, than that obtained from coal oils. The bitumen found with schists and shales he considers the result rather than the cause of petroleum — petroleum hardened by the exposure and loss of its more volatile elements.

A writer in Harper's Magazine propounds this theory: In the Chemung period of the Devonian age, an internal sea covered the central portion of the continent, its shores making the present eastern limit of the petroleum region. It was a shallow sea, as proven by the absence of limestone, with mud flats like those of New Jersey, and sandy barriers intervening, which have become the alternating shale and sandstone. A tropical heat stimulated vegetation, and an atmosphere surcharged with carbonic acid gas, fed the rank growth of salt marsh vegetation. These marshes, throwing up gigantic and fragile weeds, may have been subject to gradual subsidence, thus accumulating masses of undecayed vegetation beneath the surface. Then a sudden and heavier subsidence submerges all beneath the inflowing sand of the broken barriers, and the internal heat, which cannot consume, distils these watery weeds, separating the carbon and hydrogen, which enter new combinations, and form the oily hydrocarbons which we call petroleum. The salt water, of course, settles beneath the oil, which floats upon it, and its more volatile elements, through fissures in the rocks created by subsidences or uprisings, tend towards the surface in the form of gas.

Some believe that oil is a product of distillation perpetually in progress in the recesses of the earth, the result of internal heat; and that the withdrawal of oil only stimulates the process of condensation. Yet they confess utter ignorance of the material from which the carburetted gases are produced, which ascend from the hot depths below to the cold surface rocks, to be condensed and left to fill the interior basins of salt water.

There are those who adhere to this or a similar theory, who believe that the oil rock is limestone, and the oil a product of the carbonic acid evolved in burning.

Still other theories are afloat. One of them assumes that petroleum is produced by certain chemical combinations of salt and lime; and in support of it the fact is asserted that oil is found in localities where coal does not exist, while salt and gas are always present. It is a prevalent belief with many, that it is not a product of vegetable growth or animal decay, but a result of chemical processes in the great laboratory of the earth, wrought through the agency of internal fires; and that necessarily it will be permanent in supply — the surface cavities, in which the rising gases were caught and condensed, being again filled by escaping gases which had been repressed by the accumulation of oil and water. Upon this assumption the exhaustion of the oil in crevices, by pumping, only clears the passages leading thither, and stimulates a more rapid deposit of oil.

Believers in the vegetable theory account for the occurrence of oil remote from coal, by suggesting that, in obedience to the law of gravity, it seeks the lowest level, and finds at a distance away the geological formations with suitable cavities or crevices for containing it. It may subsequently be forced upwards, under the pressure of water from beneath, or of the accumulating gas above it, towards the surface; and if an open fissure exists, an oil or gas spring is the result.

CHAPTER XVIII.

WHERE FOUND.—HOW TO FIND IT.

GEOLOGISTS are agreed that there is no specific oil-bearing rock, reliable, wherever found, for oleaginous treasures. Oil is found in sandstone, in shales, in serpentine, and in the loose sand of the surface. In West Virginia it occurs in the coal measures overlying the Devonian deposits; in Pennsylvania, in the upper sandstones of the Devonian series; in Canada, still lower, in the Hamilton shales which overlie the corniferous limestone, and also in limestone.

The talk concerning oil belts is very loose and vague, and calculated to mislead. It has been fashionable to connect, by a continuous and very direct line, the oil region of Pennsylvania with that of West Virginia. These lines, if continued, would diverge at many an angle and embrace a wide area — at least twenty counties in West Virginia, and half as many in Ohio. And there would be some controversy about a starting point; for if Oil Creek, in Venango County, Pennsylvania, should be regarded as the oil centre of that region, the developments in several counties, east and west of that valley, would prove, not the existence of a narrow belt, but a broad area of oil.

In his survey of the coal region of West Virginia,

Professor William B. Rogers, the geologist of Virginia, gives the following description of the existing disturbances, to some extent continuous and parallel, which give color to the popular notion of "belts:"

"These anticlinal axes* met with in our great western coal region, preserving a parallel direction with those of the Appalachian belt, give rise to ranges of mountains less elevated above the general level of the surrounding region, and broader and less abrupt in their declivity than the ridges formed of the more steeply inclined strata of the Appalachian portion of the State. Yet, as might naturally be anticipated, along the summit of these broad mountains, the mantle of rocks pertaining to the coal formation, once evidently continuous in its extension over the inferior strata, has been more or less removed; and thus over their undulating tops and in their profound ravines and river gorges, the upper groups of strata belonging to the Appalachian series are not unfrequently deeply and extensively exposed. The destructive rush of waters, whose denuding power is so clearly attested by the removed summits and gashed sides of so many of these broad ridges would seem, after tearing the stouter material above, to have met with far less resistance from the soft shales and sandstones, forming the interior mass. Hence would appear to have originated the deep valleys and abrupt hills by which the space included between the flanks of these ridges is so generally characterized, and hence the deeply scooped channels of those streams, which are permitted, not merely to pass through, but to meander for great distances along the central line of the axis and in the very heart of the mountain, whose interior structure they thus contribute to disclose."

He shows that throughout the more western por-

---

* An imaginary line towards which opposite inclined strata rise, as the sides of a roof rise towards the ridge. A roof inverted would represent a synclinal axis.

tion of the coal-bearing strata, the uppermost of the Appalachian rocks are neither to be met with upon the surface or in the deepest natural or artificial exposures that exist; and that even the rocks of the principal coal measures become buried, approaching the Ohio in the region of Parkersburg and Point Pleasant, giving place to slates and shales, and sandstones, either destitute of coal or containing it in thin and variable seams. Across the river, in Ohio, these strata, thus depressed, gradually rise again, bringing in view, in reverse order, the coal, sandstones, slates, shales, iron ores, and limestones. Thus is formed a vast synclinal basin, its northern rim or edge crossing the Ohio above Marietta, the Ohio River flowing through it centrally, or a little west of the centre, and passing through its western rim near the mouth of the Scioto River. The axis of this trough, a line nearly parallel with the mountain range, being a few miles east of Parkersburg, little coal is found near the surface until, the river bending west, good coal seams appear at Pomeroy, and on the opposite shore, in Mason County.

East of this synclinal basin, and parallel with its axis, is the anticlinal axis, so frequently referred to, and so prominently marked at several points, which has been traced across the Ohio River, in the vicinity of Newport, a few miles east of Marietta, in Washington County, Ohio. It crosses the small streams, French Creek, Cow Creek, Calf Creek, and Horseneck Fork of Bull Creek, which flow into the Ohio in a direction slightly north of west; then crosses Goose Creek, at Petroleum, on the Baltimore and Ohio Railroad; Hughes River, a little west of the junction of North and South Forks; cuts the valley of Burning Spring Run, and passes across the Little Kanawha, on towards Charleston, in Kanawha County. The direction of this line is very nearly south. This may properly be considered an oil belt, but it is not the only belt in which oil exists in West Virginia. And while these disturbances, whether caused by upheavals or the subsidence of the declining strata on either side, necessarily leave cavities and fissures capable of holding oil, and lead the oil hunter naturally to expect a rich harvest, it must not be assumed too hastily that these "belts" are always parallel, or sure to yield abundant oil, or that the area between them is utterly destitute of paying deposits. Where the strata is most broken, and fissures have been produced in many directions by their mechanical fracture, more oil may reasonably be expected than where the rocks lie horizontal and unbroken.

It is assumed by some geologists that these anticlinal and synclinal waves were rolled up through the influence of subterranean forces, which moved the earth's crust in the long ages past, and caused the uplift of the Cumberland range; that the strata, thus folded over, was necessarily much broken, the amount and character of the fracture depending upon the physical condition of the several beds suffering the disturbance; that if the fissures of the anticlinals reach the oil-bearing rocks, they will permit the gas and oil generated below to escape at the surface of the earth, and the surface water to flow in and wash out and waste the oil; while the synclinals, if their fractures are deep enough to break the oil stratum, will receive and store up the product of such rocks, and will, moreover, by the divergence of the fractures, embrace deep in the earth a larger territory than that covered by the synclinal at the surface. On this theory, the centre of the synclinal basin, could it be struck, might yield unprecedented quantities of oil; yet the great cost of wells of sufficient depth, and the doubtful "if" relative to the depth of the fractures, are two potent obstacles in the way of immediate successful development. There is, doubtless, abundance of oil in the synclinals, whereever fractures exist in connection with the operation of causes producing oil; and the future enterprise of practical oil operators will undoubtedly be equal to the task of finding it.

It is upon the anticlinals, where the oil strata is upheaved, and near the surface, that fissures opening to the air are found; and here also are seen gas springs and oil springs. Such indications of the proximity of oil to the surface, are proofs that the deposits are undergoing depletion. There are many localities in Pennsylvania, West Virginia, and other States, where oil is found upon the surface, saturating shales in the beds of streams, or filling the interstices of the sand near the surface, in which wells have not been productive except at a very shallow depth. Oil has been obtained in small quantities at the depth of a few feet, when, upon going deeper, no sign of it has again appeared, and the well has proven a failure. Surface wells are not expected to produce largely, yet comparatively shallow wells have touched large basins of oil, as the Burning Springs in Wirt County, and the Horseneck Wells, especially the Gilfillan, some of which flowed hundreds and even thousands of barrels daily, it was claimed, for a short time, the flow gradually decreasing. Not only in notable instances were some of these wells sold at large figures, in the excitement attending their first flow, but their purchasers also made large profits upon their investment. Probably a clear profit of fifty thousand dollars was last year made upon the shallow wells on the Oil Run of Goose Creek, in Ritchie County — more than during any previous year since the commencement of the enterprise. Some of those wells have been worked longer than many of the deep wells of Pennsylvania; and some of them, after apparent exhaustion, and a few months' rest, have again been profitably pumped. One was pumped at twenty-six feet, and few are more than two hundred. So the statement that shallow wells are not enduring or profitable, should be received with some caution, and many exceptions acknowledged.

In the synclinal basin east of this "oil belt," is located the world-renowned asphaltum lode of Ritchie County, for facilities of communication with which a railroad is in process of construction to the Baltimore and Ohio road at Cairo station. A perpendicular fissure, three and a half feet thick, has been filled with petroleum from some great basin below, its volatile elements subsequently evaporated, and the residuum left, very closely resembling coal to the superficial eye, and yielding from one hundred and forty to one hundred and seventy gallons per ton of heavy oil. The quantity of petroleum required to produce this deposit is almost incredible, and has lead to the belief that practically inexhaustible basins of oil exist in this synclinal. There are others who have no faith in the existence of liquid oil in localities where asphaltum is found. Well boring is rife in this region, and oil has already been found. The immediate future will test the value of this locality as petroleum land. Professor Lesley says, in describing it, that "the country of the neighborhood is that of the central part of the great synclinal, which crosses the Ohio below Pittsburg, and stretches down through Western Virginia parallel to the Ohio River, into Eastern Kentucky."

The surface throughout the oil region is singularly marked with a succession of sharp hills and valleys, the elevations rising from three to five hundred feet above the valley level, their declivitous aspect in many places relieved by narrow plateaus, or "benches." These valleys were produced by drainage, when the surface formation was comparatively soft; and they are generally very narrow, though variable in width, and running in every direction, with smaller valleys, or furrowed depressions of the hills, entering the principal ones at right angles. The whole surface is a net work of valleys of erosion, varying in length, depth, and direction. The tyro in oil matters is apt to think every abrupt hill an evidence of upheaval, but soon learns that perfectly horizontal strata of rocks may be furrowed deeply as those which are depressed, upheaved, or fractured by convulsion. This fashioning of the valleys, ages subsequent to the breaking of the uplift and formation of the fissures beneath, affords a suggestive indication of the great antiquity of oil production.

THE SAND-ROCKS.

It is common to hear the remark relative to oil wells in West Virginia, that oil is obtained from the first or second sand-rock, and that great results are expected on reaching the third. Reference is had to three separate sandstone formations of the Devonian rocks, which occur so regularly in Pennsylvania, and in which the oil is found. There is no similarity in the oil-bearing rocks of the two localities. Those of West Virginia belong to the carboniferous series. If the wells should be continued a thousand feet further, the same Devonian strata might be struck. In West Virginia the strata pierced are sandstone, soapstone, and shales, variable in thickness and irregular in occurrence.

The following theory is presented by Charles S. Richardson, a mineral surveyor and mining engineer of much experience:

"A general impression prevails, that this deranged state of the formation arises from the sudden and violent plutonic convulsions, tearing asunder the strata and causing upheavals. In some instances, especially in volcanic countries, such is the case; but the upheavals of Virginia, although numerous, have not been thrown up so suddenly as many persons suppose. A close examination of the uptilted rocks and a little calm reasoning, will soon convince the diligent inquirer that the upheaval of the strata must be gradual; that they are now moving up, and have never ceased to move; that others are sinking, settling down, gradually subsiding, leaving great vacancies between their several components, and forming receptacles for any foreign matter that may chance to fall into them. Upheavals present various forms: they are sometimes curvilineal, in other places angular— that is to say, the planes of the strata present right lines to the apex; they are readily recognized by their causing the strata to form an anticlinal axis; in this operation the horizontal line becomes shortened, the rock not being elastic, breaks, and the result is a fissure whose width corresponds with the contracted lines; these fissures become refilled with sand and clay and fragments of the severed rocks; the matrix being porous affords excellent repositories for oil, gas, or aqueous minerals by infiltration; they are called 'Faults,' and in West Virginia are found to be oil-producing. In the case of Burning Spring Run, I hold an adverse opinion to that of many others of my profession: that, instead of the derangement being caused by an upheaval, it is by a 'down-throw,' and forms an abrupt depression; for the shale bed seen along the valley, several feet up in the rocks, is here, in places, found considerably below the surface. Several of the borings that I examined give evidence of having passed through a friable strata very much resembling the shale beds seen above. The comminuted particles, as taken from the sand-pump, appear identical; and it is in the numerous fissures of the sandstone rock lying below the shale, that the oil is first found. In this valley it occurs at a depth of about one hundred and fifty feet. I entertain the opinion that the oil, all along the little Kanawha, above Elizabeth, lies shallow, and that deep borings, as far as oil is concerned, will prove abortive. I may be wrong, but I think that immediately on the well intersecting the saliferous strata, there is very little hope of the discovery of any oil below it. This is not a theoretical view of the matter. I adduce the facts from practical results. We have wells in this State from one hundred and fifty to one thousand nine hundred and sixty feet deep, but I never have heard any of the operators say that they ever found oil below the middle brine spring."

Professor E. B. Andrews, of Marietta College, thus writes of the value of gas springs as an indication of oil:

"The value of gas springs is, in my opinion, less than that of oil springs. There may be large quantities of gas evolved in regions where there is little, if any, oil. In a gas works a rich cannel coal will make a large quantity of illuminating gas, but no oil, except a very little coal-tar; while in a coal-oil works, the same coal will yield a large quantity of crude oil. The difference in result is due to difference in temperature. So in the earth, the process of subterranean distillation may take place under circumstances so entirely different, that in one case gas alone is produced, and in the other, both gas and oil. But I doubt whether the gas showing itself in gas springs in Western Virginia, could have been generated without the condensation from it in the fissures below, of more or less oil. It is doubtless true sometimes, that the gas comes from the vaporization of oil already formed. I have no doubt that all the gas springs in West Virginia, prove conclusively the existence of oil, but, as in the case of oil springs, they do not indicate the quantity of oil. Wells alone can determine this. It must be remembered that the significance and value of oil and gas springs are not to be limited to the field or farm on which they are found; they may prove that the whole region for many miles around, is an oil region. Experiments have often shown that the best wells are found many miles distant from the original surface indications which first called attention to that neighborhood."

Professor E. W. Evans, of Marietta College, expresses his opinion as follows:

"Of surface signs, that which forms the most reliable evidence that the source of supply is deep, is a scum of thin volatile oil appearing on mineral springs. For example: between the two Kanawhas, along the line connecting the two burning springs, there are numerous oil and gas springs in which the analysis of the water always reveals various minerals, such as common salt, carbonates of iron and soda, muriate of lime, sulphates of soda and potash, and sometimes sulphurated hydrogen. On the common springs of pure water, whose source is near the surface, oil is not seen in this region. It comes up through slight cracks and fissures in the strata, from depths where the water has gathered its various mineral contents. The high temperature of these oil springs, as compared with the springs of pure water, is another fact indicating their deep source. These signs characterize the best oil regions generally."

Professor C. W. Wright has less faith in "oil indications:"

"The indications of the presence of oil in any particular locality are frequently deceptive. In the vicinity of Niagara it has been found in drops in fossil coral, and inclosed in rock crystal; yet no one having the proper knowledge on the subject would expect to find it in that locality in sufficient amount to make it an object of commerce. The same remarks will apply to the presence of oil on the surface of the water of springs, wells, etc., although of much importance in connection with other indications. Nor is the presence of inflammable gas in springs and wells of itself a certain indication of the presence of oil in the rocks from which it has its origin. The presence of a good quality of bituminous coal is still less so. In fact, no single indication can be relied upon as an evidence of the presence of petroleum.

"An intimate acquaintance with all the facts connected with the various localities in which oil has been found, together with a knowledge of the geology and chemistry relating to the subject, are absolutely essential before anything like a correct opinion can be formed as to the presence or absence of mineral oil in any particular formation. A familiarity with the topography of one oil region, is of little or no value of itself in enabling a person to decide as to the presence of oil in a locality remote from the one in which special experience has been acquired. Some localities which were considered the most unpromising after a superficial examination, have yielded the largest quantities of oil."

The boring of wells, and a history of their subsequent working, if accurately and intelligently noted, afford data for valuable knowledge of the peculiar structure of the rocks, the character of the fractures or oil reservoirs, and the extent and permanence of the deposit. In the light of recent experience, the

PECULIARITIES OF OIL WELLS. 203

fissures are generally seen to be more or less vertical. Adjoining wells seldom strike oil at the same depth; wells a few feet apart often yield different quantities, as well as different qualities and specific gravities of oil; salt water may exist in one, and its neighbor may yield water entirely fresh. These facts prove that a broad horizontal basin is not struck in such cases. One well may emit volumes of gas, but no oil; another may flow with oil almost pure; and a third may yield nothing but water at first, and afterwards produce large quantities of oil by perseverance with the pump. All of these conditions may exist separately, in several wells which strike the same fissure at different points respectively. The lower portion, to a certain level, contains water; oil covers the water to a certain depth; and gas is compressed, no vent existing, between the rock above and the oil and water below. If a well strikes the upper or gas level, it will yield gas only; if it pierces the oil, the pressure of the superincumbent gas, if in large volume, will force the oil through the opening to the surface; but if the water below is struck, a portion of it must be pumped out before the oil appears, which is then mixed with water, by the passage both of water and oil from distant sections of the fissure. Oil operators are more cautious now in abandoning wells which yield only water at first, after tubing. If "a good show of oil" induced a preparation for pumping, the pump is usually kept in motion night and day, till the surplus water, which comes in from water veins above, notwithstanding a most skilful adjustment of the seed-bag, is exhausted. A well on Burning Spring Run was pumped persistently for six weeks before the water was exhausted, when it produced oil in large quantity, and has proved a very valuable and enduring well. It is stated that a productive oil well has recently been obtained in Ohio, after an obstinate pumping, without intermission, for eight weeks.

Flowing wells sometimes continue for months at the same rate of production, but they usually decrease their flow gradually, until the pressure of the interior gas and the exterior air are equal, when the flow ceases. It is no evidence of the exhaustion of the reservoir that a well stops flowing, but simply a proof of comparative exhaustion of the gas; it is yet a good pumping well, and may yield as much more oil, or possibly twice as much as its previous aggregate production. There is a vast difference in the action of pumping wells. The yield of many is periodical, at intervals of a few minutes or a few hours. The accumulating gas opens the valve of the pump, and its pressure, as it escapes in volume, keeps the valve open. When the ascending gas is too weak to force the valve back, the pump resumes its action, and a fine stream of nearly pure oil often results. Flowing wells generally exhibit a similar periodicity — one upon Hughes' River has flowed once in twenty-four hours, at a certain hour each morning, for years. Others have preserved a regular daily flow; in some cases the action has been gradually deferred, by increasing intervals. Some flowing wells intermit by shorter and irregular intervals.

The selection of a site for boring is made with much care. A favorite location is at the intersection of two valleys, at or near the point where a central line through each would cross each other. Marvellous tales are told, as formerly with reference to water veins, of the magical power of the witch-hazel in the hands of a professor of the magical art. The lowest land is usually chosen; yet there are productive wells in West Virginia as well as in Pennsylvania, upon the steep hill sides. The expectation is that breaks or fissures, capable of holding oil, are more likely to exist in valleys than on the hills. As these are valleys of erosion, rather than of subsidence, there may be really no better reason for boring in them, in preference to the hills, than an expectation of reaching the oil at less distance.

CHAPTER XIX.

USES.— QUANTITY USED.

THE laboratory of the chemist is full of the wonders of petroleum, which is pouring a flood of blessings upon the world in the creation of new branches of industry. The scientific zeal of Reichenbach, in the separation of many of its constituents, is rivalled by the industry and skill of others in discovering new combinations of these elements, tending to increase the value or cheapen the cost of a multitude of life's luxuries and utilities. A visit to Professor Hedrick's room, in the United States Patent Office, will indicate a hopeless condition of "oil on the brain" of inventors. In accelerating ratio the claims for patents come in — for all kinds of machinery and implements, for processes of refining, and for useful products in substitution for other more expensive ingredients. Abundant material, in this branch of the subject alone, is at hand for a full and interesting volume. For instance, in the month of January, in 1864, no less than fifteen cases were examined, six of them for oil barrels; the others, respectively, for imparting drying qualities to oil, for lining for barrels, for making and coating pipes, for vessels for containing petroleum, for carburetting air, for roofing composition, for waterproofing paper and cloth with paraffine, for combination of India-rubber and paraffine, and for cleaning wool. In February the stream continued; there was no ebb in March or April; and in May, the number of cases had increased to twenty, for purposes as follows: generating gas (two cases), petroleum still (five cases), gas apparatus (two cases), petroleum vessels, paint for bottom of ships, paint for wood work, composition for floors, manufacture of lampblack, apparatus for carburetting air (two cases), filter for oils, apparatus for distilling, substitute for rosin, and bungs for barrels. All of these cases are found in the books of one examiner, all relating to the chemistry of petroleum.

Its use as an illuminator, now so general, and of so recent date, is not altogether new; the village of Fredonia, and the lighthouse at Barcelona, in Chautauque County, in New York, have for several years been lighted with petroleum; and it is claimed that the streets of Genoa and Parma, in Italy, have been lighted with it for two centuries. In Persia it has long been used for illumination.

In the distillation, the most volatile portion of the oil passes off in vapor, condensing into a thin, volatile liquid, called naphtha or benzine. Refined benzine is now used almost exclusively as a substitute for spirits of turpentine, in paints and varnishes; and as an illuminator, it is coming into extensive use, especially in the new process of carburetting air, which is burned in the same manner as illuminating gas, each house having its separate gasometer and fixtures. It produces a pure, steady, and mellow light, less tremulous and injurious to eyesight than coal gas, and is generally preferred by those who have enjoyed it. Those who are engaged in introducing it into public use, claim that it costs but half the price of ordinary gas, and is free from smell, smoke, or danger from explosion.

The second distillate, of a specific gravity between seventy-four and eighty-two, is also an illuminating oil. The remainder, or residuum, amounts to from five to ten per cent. of the whole.

From the published statements of experiments made by chemists, to obtain a knowledge of the comparative value of petroleum illuminating oil, it appears that the intensity of its light is eighteen times as great as that from burning fluid, six times as great as the light of sperm oil, and more than twice the intensity of camphene. The quantity of light is double that of camphene, and almost three times as much as sperm. It is a little cheaper than camphene, and costs but a small fraction of the price of sperm or burning fluid, the quantity of light being equal.

As a fuel for steamers, upon partial experiments already made, it is assumed to require scarcely one-third the bulk of coal, and only one-fifth as many men to manage it.

For lubricating purposes it is in constantly increasing demand. The heavier oil only is adapted to the lubrication of machinery; and from its comparative scarcity, and the excessive demand, it bears a high and increasing price. The Baltimore and Ohio Railroad uses nearly fourteen hundred barrels per annum, all of which is pumped from shallow wells located on less than a mile of a narrow valley, near one of the stations of the road. Much of

USES OF HEAVY OILS.

the volatile element of petroleum having passed into the air, by exposure in shallow receptacles, surface wells uniformly yield a lubricating oil. There is a wide difference in the quality of the various lubricating oils, from the finest watch oil to that applied to locomotive axles. The residuum left after extracting the liquid oils, and other useful products, yields a valuable grease for wheels. The heavy oils are also used instead of whale oil in the currying of leather, and are beginning to be used for oiling wool.

The residuum is destined to undergo an almost unending series of mutations. Its applications may prove more various than those of gutta-percha. Among the most beautiful results are the aniline colors, specimens of which can be seen in the Museum of the Department of Agriculture. The value of this product will be appreciated, when it is known that coal-tar dyes (similar if not identical with these), are produced in England to the value of nearly half a million of pounds sterling yearly, for dying the beautiful colors magenta, mauve, and various shades of blue and violet, purple, yellow, orange, and green. Among these products is a combination for coating iron and wood to preserve from oxidation or decay; a pitch for covering the bottoms of ships; material for pavements and tiles; a substitute for sealing-wax; filling for shells and shrapnell instead of sulphur; a roofing cement; a substitute for rosin in soldering; an ingredient in the manufacture of lampblack; chewing gum, as mastic and rose, in beautiful little sticks, a confection of which many tons are sold; wax used in adulterating beeswax and for making candles; moulders' facing powder; and, finally, coffins, indestructible, and claimed to be unexceptionable in all respects.

A London inventor claims to have discovered three new and important uses of petroleum — the vapors of coal oil and coal tar as chemical agents in coloring; the ignited vapors of the oil mixed with air and steam in roasting and smelting ores; oil vapors, with certain portions of air and steam, as a motive power.

Printing inks, of all colors, are made: the black superior to that made from linseed oil, at half the cost. The economy of this item represents an immense amount of money.

From the waste acid of the refineries is obtained a substance used to adulterate cream of tartar, — or a substitute for it. It is said to be used in the self-raising flour.

A half-dozen varieties of soap, from cosmetic to common washing varieties, are made with petroleum, and are held in high repute.

As a medicine, for which it was popular long before its other uses were discovered, it is an anæsthetic, a remedy for cutaneous diseases, a liniment of acknowledged virtues, a disinfectant, and a specific for consumption by inhalation of its vapors.

The increase in the production of petroleum has been rapid. The first discovery of flowing wells in 1859, and the consequent stimulation of the business of well boring, led to fears of glutting the market, and then to panic, and abandonment of all pumping wells. Oil, formerly a literal drug, became again a drug in a mercantile sense. Improvements in lamps and in the refining process had commenced; the

STATISTICS OF PETROLEUM.

people had enjoyed the benefits of cheap oil; invention was fairly aroused to a zealous competition in improvement; and the result was the same that ever follows a determined effort of the American mind. The progress, at first slow, accelerated in 1862, became extremely rapid in 1863. The striking of flowing wells of prodigious yield, during the latter year, carried the annual product to a high figure; yet the demand continued, a foreign consumption arose to keep it up, and the excitement in oil was carried to a high pitch in 1864. In the meantime, new wells were bored, but the excessive flow of some of the spouting wells began to diminish. The following is the estimate of the best informed in petroleum circles in New York, of the increase and extent of petroleum production:

Year.	Barrels, Crude.	Gallons, Crude.	Gallons, Refined.
1861	600,000	24,000,000	16,800,000
1862	1,000,000	40,000,000	28,000,000
1863	2,000,000	80,000,000	56,000,000
1864	2,180,000	87,200,000	61,040,000

It has been popularly estimated that the total value of all petroleum products of 1864 was not less than fifty-six millions of dollars — greater than the average gold product of the United States. Governor Curtin, of Pennsylvania, in his annual message, estimates the annual profit of petroleum to his State at fifty millions.—These estimates may be slightly exaggerated, but the actual value must approximate those figures.

At the close of 1864 the daily production was estimated at seven thousand five hundred barrels, or three hundred thousand gallons, of which forty thousand gallons were assumed to be the daily production of West Virginia, in territory only beginning to be developed, as the gradual breaking down of the rebellion inspired confidence in operations there.

The increase of the foreign demand is shown by the following statement of exports:

	1861.	1862.	1863.	1864.
Refined Oil, barrels,				545,525
Crude " "				232,680
Naphtha, "				16,812
Tar, "				5,187
Total, "	30,000	267,000	688,275	800,204

There is little prospect of decline in this demand, and less expectation of low prices. The enormous premium on gold in 1864 gave it a fictitious advantage which may never be enjoyed again; yet there is little prospect in the future for a lower gold value. Its introduction into new localities, its manifold and constantly increasing list of uses, and its possible employment in steam generation for long voyages, render it highly probable that the demand will fully keep pace with any increase of supply, and maintain the present prices.

CHAPTER XX.

WELL BORING. — OIL DISTILLING. — REFINING.

THE first operation in "well boring," which is really well drilling, is to dig through the soil to the cap-rock, and insert a wooden box about eight inches square — called a "conductor," because designed as a guide to the drill, through which it is inserted. Then the derrick, a square, steeple-like frame, is built, about twelve feet square at the base and four at the top, as a support for the pulley by which the tools are raised or lowered. These are rough or well-wrought, cheap or dear, at the pleasure of the proprietor, costing sometimes sixty dollars, sometimes one hundred and fifty dollars.

The tools are of various styles and curious construction. The drill is three feet in length, four inches in diameter, rounded above, champered and chisel-shaped at the point. Both rope and pole tools are used, but the rope is generally preferred for deep wells. The poles are jointed with screws, in lengths of perhaps ten or twelve feet. The poles or rope are lifted a few inches by steam-power, and allowed to drop, clipping a fragment of rock at each fall. A heavy circular bar of iron, to which the drill is attached, is suspended by the rope or poles, the whole weighing five hundred pounds or more, and thus giving the required momentum to the drill. A reamer follows the drill, breaking down irregularities and enlarging slightly the hole. Once or twice daily a sand-pump is lowered, and the mingled debris and water, which is forced through the valve, is drawn up.

After striking oil, the tube, usually two inches in diameter, is put down in sections. The seed-bag, designed to prevent the passage of water from veins above into the oil cavity, is filled with flax-seed, and placed between the tubing and outer wall of the well.

The devices for grasping tools or fragments which have been lost or become fast in the well, are very ingenious, and worthy of particular examination. Improvements are frequently perfected in this important department of well-boring.

The cost of sinking a well five hundred feet, in West Virginia, is about six thousand dollars, including engine and fixtures. Few of the wells in West Virginia have cost that amount; some of them finding oil at shallow depths, and drilled with a spring pole, requiring no engine, have cost but a small fraction of that sum. The proprietors usually supply an engine, fixtures, and fuel, and contract for the labor of drilling, paying from two dollars and a half to three dollars and a half per foot, according to the depth of the well. The cost has varied somewhat with the price of labor. Higher prices would be demanded, if the depth should exceed six hundred feet. The tools cost from three to four hundred dollars. The rapidity of boring depends upon a thousand contingencies. The first hundred feet may be accomplished in four or five days, under favorable circumstances; yet it usually takes several months, often the greater portion of the year, to complete a well and get it in operation. In cases where industry is unwearied, accidents avoided by care, and oil is fortunately struck at a moderate depth, the well is put to work in from thirty to sixty days.

Invention has been greatly stimulated in devising means for boring and pumping oil wells. The devices used and patented are of most varied forms, and adapted either to bore the rock, or by combined action to bore and pump at the same time. The main object desired to be obtained, is rapidity and certainty of execution, and to avoid difficulties occasioned by the presence of debris, in the prosecution of the work. The working of the drill produces a fine and almost pulverized powder, proceeding from the rock; and it is only by forcing water into or around the drill, that the debris is kept in a liquefied state to a considerable extent, and pumped out. The form of the cutting portion of the drill, and cutters used to enlarge the original orifice, also form the subject matter of many of the inventions.

It is known by practical experience in boring for oil, that many of the crevices in the rock, through which the oil would naturally flow, are stopped by the thick paste of the moistened pulverized rock-borings. Hence the apparent necessity of side cutters, operated from within the drill proper, and forced outwardly, by suitable power, to enlarge the area of the bore, and permit a free flow of the oil. Another device used for a similar purpose (to some extent), is the reamer attached to the drill, used principally, however, to make a smooth surface to the bore, but incidentally accomplishing the result above referred to. Since the first of May last, one hundred and thirty-four applications for patents have been filed, and seventy-nine patents granted, for devices used in boring rocks and wells.

A French invention for boring wells has been introduced into this country. The tool consists of a tubular stock of steel, with cutting edges of diamonds — not of "the first water," of course — which leaves a solid core of rock in the centre of the cut. It cuts the rock with great rapidity, and will work a revolution, it is claimed, in well boring — "cutting five hundred feet in twenty days." The core is broken off at intervals, and taken out with a clamp — serving to show the geological character of the strata more perfectly than the "bore meal" of the usual process of drilling.

The School of Mines, connected with the Polytechnic College at Philadelphia, has a set of models of improved well-boring implements, from Germany, where the art has been brought to great perfection, comprising derricks, cutters, reamers, enlargers, sand-pumps, jars, crabs, iron rods, wooden poles, and impression boxes for removing fragments of broken tools.

An "automatic well-borer" has been invented by General H. Haupt, consisting of a vertical cylinder placed directly over the well, operated by steam, with a hollow piston rod attached to a hollow piston, which moves a hemp or wire rope to which the boring tool is attached. The drill penetrates rapidly, bores a circular hole requiring no reamer to perfect it. A boiler, but no engine, is required.

Among the improvements in drilling should be mentioned prominently "Atwood's Patent Drilling Machine, with pipe-driver and hydraulic sand-pump combined," which promises to work a revolution in the business of well sinking, by its great celerity of execution, simplicity, and consequent reduction of expense. It requires no derricks, bull-wheels, Samson's-posts, reamers, sand-pumps — and occupies a space of less than five feet square, exclusive of the engine. It is on wheels, ready for instant removal to other wells. The drill is attached to the end of two-inch tubing, which is in readiness for pumping as soon as oil is struck. The drill, equally economical of results, reams as well as drills at one operation; and the sand-pump is also dispensed with, by attaching a hose to the end of the drill tube, and forcing a volume of water down it, which, discharging through openings in the drill barrel, forces the detritus or sediment up on the outside of the drill tube. This occupies but a few minutes, and is thorough, besides keeping open the small oil crevices that are so often closed up under the old system of sand pumping. Thus the work proceeds continuously, without removal of the drill, except for sharpening. It is confidently assumed by those interested in it, and with much show of reason, to be as great an improvement upon primitive practices in well boring as the perfected telegraph is upon the kite of Franklin.

It is regarded by examiner James, of the Patent Office, with great favor, and has already been introduced into successful practice. Those interested are referred, for more particular information, to S. Leland, at the Metropolitan Hotel in New York.

The refining of petroleum is a simpler and easier process than the refining of coal oil. The crude oil is placed in an under-ground reservoir, to protect from loss either by leakage or fire; and thence pumped into iron retorts or stills, which are heated by furnaces. Tubes at the top of these retorts pass through tanks, kept full of water. The retorts are subjected to heat for forty-eight hours; first the lighter, then the heavier illuminating oil, passes over in vapor. It is again heated, again evaporated, and conducted through condensing tubes into underground reservoirs. The purification is not yet complete. Being pumped into a wooden tank, chemicals are added, the petroleum is agitated violently by the introduction of a column of air injected through the bottom of the tank by a force-pump, and a thorough admixture of the ingredients is thus simply procured. It is then drawn off into shallow tanks to settle, and becomes clarified — the illuminating oil of commerce. Sulphuric acid is used, and caustic soda to remove the acid.

New processes, or modifications of old ones, are being rapidly introduced. New inventions are patented every month, affecting some of the details, if not the principles, of refining. There are several inventions or claims for refining by filtration, upon which high hopes are based.

In the distillation a very ethereal liquid, called gasoline, possessing anæsthetic properties, like chloroform, first passes over, followed by a slightly heavier liquid, about three-fourths the weight of water, very inflammable, known as benzine, useful for making paints and varnishes, and for carburetting common air, used in houses as a substitute for coal gas. It has a delicate yellow tint, samples differing from almost colorless to darker products. After these volatile products are evolved, illuminating or lamp oil is the next result of the distillation. If the lighter portion of the oil has been properly separated, there is no danger from explosion. If the oil takes fire in contact with a lighted match, it should be discarded.

After the burning oils have passed, come still heavier or lubricating oils, separated into "light" and "heavy" qualities. The residuum may also be used for lubricating. Some of these oils have proved equal to the best sperm; the lightest will not answer for machinery worked at high speed.

If the heavier portions of the oil are subjected to heat again, a wax called paraffine is produced in white scales or crystals. This is purified by agitating it in a melted state with sulphuric acid, and washing with water and caustic alkali; it is then moulded into candles cheaper and better than sperm. This is regarded by chemists as a compound substance, composed of several solid hydro-carbons.

CHAPTER XXI.

THE ERA OF OIL WELLS. — THE BURNING SPRINGS DISTRICT. — THE LITTLE KANAWHA.

THE dawning of the era of petroleum has thrown an unaccustomed light upon the quiet and lonely forest hills of West Virginia. A century since, the wild deer and the wilder Indian were undisturbed possessors; a little later, the white hunter began to encroach upon those game preserves, shooting with equal zest a fat buck or a tough Indian; then followed the pioneer, or hunter-farmer, to whom the oozing oil was a greasy fluid, useful for sprains or bruises in man or beast, and nothing more. The coal, outcropping in six-foot veins, he could mine for his own use, if he found it in his cellar or in a near hill-side; and sometimes he dreamed, that in the dim future, when forests should be scarce and railroads plenty, it might be valuable. Yet he might sell his farm, improvements and all, for five dollars an acre. His vision of enhanced values was far off and unsubstantial, dissipated by the clink of a few present dollars.

How changed the scene! In the spring of 1865, an eager crowd of strangers, on horseback and on foot, are threading those narrow valleys, climbing the steep hillsides, searching for signs of upheaval, measuring the dip of the rocks, inspecting appearances of "oil-blossom," watching for oil bubbles to rise to the surface on the margins of streams, and noting all acknowledged "indications" of oil. The soil is a secondary consideration; timber is somewhat more important, for fixtures or fuel; coal is really worth prospecting for.

The oil seeker passes unobserved the beautiful red bud that crimsons the scene with its bright blossoms; and the wild flowers he tramples carelessly under his feet. As he wanders amid the wild scenery the *coup d'œil* loses its interest in the prospect for a more profitable *coup d'huile*. If reminded that the climate is suggestive of Italy, he knows only that Parma is brilliantly illuminated; if told of Greece, he perhaps proffers an investment in the Ionian Isles. Everything is golden, because the lens which magnifies the objects of his vision is a drop of oil.

What wonder that agriculture languishes, and that the farmer either goes to drilling, or sells his land and emigrates? The local press tells truly that, "Land is seemingly changing hands by whole counties. Many tracts have been resold two or three times within the past three months — double the cost price at each sale." Many a quiet farmer has sold his hillside acres for ready money sufficient for the purchase of an equal area of rich Ohio bottom land; and he is well satisfied with the exchange. Others have leased their lands, and are already in receipt of more money than they ever expected to see; yet such cases are few as yet, and confined to two or three localities in which developments have been made. Elsewhere land-owners are hopefully awaiting the progress of the drill, confident of a fortune in the future. Nor are they building "castles in the air;" their hopes seem to be well grounded.

While West Virginia has borne with Pennsylvania a reputation as an undoubted oil region, circumstances have rendered the development of each very unequal. Either the incursions of guerillas, or the fear of them, has stopped existing enterprises, during the war of the rebellion, even in the vicinity of the Ohio River; and in the interior, on the upper waters of the Little Kanawha, upon the Elk, and Pocotalico, Great Kanawha, Guyandotte, and Big Sandy, it has been simply impossible to commence operations, and very dangerous and impracticable to prospect for the best locations, or to make purchases or contracts.

More than twenty years ago, in boring for salt on the Little Kanawha, twenty-seven miles above Parkersburg, oil was discovered. In the spring of 1860, S. D. Karnes leased from John D. Rathbone this abandoned salt well, and was remunerated for his efforts by a profitable yield of oil, at the rate of fifty barrels per day. Attention was attracted to the spot, and active operations were commenced by others. In the autumn, a well sunk by J. C. Rathbone astonished the country with a product of three hundred barrels daily, and even vastly more for a few days, the exact quantity (three thousand were reported) in the first overwhelming flow of oil, never having been precisely determined.

Other wells of great value were obtained; success added fuel to the flame of excitement; farmers, mechanics, and professional men, leaving their vocations, flocked to the oil region, the centre of which was the Rathbone farms; a village of shanties became densely populous, with derricks instead of church spires, the cooperage of tanks and barrels the only mechanical product, and the oil traffic and transport the prolific source of remunerative labor. Sharp speculative men, eager to reap the advantage which circumstances offered, waited not a moment; but floated upon the tide which promised to lead to fortune, long before it had reached its flood. They bought lands where they could; and then took leases of all that remained. The excitement spread; neighboring territory was involved; strange faces peopled every farm, and every farm-house became an inn.

A participant in this struggle for sudden wealth, who was present when the Llewellyn and Eternal Centre wells were struck, thus writes: " The desire of obtaining boring territory soon became so great that large bounties were demanded and paid. At first, one thousand dollars per acre and one third of the oil, were the conditions; afterwards two thousand dollars per acre and one third of the oil in iron bound barrels were demanded and given. The amount of oil thrown out by the Llewellyn Well, was such as to produce the impression that the surface included within a radius of one mile from that well as the centre, contained the *oil centre of the world*. Men ran wild with speculation, and the desire to sink wells within that limited locality, was boundless. A village sprung up in one month, and as the season progressed towards spring, it was calculated that over two thousand persons would be located on the ground before June."

The breaking out of civil war at this juncture, in the midst of this scene of busy life, was as unwelcome as a spectre at a wedding. The echoes of Sumter, as an evil spell, stirred to treason the hearts of "oil men"—those who believed in the right of a State to commit suicide—while the patriots, who meant that our starry flag should wave forever over a united country, prepared to do or die in its defence. Mutual repulsion was instantaneous; as oil and water separate, the loyal and disloyal element parted company, the traitors first moving South, the adherents of the Union going North, leaving derrick and drill, tank and well, and all the appointments of oil production, to the risks of violence and malice, destruction and decay.

Yet some of the principal wells, in which interests were held by persons in the neighborhood, were operated with slight interruption, although exposed to guerilla incursions, and the inconvenience of a lack of laborers, so that the production of 1861 was but four million gallons. In 1862, the war, at first believed not to be of long continuance or great severity, gathered gloom, and afforded less encouragement to oil operators than ever; yet there were three million two hundred thousand gallons sent to market from this point.

In May of 1863, the rebel General Jones, with a strong force, made a descent upon Burning Spring run, burned twenty thousand barrels of oil, tanks, barrels, derricks, houses, and fixtures, broke the engines, and filled up the wells. A considerable time elapsed before these partial operations were again renewed; and the result of the labors of the season probably did not exceed two millions of gallons.

In 1864 confidence began to revive. Well boring

was started anew; some of the old wells were put in order and found productive. A few of the oldest, which had been kept in operation a good portion of the time since 1861, showed signs of exhaustion. In one or two instances, the expedient of boring deeper was resorted to, with very gratifying pecuniary results. One of these has recently been reported a fifty-barrel well. At the close of the year the excitement was intense. Engines by scores were brought from Parkersburg to this vicinity, and the neighboring lands were purchased for future operations, or for speculative purposes. The lands of Standing-Stone, Reedy, Tucker's, Lynn Camp, Lee's, and many other creeks, and of Two Riffles, Rock, and other runs, which swell the waters of the Little Kanawha, were prospected, surveyed, sold or leased, and either "stocked" or reserved for individual enterprise. The shrewd operators upon Oil Creek, where the best lands commanded from one to ten thousand dollars per acre, seized upon these lands at fifty, one hundred, two hundred dollars, or more, according to "indications" or location. On Burning Spring Creek, indeed, the more modest of the Oil Creek figures were asked and obtained—if five thousand dollars per acre may be deemed modest.

While all this prospecting, buying and selling, were in progress, the old wells, few in number, flowed on, or were pumped industriously, yielding a quantity of oil, comparatively small, but amply sufficient to enrich their owners, and to encourage the multitude of oil operators in their efforts. The very intensity of the excitement tended to retard development. Land once sold, instead of being worked, was resold, or placed in a stock company which might be months in getting an engine on the ground, or in disposing of leases, which would involve in turn an equal delay. Yet scores of wells were commenced during the autumn, to be finished in the spring or summer of the present year; and at the present writing new wells are struck, almost weekly, on Burning Springs run and vicinity, four or five of which are yielding highly profitable results, being reported at fifty to seventy-five barrels each. And at the same time some of the old wells are making increased returns, and giving new evidence of the permanence of the oil supply. The wells which, it is morally certain, will find oil in all this region, during the summer, will deepen the popular faith in Little Kanawha oil, and probably intensify the excitement of last winter. And, what is better, they will yield more oil than was ever before obtained in this oil field, give remunerative profits to all judicious investors, and add to the productive resources of the nation.

The Standing-Stone region, although undeveloped, is very popular. Several oil companies have been formed upon it, under the patronage and co-operation of high officials and prosperous business men; and farms have been sold there at five hundred dollars per acre.

Two Riffles Run, a diminutive stream, has been the centre of a brisk trade in lands, at more than two hundred dollars per acre in certain cases.

On the south side, the valley of Reedy Creek, on "the oil belt," is a favorite field for investment; has changed hands, some of it more than once; is a finely timbered region, with some excellent farm lands. Numerous other affluents of the main stream, draining large portions of Calhoun, Gilmer and Braxton Counties, afford the most promising localities of the central oil field.

The oil of the Burning Springs wells is of average specific gravity, generally about 40° Beaumé. It is heavier than that of Pennsylvania, worth more for illumination, and bears a higher price. It is found in large quantities at a less depth, having come, in most cases, from cavities pierced at less than two hundred and fifty feet from the surface. When showing signs of exhaustion, wells have been sunk deeper, and the largely increased product has proved the existence of something more than surface accumulations in transient supply. One, deepened from one hundred and sixty feet to two hundred and eighty-five, has yielded fifty barrels daily. This fact is corroborative of the theory of Professor Andrews, that the origin of the oil is deep in the beds of bituminous shales, which are computed to contain more combustible matter than the coal measures.

A well recently struck on Reedy Creek yields a still heavier oil than that of Burning Springs — a lubricating oil of excellent quality. This affords proof, were evidence needed, of the value of the lands lying in a direct line between the famous Burning Springs of the two Kanawhas.

A good well has also been struck in Jackson County, on the Ohio River.

The surface configuration is peculiar, more abrupt, the valleys narrower, (particularly in Wirt County,) than in other American oil regions. As in other sections, the same "benches" occur, or nearly level areas, at intervals between the valleys and summits, occasioned, apparently, by land slides. The hill ranges take every imaginable direction. At many points, three, four or more ravines appear to radiate from a centre. Upon such localities oil speculators are apt to seize, and well-borers to erect their derricks; and, in truth, it is at such points, in two out of the three original oil discoveries of West Virginia, that the largest and most profitable results have been attained.

CHAPTER XXII.

THE HUGHES' RIVER REGION.—OIL RUN OF GOOSE CREEK.—
HORSENECK AND COW CREEK.

ONE mile below the junction of the North and South Forks of Hughes' River, and five miles south of Petroleum Station, on the north bank of the river, is the site of the noted "sand diggings," which supplied, for medical uses, many barrels of oil yearly; seventy-five barrels is the maximum estimate of an intelligent business man of Parkersburg, who once sent a lot to Philadelphia, and realized a little less than the freight! The diggings are now neglected, and exhibit few signs of their former fatness.

On the south side of the river, nearly opposite this point, a shallow well, little more than one hundred feet deep, now owned by Hon. J. B. Blair, has been flowing at regular intervals, one barrel daily, for five years. An engine will soon be placed there, and its capacity as a "pumping well" tested. The oil is of a superior quality. The river here exhibits oil rising from its bed, and spreading over the surface of the water.

A little higher, on the north side, near the mouth of a narrow ravine, a well has just been struck, upon the property of an Eastern company, thus described by the editor of the Parkersburg Gazette, in the issue of July 6, 1865:

"The well is two hundred and twenty-six feet deep, and cost, we presume, some fifteen hundred dollars. Just above it is an alcove, in the sand-rock, affording water for the engine. The well seemed to be only slightly affected by gas, is tubed, without a seed bag, and is being pumped quite slowly. About four hundred barrels of oil were standing in casks and tanks, and during the day we spent there the well, with its defective machinery, pumped as near as we could estimate, about forty barrels of oil. The yield of oil per day seems to be increasing. There is little doubt that when the well is properly tubed, and worked to its capacity, it will nearly double its present yield, if not more. Reckoned in cash, the well is now paying its owners at least nine thousand dollars per month, or at the rate of more than one hundred thousand dollars per year, at the present prices for oil. The oil by actual and accurate test, by Professor Barnes, is slightly over 35° Beaumé. To the above facts we invite attention, and in view of them, the intrinsic value of this locality for oil purposes is incalculable. A man can well afford to suffer forty failures to obtain one or two such wells, but we know of no place in West Virginia where a failure is less likely than at this point."

Near the forks, about a mile further east, oil has been struck, and also at the California House, the same distance west. Several wells are in progress at the latter point, two of them at least six hundred feet deep. The Vesta Company has large interests between the "sand diggings" and Petroleum; and the Bickel well, on Buffalo Run, in which it owns a half interest, created a great sensation recently, upon reaching oil, by its violent expulsion of oil, gas, water, and fragments of rock.

Other wells are in progress, further west, on Hughes'

River, Turtle Run, Goose Creek, Walker Creek, and other streams. At least thirty wells have been commenced in this region.

Upon Oil Run, a little valley winding through rocky hills, whose disarranged strata dip in every direction, at every angle of inclination, may be seen a marvel of nature and a curiosity of industry — the Virginia Oil Works — owned by a company of prominent business men of Wheeling. The works are located two miles north of the North-Western Virginia Railroad, very nearly in a direct north and south line with the oil springs of Wirt County and of Western Pennsylvania.

The oil is among the heaviest known in the country, almost destitute of benzole and naphtha, and a superior lubricator. The Baltimore and Ohio Railroad uses, as the best lubricating oil attainable, about one hundred barrels per month.

A dozen wells were working at the date of the writer's visit, all operated by a rude but effective, as well as novel, system of mechanism, driven by a single engine of fifteen horse-power, with ample power to spare for the working of many more wells. It is called a "telegraph," its continuous line of rough scantling, suspended by iron hangers between duplicate telegraph-like poles, being somewhat suggestive of such a name. The entire system, connecting the different wells throughout the narrow valley and in the ravines that make into it, requires almost a mile in length of this telegraphing, and is operated by an alternating horizontal motion — forward perhaps twenty inches, and back the same — which keeps in continuous action all of the pumps at the same time.

A dirty, greenish stream flows forth, and is borne in troughs to large wooden reservoirs, with stop-cocks near the top for drawing off the oil, and at the bottom for discharging the water. Nearly all the labor required is in running the engine and obtaining fuel for it, boring wells, making fixtures, and barrelling the oil. The oil is brought from the recesses of the earth, separated from the water, and conveyed to the barrellers absolutely without manual labor.

A good idea of the value of West Virginia oil property may be gained from the fact that these shallow wells, which average less than a barrel each per day, gave a clear profit of more than fifty thousand dollars last year, to the proprietors.

Another well has been struck this summer, upon Oil Run, near Petroleum, which has been estimated to yield forty barrels of superior lubricating oil. This run is a branch of Goose Creek, a favorite stream with petroleum hunters — the "goose" that is expected to lay many a golden egg. Operators are also busy upon its "forks," Laurel, Pigeon Roost, Myers, Ellis, and Big Run, and oil has been found in several instances.

One of the wonders of the Hughes' River region, is an immense deposit of asphaltum, known as the Great Vertical Asphaltum Lode, situated upon both sides of McFarland's Run, a tributary of the South Fork of Hughes' River. This solidified rock oil, as it seems to be, lies in a vertical fissure in a yellow sandstone rock, from three and a half to five feet in width, divided into distinct sections by an irregular partition, one portion fibrous, the other granulated, and both free from foreign admixture. It runs in a line south seventy-six degrees east, and is traced upon the surface a mile and a half. The hills on either side of the Run are four hundred feet high, and this seam runs through them, coming within a few feet of the surface at the top.

An attempt was made to find its depth; a shaft was sunk, from the bottom of the Run, nearly forty feet, when operations were stopped by water from the hills. Enough has been seen to prove the unexampled abundance of this strange mineral.

Several chemists have tested its properties. Some specimens, upon reduction and distillation, have yielded one hundred and forty gallons of petroleum per ton; other specimens have produced larger results, in one case one hundred and sixty-nine gallons. A calculation has been made, based upon mining one hundred tons per day, at ninety dollars per ton, of more than two millions of dollars profits in a single year. The specific gravity of this oil is about 30° Beaumé. The engineer in charge estimates, without reference to undiscovered depths of asphaltum, or underlying basins of oil, a yield of at least one million barrels of petroleum. It is supposed to result from the evaporation of the more volatile elements of petroleum, which has been thrown up by some convulsion of nature, at the same time that the chasm was formed; and that pits, in immense quantities, probably exist below. There are others, acknowledging the nature and value of the deposit, who reject the probability of liquid oil beneath.

A railroad, connecting these mines with Cairo Station, on the Baltimore and Ohio Railroad, fourteen miles long, is under construction.

Operations were commenced on Horseneck Run of Bull Creek, three miles from the Ohio River, and ten miles nearly east from Marietta, Ohio, in the autumn of 1863. The point selected was at the bend of the "neck," at the intersection of another valley from the north, from which the lines of boring territory diverge at nearly equal angles. The hills are high, the valley narrow, and both hill and valley in a state of nature, excepting only such improvements as derricks, tanks, rough offices and huts. In March of 1864, at little more than two hundred feet in depth, near the centre of the valley, an oil basin was pierced which deluged the whole vicinity with its astonishing flow. All the labor obtainable was put to the digging of pits and the construction of dams, which failed to contain all of this fugitive wealth, by which others were enriched, far down the stream, through similar efforts. Two or three thousand barrels were estimated as the first day's product. After the first extraordinary flow had subsided, the yield continued for a time steadily at three hundred barrels. Gradually it was reduced to one hundred barrels; then to fifty; and in April last it was still productive, pumping twelve barrels per day. The owners of the well, four in number, who leased the land at a royalty of one-eighth of the oil, sold out their interest at magnificent figures — some of them soon after the strike, and others later — those holding on realizing the most money. The owner of the land, who had been living quietly in a hut near by, after pocketing the royalty for a time, sold his little farm for one hundred thousand dollars, and purchased fine farms in Ohio with the proceeds.

Other wells were soon in operation, clustered around at a few rods apart, and all were productive, yielding twenty, forty, and sixty barrels. Two were sunk upon the side of the hill, as an experiment, by Shriver, Koonce & Co., and both were good wells; one of them produced sixty-five barrels daily for a time. Among the companies represented here are, the Horseneck, Eureka, Bergen, Calf Creek, and New York and Boston. The old wells, being very near each other, are now much reduced in product, and new ones are being bored, scattered along towards the head of the run for the distance of a mile. New and old, there are forty on Horseneck. A new strike, which promises to make a valuable well, has lately occurred.

Upon Rawson's Run, which enters Horseneck a few hundred yards below its productive wells, were seventeen, finished and unfinished, in April last; and seven more on Rawson's Fork, below the junction of Horseneck. Others have doubtless been commenced since. The most noted are those of the Tack Company, which were for a time very productive.

Bull Creek, of which the above are right-hand branches, is the longest stream in this region, with numerous forks, among which are Isaac's, Campbell's, and Laurel. On each of these, and upon the main stream, developments are in progress. Three miles south of Horseneck, on a fine, broad valley of Bull Creek, are three wells, one of them the Camden well, four hundred feet deep, with oil flowing from the conductor, though the well is untubed.

At this point Campbell's Fork comes in, affording rich but undeveloped territory.

Laurel Fork, a mile higher, midway between the Ohio River and Oil Run of Goose Creek, presents a beautiful reach of boring territory, with unmistakable oil indications, and a marked exhibition of an anticlinal axis. Messrs. Ford and Koonce, owners of the lease, have commenced boring.

Between Horseneck and the Ohio River, the line of the Burning Springs upheaval crosses Calf Creek, Cow Creek, French Creek, and one or two other small streams. Calf Creek is very rich in indications, and is being pierced at all points for oil. A remarkable evidence of upheaval, worthy of a visit from the Atlantic coast as a natural curiosity, is seen upon the summit of the ridge dividing this from the Horseneck valley. Immense masses of limestone, honey-combed as if by chemical action in the depths below, project some twenty feet above the surface, presenting to each other perpendicular parallel walls, with chasms intervening, some of them a single foot, others several feet in width. The regularity of outline and massiveness of this solitary group of projecting rock, are striking features of a remarkable landscape.

On Cow Creek, a well owned by Jackson & Pedro, a mile and a half from the Ohio River, recently flowed a large quantity of oil during the night after the vein was struck. Several barrels were gathered from hollows in the ground. A good well is confidently expected.

The wells of this Ohio section are mostly in Pleasants County. Middle Island Creek, also in this county, is a field of active oil operations, in which oil has already been found. Its precise value will be determined at an early day.

CHAPTER XXIII.

THE CENTRAL AND NORTHERN OIL REGION.

THE central district of West Virginia is daily becoming better known, and gaining high appreciation among the workers in oil. Three years ago, while gas springs and oil shows were common in this region, few people at home imagined it possible that oil in paying quantities could exist there, and nobody abroad believed in oil in West Virginia, except at Burning Springs in Wirt County, or possibly in a line extended north and south of that point — the "line of the great upheaval." That illusion is now dispelled, by heavy strikes of oil in numerous localities, east and west of that line, in West Virginia and in Ohio. In Ohio, on this line, but mostly west of it, paying wells are numerous; in West Virginia, the central oil territory, though comparatively undeveloped, with hundreds of wells commenced, or in process of boring, and giving abundant proof of oil, embraces a broad belt, which includes many counties.

Through this territory, on a line nearly parallel with the upheaval so well known to fame, operators are tracing another oil belt, which is claimed to exhibit all the signs of abundant deposits beneath, except the violent dislocation of the surface strata.

In this respect, a nearer analogy is borne to the Venango region in Pennsylvania than to the Burning Spring territory. A striking resemblance to Oil Creek, in configuration of surface, is noted in many localities in this central belt. The disruption of the regular stratification, it is assumed, is subterranean, not reaching the superficial and visible strata. And yet there are a few marked evidences of surface disturbance.

The Commissioner of Immigration, who resides in Doddridge County, and has given much attention to this subject, gives his views as follows:

"If, as conceded by science and confirmed by experience, gas vents and burning springs are indicative of petroleum in the rocks below, and that oil can only be found in the vertical fissures of dislocated strata, then a succession of these phenomena in a given direction, above the surface, may be regarded as a conclusive evidence of a pregnant line of geological disturbance below it.

"The indications most generally consulted in prospecting for petroleum, are the dips of the rocks, oil springs, gas and bubbles, whether inflammable or not, salt and sulphur springs, salt licks, and alum rock, or its crystallized exudations. The mineral belt lately explored exhibits a greater abundance and intensity of the latter indications than have so far been suspected anywhere between the lines of uplift east and west of it.

"The proximate locality of its axis may be found by tracing a line north from ten to fifteen degrees east, from the great gas springs below the mouth of Duck Creek on Elk River, to the heart of the Pennsylvania oil region in Crawford and Venango Counties, passing the noted Steer Creek and Grass Run Burning Springs in Gilmer, the salt spring, sulphur lick and alum region on branches of Little Kanawha, heading in Doddridge and Lewis counties, the burning spring on McElroy, and numerous mineral indications on Middle Island waters, the mineral region of Fishing Creek, the gas wells at Triadelphia, near Wheeling, and probably at other points in the Panhandle counties.

"Although upon the theory advanced above, this line may be regarded as one of strictly subterraneous dislocation, yet it exhibits, so far as explored, at least two instances of notable disturbances above the surface. The most remarkable of these is, a southeastern dip of about fifteen degrees in the whole visible stratification of a spur, or point, facing and shaping in its apparent axis a very acute bend in the creek, beyond which the rocks, though much fractured by vertical rents, appear in their undisturbed horizontal position. Right at the foot of this break, near the creek, gas bubbles are said to rise invariably when the stream gets over its banks, and though I did not happen there on such an occasion, I have no reason to doubt the statement. In comparing the singular geological appearance of this spot with similar ones along Elk and Little Kanawha Rivers, where the most notable gas and burning springs are to be found, the question suggests itself to me, whether the tortuousness of some of our mountain streams, so unaccountably capricious in places, might not be attributed to other causes than mere accidents of surface at the time when the running waters first began to seek their beds.

"While the topographical conformation of our territory is principally the result of gradual abrasion, and our valleys undeniably eroded by running waters, yet may not some of those short angular river bends, and perhaps much of the course of the streams, have been predetermined by rents or depressions from subterraneous disturbance, and, therefore, afford a profitable field of exploration? From several remarkable coincidences observed by me thus far, I am convinced the question is worthy some little investigation."

Among the more noticeable localities, in which gas and oil springs and other indications, have attracted the oil speculator and well borer, may be named Steer Creek, a prominent southern branch of the Little Kanawha, with numerous forks, heading up in Braxton County; the Elk, and its many tributaries, particularly rich in Clay and Braxton; Cedar Creek, of Little Kanawha, and its branches; the headwaters of the Little Kanawha, with its Oil Creek, Salt Lick, Bryant's Fork, Noll's Creek, and other small streams; the waters of Lewis County, especially some of the tributaries of the West Fork of the Monongahela, and Leading Creek, a prominent northern branch of the Little Kanawha; on the streams of Gilmer County; in Doddridge County, the headwaters of Middle Island Creek, Cabin Run of the North Fork of the Hughes' River, and other streams; and further north, in Tyler, Wetzel, and Marshall, and in some portions of the Panhandle counties. In Hancock County well boring has been vigorously prosecuted, and oil struck in one well at least.

The excitement is high in Wetzel County. Well boring is on the increase. Fishing Creek is beginning to swarm with derricks and engines; and individuals and companies are commencing operations on Proctor's Creek.

Operators in Tyler County are busy, and some of them have already struck oil. The excitement is high; and the actual value of the territory will soon be tested.

Nor is the search for oil limited easterly to this belt. Nearer the Alleghany range it has been not only sought, but found; and in Monongalia, adjoining Fayette and Green Counties in Pennsylvania, good wells have been reported during the present season, and operations have been active and exciting;

land has changed hands almost as generally as in Wirt or Ritchie County in certain neighborhoods. The adjoining county, Preston, in the Cheat River valley, has been the scene of active prospecting and purchasing, and the expression of confident expectations. As an instance indicating the feeling in this section, an undeveloped tract of two hundred acres of wild land, which a few years since was sold for five hundred dollars, last winter brought fifty-seven thousand dollars.

This interior region has been too unsafe for development during the war, so far as regards the country south of the Parkersburg branch of the Baltimore and Ohio Railroad. Except in a very few localities, and in cases in which the parties were residents, no actual operations have been commenced until recently. In such instances the drilling has generally been by hand, with a spring pole, after the ancient manner of hominy making, and the domestic method of hulling rice — the elasticity of the bent pole lifting the drill.

A fine strike of oil is reported very recently on Grass Run, a small affluent of the Little Kanawha, in Gilmer County, between Cedar and Steer Creeks, five miles from De Kalb. It was bored by two old men, with a spring pole; one of them was the owner of the little farm of one hundred acres, and had refused all offers for the property, preferring not "to be bothered" in his old age by "strange people" on his farm.

A strong show of oil is reported in a well now being bored by hand, in Doddridge County, on the headwaters of Cabin Run, which flow into the North

Fork of the Hughes' River. The oil springs of Noll's Creek, in Braxton County, have recently been satisfactorily tested.

Wells are being sunk at Dodson's Run, on two branches of Arnold's Creek, near Central Station, and also at Smithton Station. The M'Intyre Well of the Victoria Petroleum Company, commenced "gasing" at thirty feet.

On Lower Camp Run, of Elk River, ninety miles from its mouth, wells have been commenced, and high expectations of success are entertained. At Duffield's Bend, fifteen miles below Rock Camp Run, parties in this country, in France, and in Cuba, have associated themselves in the purchase of a tract of land, with reference to petroleum, iron, and coal operations.

An oil strike has occurred in Taylor County, at the depth of three hundred feet. At Clarksburg, in Harrison County, a vein of oil has been struck at two hundred feet, which is causing a great excitement by flowing a quantity of pure oil. Cultivated farms, wild lands, and gardens in town, are being leased for oil purposes. What their productive value will be, the future can only unfold. But it is morally certain that wells, in great numbers, will be sunk in every portion of the central district, during the present season; and the result may surprise the country, and intensify the general desire of enterprising men, here and elsewhere, to add to their fortunes from the overflowing treasures of petroleum.

CHAPTER XXIV.

THE GREAT KANAWHA OIL BASIN.—THE VALLEYS OF THE
GUYANDOTTE AND BIG SANDY.

MASON County, on the Ohio, at the mouth of the Great Kanawha, is participating in the petroleum excitement. Its salt has long been a valuable product; its coal fields, identical with the rich and profitable Pomeroy deposits, on the opposite bank of the Ohio, are regarded as the most valuable on the river; and the oil, of which abundant traces have long been visible, is now for the first time claiming attention and development. Nor has the effort been vain; oil has already been reached by the drill, and high expectations of its abundant presence are generally entertained.

Oil development is also progressing at other points on the same side of the Great Kanawha, with highly favorable indications. The region of the Pocotalico exhibits all the signs of oil, and shares the attentions of capitalists and well borers.

The Elk River and Blue Creek region, north of Charleston, is very promising. Operations have been commenced, and success already attained; in one instance one hundred and twenty barrels per day were reported on Blue Creek, when the well was first struck. Unimproved lands, formerly held at two, five, or ten dollars at most, command from twenty-five to five hundred. In one instance, for a lease of a tract of two thousand five hundred acres, at a royalty of one-fourth of the oil, the sum of one hundred and seventy-five thousand dollars has been paid. A correspondent, writing from that region, refers to a prediction that we should all be astonished at the changes to be wrought in a single year, and says, "but I little thought how far the facts would outrun the prediction. Less than six months have elapsed since that conversation, and I can scarcely believe that there has not been some supernatural agency at work to accomplish so much in so short a time."

At the present writing there are probably sixty wells in process of drilling, within twenty-five miles of Charleston; and in a few months this may seem a meagre statement in view of the progress then made.

In answer to inquiries relative to the experience of Kanawha salt makers with petroleum, Gen. Lewis Ruffner, who has been for thirty years engaged in the business of salt making, says that in boring the salt wells of the Kanawha Salines, a few miles above Charleston, oil was "in most cases" obtained at a depth of from two hundred and fifty to four hundred feet. The oil came mingled with salt water. A well on his premises, two and a half miles below the Burning Spring, from which salt was made thirty years ago, yielded a very inconvenient amount of oil, at least eight or ten barrels daily, for a long time; and it is not yet entirely exhausted. The most troublesome issue was when the salt water came through cavities two hundred and fifty to three hundred feet below the surface — at which time the salt water flowed into the "gum" (a hollow sycamore sunk to the rock at the depth of the river bed), and was thence brought up by a lifting pump. — These supplies were temporary; fresh supplies followed deeper boring; the tubing extended below the oil, which then ceased to be troublesome. At the depth of five hundred feet it was usual to insert suction pumps into the rock. In many of these wells, now abandoned, the oil continues to rise in small quantities to the surface. Experiments are now in progress for applying suction to the cavities supposed to contain the oil.

As the oil invariably passed off into the river, it is impossible to estimate the quantity thus lost in that vicinity. Mr. Ruffner says that "thousands of barrels" have thus passed away; and gives an instance, which he cannot vouch for from personal knowledge, of a casual demand for forty barrels, which was supplied from one reservoir in a single day. This well was but one fourth of a mile above the Burning Spring. All the great gas wells have been in that immediate vicinity, through which, according to Professor Rogers, an anticlinal axis runs.

Mr. Ruffner assumes, from observation and from inferences drawn from the geological reconnoissance of Professor Rogers, that the rocks of the coal measures, between Charleston and the mountains, are three thousand five hundred feet thick, fifteen hundred of which lie above a clay stratum of an estimated thickness of eight hundred feet, known to salt miners as the "long running rock," from the

21*

length of time that a chisel may be used in it without sharpening; and that this rock is reached at this point at about nine hundred feet; that it contains neither coal nor salt water; but that salt and coal are both found below it, some twelve hundred feet before reaching the sub-carboniferous limestone. This assumption refers only to that portion of the coal measures east of Charleston, "having no relation to the newer series nearer the centre of the basin on the Ohio River."

He believes fully that the chief source of the gas and oil must be sought beneath that "long running rock;" and that its existence in the porous or cavernous upper strata hitherto supplying it, is accounted for by its efforts to reach the surface, impelled by the gas below, through fractures of the intervening strata. As evidence of the truth of this theory, he gives a single instance in which the oil-bearing rocks below the clay stratum have been reached. A well was bored eighteen hundred feet below the bed of the river, when gas was struck, and for a time oil and salt water were thrown out. When it ceased flowing it was abandoned, because it required too long a suction-pump to raise its contents. All the great gas wells were reached by boring *to* this "long running rock," or (in two cases) *into* or *through* it; and in the latter cases the gas was accompanied with oil. The only well now furnishing gas for fuel, and which has continued gas-producing for the greatest length of time, was bored at least to that rock. When the well was first bored, some fifteen or twenty years since, gas was struck in very large quantities, which threw up salt water, and supplied fuel for its evaporation. After flowing for a few months, it suddenly ceased. Suction was applied at the depth of a hundred feet, and it was worked by steam a few months longer, when, as suddenly as it ceased, the gas commenced again. The most singular feature of its action is, that while no oil was produced in the first evolution of gas, or in the second for months after its revival, it then flowed in such quantities as to cover the reservoir, several inches if not feet in depth, as avouched by the manager of the works—and was allowed to run off into the river. As much was saved as was called for by curiosity or use. This well continued to produce gas, oil and salt for years, gradually diminishing in quantity. This is known as the Dickinson and Shrewsbury well, situated nearly opposite the Burning Spring, which it eventually tapped, at a comparatively recent date, and destroyed its issue of gas. Its history is certainly suggestive to intelligent theorists upon the origin of rock oil.

The following, from a correspondent of the *Pittsburgh Commercial*, in corroboration, refers to some of the salt wells in this vicinity:

"Oil was usually reached at a depth ranging from two hundred and fifty to three hundred feet, and in some wells the flow of gas and oil was in such large quantities as to prove very 'troublesome' and 'annoying' to the operators. On Field's Creek, thirteen miles above, on some property now owned by Mr. John McConihay, and on which he now resides, a well for salt water was in process of being bored, in April of 1815, and when at a distance of three hundred and seventy-five feet from the surface, a vein of oil was struck, which flowed over the top of the 'gum' as thick as a man's arm, and ran down the bank like a branch, spreading half way across the river in beautiful iridiscent colors, whence it continued to flow until some time on the following day, when they succeeded in tubing it out. Mr. McConihay, from whose lips I obtained the above, is a gentleman of unquestionable veracity and honor, and much respected by his neighbors, and the above description is as nearly as possible in his own words. He was assisting at boring at the time the oil vein was tapped, and he very humorously detailed the actions and expressions of the supposed 'ruined' owner. After looking at the changeable colors of the oil spread out upon the water, for a little over an hour, and having an eye to the useful and ornamental, he 'tipped the wink' to another young workman, when they got their rifles and went away to hunt, leaving the 'old man' disconsolate over his 'bad luck.'

"Many other well-borers have had a similar experience, which would occupy too much time to enumerate, but it would be safe to say that, out of one hundred and fifty wells that have been sunk in this region, two-thirds have been greatly 'bothered' with oil. In many of the old salt wells at the present time, petroleum can be dipped out in quantities of half a barrel and upwards, whenever the river is low. This is especially the case in an old well near Reynold's Furnace, owned by Mr. William D. Shrewsbury, of Malden. There is a well on the Hurt property, which was notorious for its yield of oil; hundreds of barrels of oil were run into the river, and until it was tubed out, it was almost impossible to use the well for salt. Oil is obtained from this well now by pushing down a cloth plug three hundred and fifty feet, and withdrawing it suddenly — oil will follow the plug to the extent of several gallons each time. The oil, as taken out of the wells, is used by the miners in the coal banks, and for lubricating their machinery. I have examined the oil of several of the wells, and find it like in color to the petroleum of Oil Creek, but with a much less pungent odor. In testing the gravity, I found it 40° Beaumé.

"A ludicrous story is told of a citizen, well known for his positive assertions, bordering on profanity, who, on sinking a 'gum,' vowed he would either get salt water or bore to 'Pandemonium.' He had but little knowledge of oil or gas, and after going down a certain depth, the drill was violently thrown in the air, followed by which, by some means, took fire and exploded, making the man believe his rash vow was being fulfilled, and terrifying him almost to death. This occurrence happened right back of this city, and is well authenticated."

On the north side of the Great Kanawha River, seven miles above Charleston, a strike is reported on the property of the Great Kanawha Oil Company.

In Cabell County, at the mouth of the Great Kanawha, well boring is rife — on the Guyandotte River (where oil has lately been obtained), Seven Mile, Four Pole, and Tom's Creeks, on the Porter Farm near Salt Rock, in the vicinity of Barboursville, and elsewhere. A large proportion of these enterprises are just commencing, some of them obtaining a fair show of oil at less than sixty feet. The Guyandotte has many tributaries, with rich surface indications, and abundant proof of oil in former salt wells, and will certainly be prominent as an oil field. A large portion of the land in this county has either been purchased or leased.

The territory south of the Great Kanawha, upon the net-work of streams flowing into the Guyandotte and Big Sandy Rivers, will be the scene of much excitement and busy labor, in the immediate future; and it will undoubtedly be found, at no distant day, very productive in oil. Almost all of it has been under the complete control of guerillas until very recently, the Union men either driven out or intimidated, and all enterprise suppressed, and all labor, except for the production of supplies for the most pressing wants.

CHAPTER XXV.

PETROLEUM COMPANIES OF WEST VIRGINIA.

IN exceptional cases a well is bored and pumped by an individual. The almost invariable rule is, the establishment of a partnership, or the formation of a stock company. As prices advanced, the latter course became a necessity. As in Pennsylvania, the practice, of doubtful expediency, has obtained, of giving the capital stock a nominal price, and selling it to original stockholders at a lower rate. The plausible pretext was, that good oil property, when developed, appreciated so greatly, that it was best to fix upon a fair estimate of prospective actual value.

The stock of West Virginia companies is not based upon unreasonable values. There may be those which will prove unproductive, but the failures will probably be less than those of any other oil region.

It would be impossible even to mention them all. New ones are in progress of organization; divisions of the property of old ones are frequently occurring; the names of many are not published; it is therefore proposed to notice a few owning large tracts of land, and give a list of the others, as far as opportunity to note their existence has been enjoyed.

The "Little Kanawha and Elk River Petroleum and Mining Company," recently organized, with headquarters at New York, is based upon sixty-two thousand eight hundred and sixty acres of valuable mineral and agricultural lands, situated in the geographical centre of West Virginia, upon the headwaters of the two rivers named, in the immediate line of the proposed Central Railroad, already chartered, and undoubtedly soon to be built. Its organization is as follows:

Oliver E. Wood, President; James Cruikshank, Vice-President; Charles J. Martin, Treasurer; James Wadsworth, Secretary; E. R. Blackwell, Consulting Engineer and General Superintendent. Paul N. Spofford (of Spofford, Tileston, & Co.); Charles J. Martin, President Home Insurance Company; Hon. Roger Averill, Danbury, Connecticut; Hon. Albert L. Catlin, Burlington, Vermont; James Cruikshank, 55 Broadway; Oliver E. Wood, 26 Barclay Street; James Wadsworth, 61 Cedar Street (of James Wadsworth & Co.); John W. Strong, Detroit, Michigan; Edward M. Morgan, 2 Pine Street—Trustees.

Among the stockholders are some of the first business men in New York. Arrangements are in progress for developing, upon an extended scale, the varied resources of these lands, which are situated in Braxton and Gilmer Counties, forty miles from the Burning Springs of the Little Kanawha, and seventy miles in a direct line from Parkersburg. Practical geologists have testified to the high value of the oil-producing capabilities of this tract. Among its minerals are cannel and other coals, iron and salt; in all of which it abounds. Its forests are of white oak, poplar (white wood), black walnut, cherry, and other woods. The soil is of excellent quality;

the surface less mountainous than other portions of the State; and the climate healthful as that of any portion of any other State in the country.

Numerous wagon roads, two turnpikes, navigation by two rivers in the winter season, and by one creek at high water, furnish facilities for getting the products of industry to market. The opening of the railroad, connecting the Ohio with Charleston and the Baltimore and Ohio road, will give instant enhancement of value, and high prominence as a point of profitable settlement, to these lands. The probable construction of another road, down the little Kanawha to Parkersburg, will add greatly to these values. With such facilities for inter-communication, the central position of Braxton would make it a formidable rival with the most favored section in the location of the State Capital.

A few brief points, in description of this valuable tract, will illustrate the natural wealth of the central counties. On Otter Creek, a branch of the Elk, is a tract of six thousand acres, two miles in width at the river, seven at the other end, and nine in length. An oil spring of considerable strength is reported near the mouth of the creek, and the water in a well near by is too greasy in summer to be fit for household use. North from this spring, in a branch over the hill, a similar spring is found. Numerous indications of oil are discovered on Rusk Creek, and in other valleys, all in close proximity to Elk River, which furnishes facilities for transportation to Charleston, on the Great Kanawha. In the valleys of parallel streams, as the Sycamore, Sugar, and Rock Camp Creek, gas and oil are abundant, in one of which the emission is particularly constant and strong.

Numerous oil springs are also reported on Grannies' Creek, and old Old Woman's in the vicinity of the main tract of the Little Kanawha and Elk River Company. C. S. Richardson, a mining engineer, who knows this county well, writes thus:

"We now make our way up towards Bulltown, distant seventeen miles, and pass through many promising locations for oil wells. Gas springs abound, and so strong is the pressure at times in some of them, that it creates a noise under ground, the people say, resembling the rumbling sound of a wagon over a rough country road. This can easily be accounted for. When the summer season sets in the creeks and branches become dry, and the fissures and joints of the rocks, which in winter are filled with water, become drained and form vacuities. The noise of the gas as it bubbles up through the water in the lower depths of these fissures, produces an echo, resounding through these cavernous spaces; hence the rumbling sound spoken of. A few winters ago, an outburst of gas, very singular in its results, happened in the river while it was frozen over. An air hole had been noticed in the river for some time, but one morning a large column of water, mud, coal, shale, and oil was thrown up several feet in the air, and covered the surrounding sheet of ice for yards. This spot was about opposite, and thus in a line with Otter Creek Springs, and no doubt belongs to the same group of cleavages."

Salt Lick Creek, a tributary of the Little Kanawha, courses along the northeastern boundary, exhibiting .evidences of gas and petroleum. Its brine is so strong that salt can be obtained by evaporation in kettles; and was thus manufactured by the Indians. In Cowpens Run and Duck Run, the hills are much denuded, great slides have occurred, shale beds occur, evidences of a great subsidence are seen, and the surface shows much disturbance of the strata. Steer Creek is somewhat noted for two gas springs, which are claimed to equal any in West Virginia. One of the main branches of this creek traverses the company's property for miles.

A six-foot vein of coal passes under the mountain ridge through the estate. The seam is pure coal, free from sulphur, and highly bituminous, making superior gas and fine coke. A practical engineer, making a survey of it, found the seam considerably to exceed six feet in some cases, and in one to fall short of it. Another seam exists higher up the mountain.

The iron ore is a brownish oxide, yielding thirty-three per cent. It is abundant and easily mined. No iron works are yet in existence. An argillaceous limestone is found on the elevated ridges sufficient for all the requirements of iron furnaces.

The capital stock of this company is six millions. The sum of one hundred and fifty thousand dollars is reserved in its treasury for the development of these magnificent resources. With all the speculation, not to say swindling, charged upon oil companies — and justly charged, it may be, in some cases — who will say that the actual price of stock, representing such land at less than ten dollars per acre, is too high? Or that even the nominal value of the stock, at eight dollars for one, may not be far more than realized? The best lands of the Sciota and Miami Valleys, are held to be cheap at one hundred dollars per acre. Are not lands fat with oil, abounding in coal and iron, covered with fine timber, and with a fruitful soil, worth at least as much?

Another organization, embracing a large territory, and involving heavy operations, is the Virginia and Ohio Mining and Petroleum Company, formed for the purpose of developing upon a grand scale the real capabilities of this region. Its lands lie in the centre of the West Virginia oil basin, and embrace no less than sixty-seven different tracts, varying in size from two acres to six hundred, and making an aggregate of seven thousand acres.

It is becoming common for shrewd, practical men, who are experienced in oil production, to leave the high-priced lands of Pennsylvania, where one great success has gone in company with several failures, and select lands as yet undeveloped, but possessing acknowledged value as oil territory, where almost every well that has been drilled in the past has been oil producing. They have purchased, entered and improved them wisely, with every prospect of reaching results worthy of their efforts. This is one of the working companies.

It was organized under the laws of New York — its capital stock one million dollars — one hundred thousand shares at ten dollars each.

Its officers are as follows: President, Bradhurst Schieffelin (of Schieffelin, Brothers & Company); Treasurer, William E. Rider (of Rider & Clark); Mining Superintendent, Charles D'Hervilly. Offices, 51 Broad Street, New York; 98 Water Street, Pittsburg; and 21 Front Street, Marietta.

These lands are located in the heart of the petroleum region, within a radius of about thirty miles from Marietta, Ohio, on the various creeks and runs flowing into the Ohio River; in Washington, Perry, Noble, and Morgan Counties, in Ohio, upon a dozen different creeks; and in Wood, Pleasant, Ritchie, and Wetzel Counties, in West Virginia; on Bull and Fishing Creeks, Laurel Fork, Wellington, Stillwell, Bull, and Big Runs. They were selected with care, in advance of the great influx of petroleum seekers in this region, by the Mining Superintendent of the Company, Mr. D'Hervilly, a gentleman of much experience in locating and working oil lands.

The petroleum from this section being about 40° Beaumé gravity, and very free from sediment, is much sought after by refiners, and readily commands, it is claimed, about two cents per gallon more than that from Oil Creek. In addition to the light oils used for refining, a heavy oil of about 28° to 30° Beaumé is found at the depth of sixty to one hundred feet, unequalled as a lubricator, and used extensively on railroads, steamboats and stationary engines, and sought for beyond the limit of present production. This oil readily commands, at the present writing, twenty dollars per barrel at the wells — a price double that of the lighter oils.

Scores of derricks have been erected, preliminary to boring; many wells are being bored, in most of which are indications of oil; several are completed and working. The company owns numerous steam engines, many sets of boring and other tools, tanks, etc. The wells now finished will alone pay a fair dividend on the amount of stock issued.

The West Virginia properties, in the heart of the most successful oil producing region, and in the vicinity of some of the most productive wells, make an aggregate area of nearly two thousand acres, of which two hundred and twenty-five acres are on Laurel Fork, Wellington Run — four hundred acres on Bull Creek — four hundred and fifty acres on Stillwell Run, forty acres on Big Run, and seven hundred and thirty on Fishing Creek.

The Company holds fifty thousand shares of its capital stock, the proceeds of which are to be used in developing the property. If all shall not be wanted for that purpose, the remainder will be divided *pro rata* among the stockholders.

A limited number of these shares has been sold, for this purpose, at five dollars — par value ten dollars — and will be.

The Vesta Petroleum and Refining Company, incorporated under the laws of New York, has the two-fold object of developing and refining petroleum. Its organization is as follows: John H. Hebert, President; John Caldwell, Secretary; John H. Hebert, Louis Dagron, James M. Leavitt, George W. Randall, James C. Daniels, Henry B. Hebert, Trustees. Office, 4 Cedar Street, New York.

Their property consists of the undivided half of nine hundred and twenty acres, in Ritchie County, lying between Petroleum Station and the junction of the forks of Hughes' River, on the waters of Buffalo Creek. They also own two hundred and eighty acres on Pithole Creek, in Venango County, Pennsylvania, three miles east from Oil Creek, and seven miles southeast from the railroad depot at Titusville.

The operations of this company are not speculative, but practical. Energetic, prompt measures for development were initiated at once upon its organization. In addition to the wells in progress in Pennsylvania (five or more), there were in progress, on the tenth of June, in the West Virginia division, the following wells: the Bickel Well, down six hundred feet, with a good show of oil and gas; the Broom Well, three hundred and fifty feet, with similar indications; the Patterson Well, seventy-five feet; and another just started on the "Plowman Lease." The writer, in his last visit to West Virginia, saw the Bickel Well just after it had struck oil, when the indications seemed very favorable, exciting great expectations. Gas, water, oil, and fragments of rock, were blown out with great violence.

This locality is on a line direct with the Burning Springs, Oil Run, and Horseneck Wells, in the centre of the famous "Oil Belt," hitherto so popular and so productive.

The Hughes' River Petroleum Trust Association owns, in fee simple, a tract of six hundred acres of valuable oil lands, lying on the South Fork of Hughes' River, opposite the mouth of Spruce Creek, in Ritchie County. It lies within three miles of the celebrated Gas Springs; six or eight miles from the great asphaltum deposit on McFarland's Run, in the neighborhood of the Burning Spring, and a short distance from the old sand diggings, near the junction of the two forks of the Hughes'. It is in a direct line with the upheaval of shale, among the fissures of which crude asphaltum is found in immense quantities.

This site early attracted the attention of oil operators. In 1861 preparations were made for sinking wells in the vicinity, but discontinued during the war, which has made oil developments impracticable until the present season. It is certain that petroleum abounds here, probably in immense quantities.

The tract is remarkable for the extent of its ravines and bottoms suitable for boring, in which also, at many points, gas springs and surface oil shows occur. More than a mile and a half of river frontage, and almost as great a length of creek bottoms, afford numerous sites for wells, some of which have attracted the marked attention of those versed in the lore and labors of petroleum.

Three hundred acres of the tract have been in cultivation; four houses and a barn are among the improvements; the remainder is covered with a heavy growth of oaks, ash, hickory, black and white walnut, sugar maple, whitewood, and chestnut.

In this region a confidence is felt that a great oil deposit exists beneath the "asphaltum lode." Mr. Stovin, mining engineer of that property, reports a discovery of bitumen, more remarkable than the original, which he says "puts at rest forever any doubt that could have existed as to its having been liquid."

Hon. Amos Myers, of the Twentieth (Venango) Congressional District, of Pennsylvania, on whose advice the tract was purchased, has recently visited it, and thus writes of its capabilities:

"It is the best looking land for both farming and oil purposes, as well as for a town, that I have seen, and an old citizen say it is the best on the South Hughes' River. The soil is equal to prairie, and that too on the hills, and every tree is a giant of its kind. The bluffs, the bottoms; the rocks, ravines, and breaks; the timber, oil, and springs — all indicate oil. This is my honest, candid opinion. I could not, if I desired, resist the conviction."

The capital stock of the association is one hundred thousand dollars, in twenty thousand shares, at five dollars each, and the officers are the following well known and reliable residents of Washington, where most of the stock is owned. Trustees, James C. Lewis, Edward Young, William Stickney; Treasurer, J. C. Lewis; Secretary, M. L. Story; Advisory Committee, Francis Jordan (Penn. Military Agent), John S. Poler, J. E. Forbush, Martin King, W. S. Bailey.

Incorporated companies and private partnerships, in multiplied forms, involving interests of varied magnitude, exist in all parts of the country, upon a basis of West Virginia oil property. So far as those interested have responded to calls for information, or kept their organization or operations before the public, they are brought here to view; yet this must not be considered a complete exhibit of the organized capital and labor engaged in the petroleum business of the State. New companies or partnerships are daily organized, and new and promising fields of labor daily explored. The following is a list of Philadelphia companies, so far as their names have been obtained:

Blair Oil Company; capital, $1,000,000; $5 per share. Office, 305 Chestnut Street.

Blue Creek Oil Company; capital, $500,000; $10 per share. 407 Walnut Street.

Bull Creek Oil Company; capital, $1,000,000; $10 per share. 309 Walnut Street.

Burning Spring Oil Company; capital $1,000,000; $10 per share. 113 Chestnut Street.

Burning Spring and Goose Creek Oil Company; capital, $125,000; $1 per share. 311 Walnut Street.

Buck Run Oil Company; capital, $150,000; $1 per share. 201 Callowhill Street.

Calf Creek Oil Company; capital, $1,000,000; $10 per share. 240 North Front Street.

Clouston Oil Company; capital, $200,000; $3 per share. 407 Walnut Street.

Cow Creek and Stillwell Run Oil Company; capital, $500,000; $5 per share.

Cow Creek Oil Company. 221 South Fifth Street.

Eureka Oil Company; capital, $1,000,000; $10 per share.

Elk River Oil Company. 208 South Fourth Street.

Elk River and Blue Creek Oil Company; capital, $1,000,000; $10 per share. Merchants' Exchange Building.

Fee Simple Petroleum Company. 150 Front Street.

Ferguson Oil Company. 417 Walnut Street.

Government Oil and Mining Company; capital, $200,000; $1 per share.

Horseneck Oil Company; capital, $500,000; $50 per share.

Horseneck and Burning Spring Oil Company; capital, $500,000; $5 per share. 424 Walnut Street.

Hughes' River Oil Company. 605 Walnut Street.

Imperial Kanawha Valley Oil Company; capital, $600,000; $10 per share.

Kanawha and Hughes' River Oil Company; capital, $1,000,000; $10 per share. 208 South Fourth Street.

Kanawha and Riffles Run Oil Company; capital, $250,000; $2.50 per share.

Kanawha River Oil Company; capital, $375,000; $10 per share. 112 South Fourth Street.

Kanawha and Ohio Oil Company. 424 Walnut Street.

Kanawha Valley Oil Company. 108 Walnut Street.

Lick Run Oil Company; capital, $100,000; $2 per share.

Little Kanawha and Bridge Run Oil Company; capital, $250,000; $1 per share. 383 Walnut Street.

Little Kanawha and Spring Creek Oil Company; capital, $250,000; $1 per share.

Lynn Camp Oil Company; capital, $500,000; $10 per share. 228 South Third Street.

Logan Oil Company; capital, $500,000; $10 per share. 309 Walnut Street.

Mutual Oil Company. 332 Walnut Street.

Mutual and Beneficial Mining Company. 274 South Third Street.

North Fork of Hughes' River Oil and Mining Company.

Mount Farm Oil Company; capital, $750,000; $5 per share.

Old Burning Springs Oil Company; capital, $1,000,000; $10 per share.

Rathbone Oil Company; capital, $500,000; $5 per share. 206 South Fourth Street.

Rock Run Oil and Mining Company. 108 South Fourth Street.

Reedy Creek Oil Company. 112 South Fourth Street.

Standing Stone Creek Oil Company. 233 South Third Street.

NEW YORK OIL COMPANIES.

Tack Oil Company. 215 Walnut Street.

Victor Mutual Petroleum Company. 429 Chestnut Street.

Volcanic Oil and Coal Company; capital, $1,000,000; $10 per share. 417 Walnut Street.

Vulcan Oil and Mining Company; capital, $200,000; $1 per share. 417 Walnut Street.

West Virginia and Ohio Oil Company. 206 Walnut Street.

West Virginia Oil Company. 411 Walnut Street.

West Virginia National Petroleum Company. 5½ South Sixth Street.

Wetzel County Oil Company. 309 Walnut Street.

Wirt County Oil Company.

The following companies have their headquarters in New York City:

Bergen Coal and Oil Company; capital, $2,000,000; $10 per share. Office, 416 Broad Street.

Big Sand Creek Oil Company. 13 Broad Street.

Burning Spring Oil Company.

Chemical Oil Company; capital, $250,000; $5 per share.

Dutchman's Run Oil Company; capital, $1,000,000; $10 per share. 71 Broadway.

Great Kanawha Oil Company; capital, $300,000; $10 per share.

Hancock Oil Company.

Kanawha Petroleum Company; capital, $500,000; $10 per share. 154 Front Street.

Leading Petroleum Company; capital, $500,000; $5 per share. 80 Broadway.

New York and Boston Petroleum Company. 11 Wall Street.

New York and West Virginia Petroleum Company; capital, $500,000; $5 per share. 137 Broad Street.

New World Petroleum Company; capital, $500,000; $10 per share. 155 Maiden Lane.

North American Petroleum Company; capital, $1,250,000; $10 per share. 73 Broadway.

Old Dominion Oil Company; capital, $500,000; $10 per share.

People's Mutual Oil and Mining Company. 6 Wall Street.

Rathbone Oil Tract Company. 69 Wall Street.

Ritchie County Oil Company; capital, $800,000; $5 per share.

Second National Oil Company; capital, $500,000; $10 per share.

Tack Oil Company; capital, $500,000; $10 per share.

Vesuvius Oil Company.

Virginia Oil Company; capital, $500,000.

West Virginia Coal and Oil Company; capital, $3,000,000; $10 per share.

Many other companies are located in Pittsburg, Cleveland, Cincinnati, and other places beyond the limits of West Virginia; while still others have offices in Wheeling, Parkersburg, and other points within the State. The enumeration already made will suffice to show the prevalence and comparative extent of the petroleum excitement, as it existed early in the present season. A temporary lull succeeded, followed by renewed activity, which promises to embrace the central and southern portions of the State in its operations.

CHAPTER XXVI.

PETROLEUM PROSPECTS.

"WILL the oil product of the country decrease?" is the anxious inquiry of interested parties. So far as West Virginia is concerned, it may safely be asserted, that this species of mining is in its infancy. To persons unacquainted with the peculiarities of the business, the assumed decrease in production, during the past winter and spring, in Pennsylvania, and to some extent in West Virginia, has given color to such a view. There is little real ground for such an assumption. While a given well may reasonably be expected to suffer partial exhaustion in a few years, and in some instances in a few months, that single well usually drains but a small space — a cavity, imperfectly connected with others by fissures liable to obstruction — or a single crevice, possibly extending a long distance, but entirely unconnected with another parallel to it and a few feet from it. Wells may therefore be increased indefinitely, and if the sources of supply in some of them shall be tapped by others, there will be many still to yield a handsome return.

The production has been sensibly diminished by the speculative operations of the past year. Productive lands were sold, once or twice, perhaps many times, causing a cessation of drilling, tubing, and even of pumping finished wells; while companies were organized, stocks sold, and new machinery placed upon the ground and put in operation. Many of these companies have remained inactive for months, and some may never commence development. The business of making and selling stocks is one thing; that of drilling wells and pumping oil quite another. The excessive multiplication of companies may eventually favor increased production; but their immediate effect was the reverse.

Immense damage has been occasioned, in districts where wells are most numerous, by carelessness in tubing off the surface water, by defective seed-bags or their improper location, or negligence in leaving open abandoned wells. By such means the oil reservoirs have been flooded, and the oil driven back to higher levels, whence it cannot force its way through accustomed avenues to the well. Early in the spring of the present year, a disastrous flood occurred in the most productive localities in Pennsylvania, which demonstrated conclusively the fatality of this faulty and negligent practice. That "haste makes waste" was again proven to the sorrow of luckless wights impatient to be rich. An almost total cessation of oil production followed in the flooded districts, particularly on Oil Creek; but an immense increase on Pithole Creek gave evidence, as believed by operators, that the oil had been driven outwards in that direction. Persistent and long-continued pumping was at length rewarded by the return of oil, at first much diluted with water, yet improving as the superabundant water was withdrawn.

The natural effect of these causes, joined with the reduction in the price of gold at the close of the war, was a panic among holders of oil stock, many of whom had bought with as little discretion as they now manifested in selling. Wise capitalists held what they knew to be valuable, and some took occasion to buy more stock and territory. The panic affected shares far more than lands. The best locations were held with almost as firm a grasp as ever; and the price actually advanced in portions of West Virginia which had but just before been practically inaccessible. Prices are still advancing in such localities. Development is talked of, in a few instances commenced; and when oil shall be found, as it doubtless will be, a new circle of excitement will be opened to the votaries of oil.

Among the many companies based upon West Virginia lands, it is possible that some may prove worthless. Where millions awaited the efforts of judicious enterprise, it would be strange if dishonesty had neglected so favorable an opportunity; yet the investments made have proved singularly satisfactory, and few charges of swindling or misrepresentation are preferred.

The conviction in intelligent minds is strong that a brilliant future awaits the continued prosecution of the business. The existence of oil in large quantities is demonstrated; equal evidence proves the supply to be widely diffused; and practical results affirm the necessity of energetic and well directed efforts, except in isolated cases, to insure large and enduring success. While the profits are often greater, in proportion to expenditure of money or labor, than in gold or silver mining, the same energy and experience required in such enterprises are equally requisite and certain of adequate remuneration. The fall of gold affected the price of the product less than most other articles of export; the increase in demand and diminution of supply served to sustain its price in an appreciated currency. There need be no fear of low prices, while a multitude of new uses for petroleum are originated almost daily, and substitutes are consequently becoming scarce and costly. The business will advance in importance for many years, and much of the permanent prosperity of West Virginia, as well as of other States, will result, directly or indirectly, from the developments now in their incipiency.

The expensive schooling of experience — the mistakes in locating and boring wells, in construction of fixtures and machinery, and in misconceptions through false theories — will facilitate and cheapen future operations, and render success far more certain. The errors in management of companies, and even the swindles perpetrated by the dishonest, will all prove beacons to warn against the dangers of the past. The cost of labor is in process of reduction, and the price of tubing tools and machinery. Every new business involves a laborious and costly apprenticeship; this is no exception, though the enormous production of such wells as the Llewellyn or Gilfillan might defy the losses of inexperience and folly.

Fortunately the mania for buying "shares," in companies of which nothing was known, at whatever prices cupidity might demand, has subsided. The legitimate purchase of lands, positively valuable and promising great productiveness, by parties intending either to develope or hold for further action, is not likely soon to cease, unless prices should be rapidly and generally enhanced to a much higher point than at present. Judicious investments are constantly made, and will yet be found in the petroleum sections of the State.

To those seeking such investments, the following advice is appropriate: Seek lands with good titles, not too remote from railroad or navigable stream; give personal attention to development, individually, or in small partnerships of reliable men, or small companies originated for work rather than speculation; work economically, as in any other business enterprise, and quietly persevere, overcoming all obstacles, and securing a gratifying success, which will prove equally sure and full, when followed with such judgment and tact as that which attends the average of business enterprises. Investments in large companies may prove equally profitable, when fairly constituted and properly managed. An acquaintance with the officers and property basis of such companies should precede investment.

The following conclusions, relative to the oil region of West Virginia, may be safely reached:

That oil production is in its infancy, and the daily product small in comparison with the future of the enterprise.

That the oil region of West Virginia embraces a much wider area than that of Pennsylvania.

That the southern portion of the State, hitherto undeveloped, promises as rich rewards to oil enterprise as any other.

That the business will prove a permanent and highly productive element of the industry of the State.

The value of this and other interests of West Virginia is prominently shown in the enhanced prices at which lands are held and sold, amounting to an aggregate appreciation, within a single year, to tens of millions of dollars. Nor has the average valuation attained a point above its intrinsic worth. Except in a few instances of wild investment in untested petroleum lands, the price is still rising, and will continue to increase. Judicious investors will still secure a good advance and large profits.

The coal, iron, salt, and other minerals; the dense virgin forests, of almost all the woods wrought by manufacturers, or indigenous to North America; the fruitful soil and genial climate, so peculiarly adapted to the most profitable branches of agriculture and horticulture; all will conspire with petroleum to draw from other States, and from beyond the sea, population and capital, and to give to labor abundance, and ultimately clothe the land with beauty, and bless it with the adornments of taste and art. With the added influence of churches and schools, rendering the moral atmosphere as pure as the physical, and making "the waters of life" as free as the perennial springs of the everlasting hills, the homes of West Virginia may equal in attraction the most favored upon the continent.

INDEX.

A.

ADMISSION into the Union	Page 12
Agricultural College,	22
Altitude,	55
Anticlinal Axes,	193, 196
Asphaltum Lode,	197, 232

B.

Baltimore and Ohio Railroad,	152
Barbour County,	134
Berkeley County,	70
" Sir William, on Schools,	36
" Springs,	71
"Blue-laws" of Virginia,	28
Boone County,	124
Boring, Site for,	204
Braxton County,	139
Brooke County,	97
Bull Creek,	235
Burning Spring,	183, 222
" " Washington's,	179

C.

Cabel County,	125
Calhoun County,	137
California,	230
Caudy Castle,	73
Central Counties,	128
Central Oil Region,	237
Central Railroad,	159
Clay County,	141
Climate,	54
Coal,	162
Copper,	174
Corporations, Law Relative to,	19
Covington and Ohio Railroad,	158

Cow Creek, ... 236

D.
"Devil's Garden," 76
Doddridge County, ... 136
Drilling Machine, Atwood's, . . . 217

E.
Emigration, Reasons for, . . . 25

F.
Fayette County, ... 117
Fertility of Soil, ... 45
Finances, ... 20
Flowing wells, ... 204

G.
Gas Springs, Value of, ... 200
Gilmer County, ... 138
Great Kanawha Oil Basin, . . . 243
Greenbrier County, ... 115

H.
Hampshire County, ... 72
Hancock County, ... 100
Hanging Rocks, ... 74
Hardy County, ... 75
Harrison County, ... 135
Hempfield Railway, ... 158
Horseneck, ... 234
Hughes' River, ... 229

I.
Ice Mountain, ... 72
Incorporation, ... 19
Indian Mound on Grave Creek, . . 89
Internal Improvements, . . . 148
Iron, ... 168

J.
Jackson County, ... 105
Jealousies, Sectional, ... 9
Jefferson County, ... 70
Judicial System, ... 14

INDEX. 273

K.
Kanawha County,	118
Kanawha Valley,	112

L.
Land Rights,	29
Lands, Enhanced Value of,	42
Laws,	17
Lead,	173
Legislature,	13
Lewis County,	136
Limestone,	171
Little Kanawha and Elk River Petroleum Company,	250
Live Stock, Statistics of,	146
Logan County,	126
Location of West Virginia,	39

M.
Marion County,	133
Marshall County,	88
Mason County,	119
McDowell County,	126
Mercer County,	115
Mineral Waters,	174
Mineral Wealth,	160
Monongalia County,	133
Monroe County,	115
Morgan County,	71
Mountain Group,	79

N.
Navigation, Slackwater,	151
New York Petroleum Companies,	263
Nicholas County,	140

O.
Ohio County,	90
"Oil Belt,"	194
Oil Run,	231
Oil-wells, Characteristics of,	203
Organization of the State,	11

P.

"Panhandle,"	87
Parkersburg,	106
Pendleton County,	74
Petroleum,	176
" Boring for,	213
" Companies,	250
" Distribution of,	177
" in Salt Springs,	180
" Its Discovery in West Virginia,	183
" Origin of,	185
" Prospects,	265
" Refining of,	218
" Statistics of,	211
" Uses of,	206
" Where to Find,	192
Philadelphia Petroleum Companies,	260
Pioneers, Domestic Implements of,	32
" Wedding Customs of,	33
Pioneer life,	30
Pocahontas County,	81
Political Convulsion,	7
Population,	24
" Table of,	38
Preston County,	82
Production, Statistics of,	142
Putnam County,	119

R.

Railroads,	152
Rain-fall,	61
Raleigh County,	117
Randolph County,	81
Regurgitory Spring,	76
Ritchie County,	136
River Counties,	101
Roane County,	138

S.

Salt, Kanawha,	170
" Mason County,	171
Salubrity,	62
Sand-rocks,	199

Scenery, ... 64
School System, ... 17
Settlement, ... 23
Settlers of West Virginia, . . . 9
Sheep Husbandry,. 44, 98
Shenandoah Valley, ... 68
Slavery, Abolition of, ... 12
Soldiers of West Virginia, . . . 21
Southern Counties, ... 123
Standing-stone Creek, . . . 226
Statistics of Kanawha Valley, . . . 121
Statistics of Production, . . . 142
State Officers, ... 16
State Seal, ... 15
Steamboat Navigation, ... 151
Stock Farming, ... 43

T.

Table of Farm Products, ... 148
Taylor County, ... 133
Tea-table Rock, ... 74
Temperature, ... 58
Tucker County, ... 82
Turnpikes, ... 150
Tyler County, ... 105

U.

Upshur County, ... 140

V.

Value of Farms, ... 41
Vesta Petroleum and Refining Company, . 257
Virginia and Ohio Mining and Petroleum
    Company, ... 255
Vineyards, ... 91

W.

Washington's Lands, ... 44
Wayne County, ... 125
Webster County, ... 140
Weddings of Early Days, . . . 33
West Virginia, Abolition of Slavery in, . . 12
   "   " Admission of, . . . 12
   "   " Agricultural College, . . 22

West Virginia,	Climate of,		54
"	"	"Blue Laws" of,	28
"	"	Compared with New Hampshire,	51
"	"	" " Minnesota and Maryland,	54
"	"	" " Ohio and Pennsylvania,	53
"	"	Corporation Laws of,	19
"	"	Emigration from,	25
"	"	Fertility of,	35
"	"	Finances of,	20
"	"	Judicial System of,	14
"	"	Kanawha Valley in,	112
"	"	Land Rights,	29
"	"	Laws of,	17
"	"	Legislation of,	13
"	"	Location of,	39
"	"	Mountain Counties of,	79
"	"	Organization of,	11
"	"	"Panhandle,"	87
"	"	Population of,	24
"	"	River Counties of,	101
"	"	Scenery of,	64
"	"	School System of,	17
"	"	Settlement of,	23
"	"	Sheep Husbandry in,	98
"	"	Soldiers of,	21
"	"	Southern Counties of,	123
"	"	State Officers of,	16
"	"	" Seal of,	15
"	"	Stock Farming in,	43
"	"	Value of Farms in,	41
"	"	Vineyards of,	91
"	"	Washington's Lands in,	44
Wetzel County,			105
Wheeling,			93
White Sulphur Springs,			116
Wirt County,			137
Wood County,			105
Wyoming County,			126

THE END.

www.ingramcontent.com/pod-product-compliance
Lightning Source LLC
Chambersburg PA
CBHW031941230426
43672CB00010B/2006